WPB

EDGAR CAYCE'S PREDICTIONS For The 21st CENTURY

EDGAR CAYCE'S PREDICTIONS For The 21st CENTURY

MARK THURSTON, Ph.D.

WE PUBLISH BOOKS

For further information, you may write or e-mail:

We Publish Books
P.O. Box 1814
Rancho Mirage, CA 92270

www.WePublishbooks.com
E-mail: WePublishBooks@gmail.com

Cover Artwork by Daniel L. O'Byrne
Cover Design by Rhonda Clifton Lyons

Library of Congress Control Number: 2005922848

Thurston, Mark
Edgar Cayce's Predictions For The 21st Century

Printed in the United States

Body, Mind & Spirit-General OCC000000

ISBN 1-929841-03-5   Paper Back
ISBN 9781929841035   Paper Back beginning 2007

First Printing, 2005

CONTENTS

Author's Preface ix
Introduction *xi*

PART I EDGAR CAYCE AS VISIONARY

1 Edgar Cayce: Visionary of the 21st Century and Beyond 3

2 Cayce's Prophecies of Earth Changes 21

PART II PROPHECIES OF A WORLD IN DISORDER

3 The Many Streams of Prophetic Wisdom 37

4 A New World Order for the 21st Century 65

5 Visions of Atlantis, Weather Changes, and the Second Coming 95

PART III A PRIMER FOR LIVING IN THE 21ST CENTURY THAT CAYCE ENVISIONED

6 Understanding the Inner Shift of the 21st Century 119

7 Cayce's Visions for Five Ancient Riddles 145

8 A 21st Century Approach to Guidance and Decision-Making 159

9 Spiritual "Work" in the 21st Century 171

10 Meditation: The 21st Century Key to Powerful, Healthy Living 197

11 We Can Make a Difference 221

Postscript Edgar Cayce's Work for the 21st Century 235

About the Author 237

About Daniel L. O'Byrne – Creator of Cover Artwork *239*

AUTHOR'S PREFACE

Prophecy is an unfolding topic. We cannot understand it otherwise. As soon as we try to set a prophecy "in stone" – for example, "such and such" *will* unavoidably happen – then we have already missed the deeper sense of how a visionary does his work. The seer truly operates at the level of what Edgar Cayce called the "Creative Forces" – those dynamic energies that are always involved in shaping a future that isn't sure until it manifests.

Consider how oftentimes a prophet will amend or edit his visions over time, maybe because conditions have changed or maybe because he is starting to see the future in a new way. In our study of prophecy we find that what a seer or clairvoyant says one year as he (or she) looks into the future may then be followed by new statements by that same psychic as the date in question draws near at hand.

It happened with Edgar Cayce on more than one occasion. For example, in 1934 he made certain prophecies about things to come in 1936. But in January, 1936, he made new pronouncements that backed away from some of his previous predictions.

Just as surely the *interpretation of* prophecy is an unfolding matter, too. Our understanding of the meaning, value and accuracy of prophecy is something that develops over time.

Edgar Cayce's Predictions for the 21st century – is a sequel. It is the follow-up book to my previous publication *Millennium Prophecies,* which was published in the 1990s when we were still looking at Cayce's pronouncements from "the other side" of 1998 and the turn of the century. But now, here in the first decade of the new millennium – no longer just speculating about what it might be like to live in the years 2001 and beyond – we can take a fresh look at this remarkable man Edgar Cayce and what his teachings have to offer.

In this sequel book the reader will find that my interpretation and understanding of the Cayce prophecies is an unfolding thing. Many matters I see in a different way than I did more than a decade ago as I was preparing that previous book.

And so, in a similar way, *Edgar Cayce's Prophecies for the 21st Century* includes my unfolding understanding of the prophetic material of this important man. Some of that unfolding understanding is, of course, simply a matter of the passage of time. We are now on the 21st century side of the years 1998 and 2001 – dates for which Cayce indicated certain things might be expected to have taken place. The first book, *Millennium Prophecies*, attempted to understand and interpret Cayce as we were still approaching those pivotal years. Now a new book is in order – one that addresses prophecy in light of the fact that we are already living in the 21st century.

The need for a sequel became evident to me immediately after the year 2001 had come and gone. Surely it was a traumatic year for the world, and for the United States in particular. But it wasn't just the terrorists tragedies that made me feel that a sequel was needed. I recognized that people were starting to look at the Cayce material in a new way. They were confused about whether or not the man's work still warranted belief, especially since certain predictions seem not to have come true. Yes, a book about the 21st century, *written in the 21st century*, would provide a chance to take a fresh look at the man, his prophecies and his value to our own era.

And so, let's begin – starting even with an example of how the daily newspaper often offers new ways for us to see and interpret this man's mysterious talents and teachings.

INTRODUCTION

It was a startling headline and story in *The Virginian Pilot*, the newspaper for Virginia Beach, which was Edgar Cayce's hometown for the final 20 years of his life. "Earth's Declining Magnetic Field Could Be Sign of Shifting Poles," it warned ominously on July 13, 2004. Cayce had been dead for nearly 60 years, but one of his predictions quickly came to mind for anyone familiar with his work. The newspaper article then went on to describe the latest scientific concerns about what could well be the first stages of a dramatic reversal of the magnetic poles – something that last happened 780,000 years ago!

This news was bound to get the attention of those who had once been fascinated with Cayce's teachings, but perhaps in recent years had come to question the accuracy or relevance of what he had had to say during the 43 years in which he presented clairvoyant insights about hundreds of different subjects – dramatic earth changes being just one. But now a news story – front page, no less, and reported by newspapers and television worldwide – had the potential to rekindle interest in Cayce's prophecies for the 21st century and beyond.

In fact, only a few years ago – as we stood on the threshold of the new millennium – countless prophets and would-be-prophets warned of disasters and catastrophes. But then things predicted didn't take place. The Y2K computer glitch that never quite panned out. A pole shift of the Earth that never got around to happening. It finally began to seem like "much ado about nothing."

In some ways it had all been rather disappointing. For serious students of the Edgar Cayce predictions there were great expectations for the year 1998, as the culmination of a 40-year time of great change and testing. Other prophets had targeted 2000 or 2001. But looking back, one might feel duped. There was no sudden shift to a new age. And even now, there doesn't seem to be a whole lot more enlightenment in the world than there was, say, 10 years ago.

Maybe the problem isn't so much a matter of unreliable psychic information, but instead what it is we are looking for. It may well be that only by getting on this side of the years 1998 or 2001 that we can really begin to appreciate the prophetic work of a man like Cayce.

Now that we are free of the hype and the sensationalism of the end of a century and the end of a millennium, we can step back and really appreciate the teachings of this remarkable spiritual philosopher, mystic, and intuitive healer and we are likely to find an extraordinary picture of what life in the 21st century and beyond can be all about. In fact, we may even come to decide that Cayce's images and vision for life *after* 2001 is really much more important than anything he had to say about the decades we have just passed through.

To see the power of his message we need to consider two words that are related but different: "prediction" and "prophecy." This is a relationship that we will explore in more depth later in the book. But for now suffice it to say that predictions are statements about what is likely to happen in the future. The tone is that things are more or less set, and here is a sneak preview. On the other hand, a prophecy is more conditional. A prophecy indicates what *might* happen in the future, but it retains the sense that *the future is still in the process of formation*. And because the future is still fluid, we can still have an impact. In fact, that's the whole point of *biblical* prophecy: something dire may come to pass, but there is still time to change your ways and have things turn out different.

Prophecy therefore is empowering. It shows us the momentum that currently exists and where that momentum is likely to lead. At the same time, prophecy reminds us of our own free will and our own capacity to co-create conditions for the future. Edgar Cayce was a prophet and he was a predictor. Admittedly, there may even be times in this book where the two words seem to blend and become virtual synonyms. But we don't understand the depth and scope of Cayce's teachings unless we remember that he usually took that extra step beyond just predictor and became a prophet, that his philosophy was always intent on reminding us of who we are *and* of our inherent capacity to shape a positive future – for ourselves personally and for the planet collectively.

And so, yes, some of the statements that Cayce made in his psychic readings don't seem to have come true. There were events and conditions that he felt would manifest before the 21st century began, and some of them don't seem to have happened, especially certain earth changes. But we must keep some perspective here, especially if we want to be able to see how useful and influential his teachings can be for us in the 21st century. First of all, let's recognize that less than two-tenths of one percent of all his readings dealt with catastrophic earth changes. So what about the other 99-plus percent of his teachings, what did they tell us about the new world that we have in this new millennium? What's the very heart of Cayce's prophecies and what does it mean to us *today*?

Essentially Cayce had a very hopeful view of the world for beyond 1998 or 2001. And much of this book will focus exactly on that hopeful message – the teachings about how we can creatively shape a new culture for the 21st century, one that is based on our extraordinary inner faculties.

As we traverse together the timeline of history and stand on this side of the turn of a new millennium, here is what we can see and appreciate about the Cayce prophecies.

Ten essential themes stand out:

1. **A new form of medicine will emerge** – a kind of transformational healing – that is rooted in holism and deals with the body as an energy system. Each of us has a body, mind and spirit that interconnect. For healing to be complete and lasting, we will have a new kind of medicine that works toward the integration of all three elements. That means having not only physical treatments and procedures to promote healing for the body, but also having methods to transform attitudes and emotions, as well as disciplines to keep spiritual ideals and purposes clearly in focus. (Later in this Introduction we will look at one aspect of his health and healing predictions – longevity.)

2. **Intuition and psychic abilities will become the norm.** As Cayce envisioned it in one statement about the essence of "Aquarian Age consciousness," people of the future will have "the full consciousness of the ability to communicate with, or to be aware of, the relationships to the Creative Forces and the uses of same in material environs." (#1602-3) In generations to come, individuals will be able to have a personal and direct connection with the spiritual

world; and what's more, in ways that allow that connection to bring practical application into material life.

3. **Science and spirituality will cease to be antagonists.** The convergence of these two great streams in human history will transform culture. "Research" and "enlightenment" will become partners, making possible a science of the spiritual world *and* a new sense of sacredness to the material realm. Perhaps the most powerful way this will manifest in the new millennium is through individual seekers, rather than in sterile research labs. The science of consciousness can be carried out in our own homes. Chapters 8, 9, and 10 especially will outline the methods of consciousness-expansion that Cayce predicted would be the norm in the generations to come.

4. **Dramatic changes to the geography of the earth will take place**, including very significant changes in weather patterns. In fact, it may well be that what Cayce saw in many of his earth change prophecy readings, in regard to earthquakes and floods, may actually pertain to drastic changes in *weather* patterns to occur in the 21st century and beyond.

5. **There will come to pass on a worldwide scale a kind of social "leveling."** This is very likely to be a difficult, painful, and even violent process, but conditions cannot continue whereby "there [is] one measuring stick for the laborer in the field and the man behind the counter, and another for the man behind the money changers." (#3976-18)

6. **Leadership on the international scene will move to the Orient, and even to central China.** China will one day become the cradle of Christianity; and "civilization must wend its way westward - and again must Mongolia, must a hated people, be raised." (#3976-15)

7. **Archeological discoveries about ancient civilizations will radically alter our sense of human history**. What's more, these discoveries will show us the ways in which our ancient ancestors found ways to integrate science and spirituality.

8. **The continuity of life will be fully accepted as an indisputable fact.** There is no death – merely a transition from one state of consciousness to another. The fear of dying will be eradicated as a central human motivation.

9. **The principle of oneness will become paramount in human affairs.** The oneness of God will guide all religious traditions, the oneness of all energy will guide science, and the oneness of all

humanity will direct politics.

10. **Christ will reappear directly in earthly life.** The so-called "Second Coming" is perhaps a misnomer because the Christ Consciousness has never left us. Cayce envisions, however, the physical appearance of the soul who came two millennia ago as Jesus. No date is given, but the prophecy is found many times in the Cayce readings.

Taken as a group these ten prophetic themes are an inspiring vision of the purposeful world in which we live. And perhaps in many ways it is a good thing that the years 1958-1998 have come and gone without some of the dire predictions having been actualized. Now we have the chance to step back and get clearly in view a bigger picture of what Cayce prophesied for the new century and for centuries to come.

What's Ahead in This Book

Edgar Cayce's Predictions for the 21st Century is a careful examination of all the prophecies that Cayce made. Some were very far reaching. They spoke about the direction in which humanity will evolve, and clearly it is a matter of many decades (or even many centuries) to reach those conditions. Other prophetic statements were much more focused and even had short timelines. They were attempts to see what lay just ahead for people living in Cayce's own era. In those cases we already know whether the statements came true or not.

In some ways it might be tempting to skip over the "old prophecies" and have a book like this one deal exclusively with matters of the long timeframe view. But it's crucial to consider *all* of Cayce's prophecies. First, the comprehensive view allows us to see all the factors and dimensions that are a part of Cayce worldview. What's more, some of the "old prophecies" that don't seem to have come true *may yet* come to pass. Perhaps Cayce's timing was simply off. It's surely worth looking closely at the whole package, not just the direct and explicit hints and peeks he offers of the 21st century and beyond.

The upcoming chapters of our exploration are divided into three major sections or "Parts." Here is a description of the purpose for each Part and an overview of the chapter topics making up each one:

Part I, "Edgar Cayce As Visionary," is the portion of the book that addresses most directly the specific prophecies for change in the Cayce readings. Here we will look at how Cayce did his psychic work, and we will examine the details of what he said might happen in the latter part of the 20th century and into the 21st century. This section of the book will make only minimal reference to other prophets and futuristic traditions (an important aspect of this book, but largely confined to Part II). Within Part I are these two chapters:

Chapter 1, "Edgar Cayce: Visionary of the 21st Century and Beyond," takes a look at how Cayce gave psychic readings. The chapter starts with a reading given in 1936, offering some of the most dramatic prophecies ever to come from Cayce, including a possible view of life one hundred and fifty years from now, in the 22nd century. Chapter 1 also presents examples of Cayce's talent for prophecy, such as statements warning of the Great Depression, as well as World War II.

This initial chapter also explores the question of what it means to live in times of change. And, what is this "new age" that Cayce predicted really all about? It was a world-in-transition that Cayce said we would be living in. So, how do we respond to life when everything seems to be changing, how do keep from having circumstances pull us apart? Those questions will be central themes *throughout* the book, and they begin to come into focus here in Chapter 1.

Chapter 2, "Cayce's Prophecies of Earth Changes," looks at some of the most dramatic statements in the Cayce readings. They are his predictions for geophysical changes on a huge scale. But these statements by Cayce are some of the most often misquoted and misunderstood aspects of his work. In this chapter, we examine all of the earth change prophecies in the chronological order in which Cayce gave them.

Part II, "Prophecies of a World in Disorder," provides an overview of Cayce in comparison to many other prophetic traditions. Included in this Part is also the material that Cayce gave about a changing world, politically and spiritually. The three chapters of Part II are:

Chapter 3, "The Many Streams of Prophetic Wisdom" is a fascinating exploration of many other sources of prophetic tradition, including Nostradamus, some North and South American Indian Peoples, and another respected clairvoyant, Irene Hughes. As Cayce himself often indicated about education, we learn best by making comparisons and looking for correlations. There is much to be discovered in these highly respected prophecies that stand alongside Cayce's own.

Chapter 4, "A New World Order for the 21st Century," explores the Cayce prophecies about a tremendous shift in consciousness for humanity – something so different that it could be labeled as a new order of being or "root race" (a new "race," not in the sense of skin color, but instead in the level of awareness). This chapter also examines the prophecies concerning social change and the destiny of the nations – the so-called "World Affairs" prophecies – plus, Cayce's visions about health care in the 21st century and beyond.

Chapter 5, "Visions of Atlantis, Weather Changes, and the Second Coming" looks at other crucial parts of the Cayce prophecies. First we will explore the possibility that the hundreds of readings Cayce gave about Atlantis might not have been so much retrocognition (i.e., clairvoyant views of an unrecorded time in history) but instead *precognition* – prophecies about what may be in store for us in the 21st century and beyond.

Then we will examine the possibility that Cayce's earth change prophecies are best understood as events that may occur in the 21st century as the result of dramatic alterations in the weather. Climate change could trigger much of what he describes.

Finally, this chapter addresses Cayce's most profound prophecy: a Second Coming. Can we expect the Christ to return, even in our own lifetime? Cayce holds out this intriguing promise in some of his prophecies, but he always suggests certain contingencies (i.e., things that have to happen first). But maybe just as important as understanding these contingencies is the recognition that a "Second Coming" may not be quite what we expect. Rather than Jesus merely showing up on the Earth, perhaps it has more to do with new ways in which the Christ Spirit will be actually *lived* by people in the 21st

century and beyond.

Part III, "A Primer for Living in the 21st Century That Cayce Envisioned," is probably the most important part of this book, although most readers will have obtained this volume for reasons more closely linked to the two previous Parts. However, here in the final section of the book we get to the most essential aspect of the Cayce prophecies – namely, a new way of living on the Earth in the 21st century will create a revitalized, transformed planetary culture. It's the positive potential in all the Cayce prophecies. It's the hopeful message that we can take from this book. Although his visions of the future included difficult times for us – inwardly and outwardly – there was always a kind of optimism in his prophecies, a hopefulness that humanity will rise to the occasion and be renewed by these challenges.

This "primer" for living in the new millennium is made up of five chapters, each offering a piece of the fascinating mosaic found in the Cayce material. That "big picture" is an empowering description of exactly how we, as individuals, can go about helping to shape a new society for the Earth.

Chapter 6, "Understanding the Inner Shift of the 21st Century," is a chance to take a careful look at how Cayce's prophecies about earth changes are just as relevant to our *inner* lives as they might be to the *outer* world. What happens inside of us when society's most treasured values and assumptions no longer seem valid? How do we respond to the growing evidence of the need for a dramatic "paradigm shift?" The options will be clearly spelled out.

Chapter 7, "Cayce's Visions for Five Ancient Riddles," is like a handbook of Edgar Cayce's spiritual psychology for the 21st century. It takes five mysterious problems of the human condition and presents a fresh way in which we can live freely and creatively on the Earth. These riddles are problems with which humanity has struggled for millennia. And it is not to say that in the 21st century these ancient challenges will suddenly disappear. But Cayce's holistic psychology – a skillfull interweaving of body, mind and spirit – offers a new perspective on these old issues:

• The nature of time;

- The problem of good and evil;
- The question of how spirituality and healing can interface;
- The question of how we can really help someone else along the spiritual path;
- The question of what to do with anger and aggression.

Chapter 8, "A 21st Century Approach to Guidance and Decision-Making," focuses on our power to choose. Ultimately the kind of future we will have in the new millennium boils down to the results of lots of little choices made by billions of people. Just as free will is the key to individual soul-growth, so too is decision-making the key to the creation of a new planetary culture. We must learn how to use the spiritual gift of free will in a healthy, constructive manner. This chapter provides a theory from Cayce about free will, along with a practical, 9-step program for making a spiritually-directed decision. Without a doubt, it is one of the most important chapters of the book, particularly if we approach this book as a guide to creating the sort of world that Cayce's visions said is possible.

Chapter 9, "Spiritual 'Work' in the 21st Century," examines a practical issue. What does it mean to have purposeful vocation in the modern world? What's involved in actually living one's soul-purpose, one's mission in life? The second most frequently-requested type of reading from Cayce was a "life reading" (second only to the health readings in which clairvoyant medical diagnoses were offered). Those life readings were often a kind of "personal prophecy" for individuals. That is to say, rather than making predictions about coming earth changes or world events, Cayce used his clairvoyance to help the individual chart a personal course for the future – one that involved identifying a soul-purpose and then moving forward to *live* that mission. His strategies and approach as a spiritual psychologist in this way can be adapted and used by each one of us today, and this chapter provides the outline of exactly that process.

Chapter 10, "Meditation: The 21st Century Key to Powerful, Healthy Living," is a fitting final chapter. Without meditation, the habits and conditioning of our wounded personality selves take over – individually and collectively. Without meditation, the world of the 21st

century and beyond can look forward only to deep expressions of discord and suffering. But with the widespread growth of meditation as a daily discipline, the opportunity for planetary cooperation and transformation becomes a very real possibility. Unless we learn to meditate and practice it regularly, there is really little point to studying the other prophecies that Cayce presented.

And finally, *Chapter 11* entitled *"We Can Make A Difference,"* serves as a capstone to this book. It covers the most important prophecy of all. We will shape the future, and there is a specific way to understand exactly how that creative power can operate.

Taking a Deeper Look at Cayce: What That Means

As we move through the topics of these upcoming eleven chapters, it will mean looking deeply at Cayce's extensive teachings. But too easily, when we study the works of a man like Cayce, we end up wanting quick answers. It can all seem just too time consuming to wade through the vast amount of information. Especially in our modern, impatient era, we want the "bottom line solution" and prefer to skip over the more complicated, subtle or paradoxical answers that a man like Cayce often presented.

This pattern is particularly true when it comes to something complex like a look into the future. "What's ahead for us on this planet?" we wonder. And we'd like to get a straightforward answer – a direct prediction. But instead we often find Cayce speaking about probabilities or reminding us of the free will that determines much of what's in store for us – individually and collectively. Let's consider one example here in this Introduction, knowing that there will be many similar cases to be explored later in this book – many additional instances where a glimpse into the future requires us to look at ourselves holistically (body, mind and spirit) and to recognize how important our free will choices are going to be.

Consider this question, "In the 21st century and beyond, how old will people live to be – what will be the human life expectancy?" Medical researchers are now beginning to believe that by the mid-21st century, human life expectancy – for those people who have access to the best of medical care – will reach up to 150 years old. This bold prediction is reminiscent of statements by Cayce about longevity, suggesting life expectancies of 120 to 150 years. For example, to one person who asked how long he would live, Cayce replied, "To a hundred and fifty! If there is the turning." (#866-1). Another man was told by Cayce, "And if you set your life to be a hundred and twenty, you can live to be a hundred and twenty-one!" (#2533-6).

What are we to make of such a prospect? How many of us would even want to live that long? Breakthroughs in medical research – especially related to gene manipulation – may well be able to create a highly efficient body-machine that can live twice as long as today. But the fascinating prospect that "We can live to be 150 years old" may cause us to get too focused on the number "150" instead of the word "live." What's the quality of life that we are talking about when imagining such long lives? Do our efforts at life extension come from a fear of dying – i.e., that we want to put off the inevitable for as long as possible?

Consider that life extension is really a *three-way challenge*. There are physical, mental and spiritual components. If it were merely a question of how many years the body can be kept alive (unfortunately, the way that medical researchers may be thinking about it), then it's a one-dimensional matter – like a timeline that we find a way to make a little longer. And when we hear about prospects that we might live to be 150 – either in this lifetime or the next one – we probably think one-dimensionally at first: What would I do with all those extra years? Will I get bored?

Something changes, however, as soon as we introduce a bigger picture and look at the topic more holistically. Instead of a one-dimensional timeline getting longer, imagine instead a sphere (i.e., something with three spatial dimensions of height, width and depth) expanding into a much larger sphere. Now we have a model for life extension that is three-dimensional, with the additional components – the deepenings of our mental life and our spiritual life. Now we can explore what it would really mean to *live* with new parameters and expectations. The emphasis becomes the quality of life rather than the number of birthday anniversaries we pass before dying.

What would be the equivalent in the *mental* realm of doubling the physically body's longevity? In other words, what would be an equally dramatic extension in the arena of the mind? Perhaps the development of intuitive consciousness – interestingly, another of the ten prophetic themes for the 21st century. If we could more directly experience our connections with other people – empathetically and psychically – then it would profoundly alter the quality of our lives, maybe making the prospect of living to 150 seem more appealing than it does now.

Another possible expansion of life in the mental realm is a new understanding of death and dying. So much of our modern attitude and life-style revolves around our fear of death. Cayce suggests that the symbolic prophecies in the Great Pyramid, including an empty sarcophagus, point to the dawn of a new human consciousness that doesn't fear death: "That there will be no more death. Don't misunderstand or misinterpret! But the *interpretation* of death will be made plain." (#5748-6).

And then, what kind of *spiritual* expansion is possible for us by the mid-21st century that would make living to 150 years old be something to look forward to? Since Cayce's spiritual psychology so often links "values and ideals" to the spiritual dimension, let's consider what would make for a significant expansion that way. To paraphrase the Cayce adage "Don't just be good; be good *for* something," we might also say, "Don't just live a long time; live a long time because you are doing something *worthwhile for others*." Or, as the readings more bluntly remind us, "We are our brother's [and sister's] keeper." Even though we are not responsible "for" others, we are responsible "to" them.

With a spiritual value system based on that deep sense of purposefulness, we have a third kind of expansion; and now our sense of "life extension" takes on a much different meaning than just living longer and collecting social security to an older age. Now each incarnation becomes an even richer opportunity to experience what souls are here in the earth to do. This gives us a deeper and more accurate picture of one of the Cayce prophecies for our century and the centuries to come. We will want to approach many of the Cayce prophecies in this holistic way.

The Purpose Of This Book

Prophecies of human life expectancy are, of course, just one small example of how important it is to consider body, mind, *and* spirit as we study the material in Cayce's teachings. But that's what makes this man's work so fabulous. It never settles for superficial or simple answers. It requires that we holistically look at topics – and even more important, that we look at them in terms of *our own personal role in shaping our experiences.* We shouldn't just sit back and wait for the future to happen to us; we can be directly involved in its co-creation. That's the heart of "prophecy" at its best – an invitation to co-create.

The purpose of this book is to make a deep examination of exactly what Cayce said about the times in which we now live. The exploration is, of course, strengthened by considering parallel resources. And so, throughout the book, you will find comparisons to ancient prophetic traditions, as well as some of the most creative-thinking futurists of recent years. Consider just one example here in this Introduction. The ancient Mayans constructed calendars of extraordinary accuracy. And yet, from all indications, their projections about the destiny of the world don't extend past 2012 – or, some would argue, they had the sense that the world post-2012 was undeterminable and was left to what we would collectively choose to create. Although Cayce himself did not target 2012 for any specific event, there *will*, in fact, be an extraordinary astronomical event in 2012: a transit by Venus of the Sun. (That is to say, from the Earth's perspective, Venus will pass directly in front of the Sun.) These rare transits by Venus occur in pairs, and we recently experienced one in 2004. But after the one 2012, it will not happen again until 2117.

Some interpreters deduce great significance to this coincidence of the Mayan calendar ending in 2012 and the transit of our "sister planet" Venus with the Sun in the same year. They see it as an astronomical sign of the very kind of global transformation that Cayce spoke of in his prophecies.

And global transformation is the essence of the Cayce prophecies – a transformation that we have a role in helping to shape. This book can be read as a handbook for co-creating a future that Cayce and other great visionaries have seen as a very real and lively possibility for humanity in the 21st century. Some of the chapters will be informational; others will be directed more pragmatically towards things you can start doing in your life. It's even possible to read the chapters out of order, depending on where your strongest interests lie. But no matter how you approach the reading of this book, try to remember that it is only in *application* that these ideas come alive and make a difference.

PART I

EDGAR CAYCE AS VISIONARY

Edgar Cayce

Born: **March 18, 1877   3:03 p.m.**
Died: **January 03, 1945   7:15 p.m.**

CHAPTER ONE

EDGAR CAYCE AS VISIONARY OF THE 21ST CENTURY AND BEYOND

Edgar Cayce was America's most famous intuitive healer and mystic philosopher. And yet, for millions of people, it is not his holistic healing remedies or his practical methods for personal spirituality that make him noteworthy. Instead, it's his visions for the future.

If we look at Cayce's psychic work as a whole – 14,306 discourses given over a 43-year period – we find a central principle that links his ideas and philosophy of life. He felt that we should all feel honored to live in times like these. Being in a physical body at this special time in human history is a tremendous opportunity. Admittedly, there are many stresses that come from living in times when things are changing all around us. But if we can see past the obvious difficulties of living in uncertain times, then we can perceive what a wonderful moment in human history we now face.

Building on that central principle, Cayce also asserted time and time again that each one of us potentially can play a very constructive role in shaping the future that lies just ahead. A clairvoyant like Cayce can actually read only the trends and possibilities. What really unfolds as physical reality is largely the product of human choices and deeds. And it's our decisions and actions that will have a huge impact on the course of history, profoundly influencing the course of events for many generations to come.

So how do we respond to such a challenge? Are we ready to take responsibility for being among those who create a "new age," as Cayce sometimes called it? Here in the early years of a new millennium, can we muster enthusiasm for the task at hand? Can we get past some of the prophecies that sound dire, and by getting past them can we see the hopeful side of what Cayce and others have envisioned for the 21st century and beyond?

How Cayce Gave His Readings

As curious as the Cayce *information* often seems to be, some would say that the *process* through which it came was even more unusual. Cayce discovered by accident at the age of twenty-four that he had the remarkable ability to tap into wisdom from his own unconscious mind – and even beyond that to the unconscious minds of others and also to a universal mind, with virtually unlimited resources of knowledge and wisdom.

At first the process of giving a reading was via hypnosis. In fact, the Preface to Thomas Sugrue's biography of Cayce, *There Is A River*, begins with the words, "The story of Edgar Cayce properly belongs in the history of hypnosis." A curious illness had left the young man Edgar Cayce with chronic laryngitis, and it was only when a traveling stage hypnotist visited his hometown of Hopkinsville, Kentucky, that Cayce experienced once again the capacity to talk normally. Under hypnotic trance his voice – impaired for months – was mysteriously restored. But something even more remarkable ensued. Since the illness re-emerged once Cayce was out of the hypnotic trance, further sessions were tried, with more than one hypnotist. Eventually it was discovered that while he was hypnotized Cayce could do something far more significant than just talk in a normal voice: He could tap into sophisticated medical knowledge about his own condition and even recommend a strategy for how to effect a healing. What's more, when that strategy was employed, Edgar Cayce got well. His gift for medical clairvoyance had revealed itself, and it wasn't long before there were remarkable demonstrations that Cayce could give accurate medical diagnoses and effective treatment plans for other people's ailments, too. This gift was nurtured and developed, and Cayce discovered that he didn't even need a hypnotist to be present. Instead he could put himself into the altered state of consciousness from which these discourses – or psychic readings, as they came to be called – could be obtained.

For the first twenty years of his psychic work, Cayce gave only medical clairvoyance readings, and even then it was only part-time work, as he supported his family as a photographer. But in the 1920s his work began to expand, and he started to give other types of readings: mental and spiritual advice readings, dream interpretation readings, business guidance readings, and the so-called "life readings" which gave individuals a description of the purposes for the current lifetime and clairvoyant descriptions of past lifetimes.

Among those non-medical readings, this book is especially focused on Cayce's prophetic discourses. Usually those prophecy readings came in response to a direct request from an individual asking questions about the future, or from a group of Cayce supporters who were interested in getting discourses on matters of national and international concern (a series of readings that came to be called the "world affairs" readings). But occasionally Edgar Cayce's own curiosity about the future was the impetus for a prophetic reading to be given.

One excellent example is from June, 1936. It makes an especially appropriate starting point for our consideration of the Cayce prophecies, simply because in this reading Cayce looks farther into the future than he did in any other reading. His vision extends out to the year 2158.

First a little background about how this reading came to be. Like all of us, Cayce was a dreamer – not just visionary about the possibilities of what could be, but also a dreamer at night as he slept. And some of his most important psychic and spiritual experiences came through his own dreams. But one dream that had come some three months earlier had continued to haunt Cayce, even to the point that he felt it was necessary to ask for a reading in which this very dream could be interpreted by Cayce's own higher mind.

The context for this dream is particularly important. It had come to him on March 3, 1936 as he slept on a train bound from Detroit back to his home in Virginia Beach, Virginia. But this trip home was no triumphant return. The good work that he had intended to do in Detroit, giving readings to a variety of interested people, had turned out a disaster. On November 23, 1935 he had been arrested for practicing medicine without a license and even jailed briefly. When he was finally able to clear up his legal problems and head back to Virginia, he was deeply discouraged about this work. So much had gone wrong in the previous five years that it was hard to see much to be hopeful about. The Edgar Cayce Hospital suffered financial collapse. And the small educational institution he had co-founded, Atlantic University, had been closed. Now this humiliating arrest and jail time.

But suddenly on that train ride home, a dream comes to put all of these trying events into a bigger picture. The dreaming Cayce finds himself in the future. It is the 22nd century. Somehow he even knows that the year is 2158 and he has reincarnated, living in Nebraska. But it's not Nebraska as we know it today. Big changes have happened because Nebraska has seacoast. This is not the coastline of an inland sea, such as one of the Great Lakes. In the dream Cayce realizes, "the sea apparently covered all of the western part of the country, as the city where I lived was on the coast."

In this dream as a boy, he remembers his past life as Edgar Cayce and tells others about the memory. Perhaps reincarnation is taken more seriously in the Nebraska of the mid-22nd century than it is in the early part of the 21st. An investigation of his past life memory is initiated. "Scientists, men with long beards, little hair, and thick glasses, were called in to observe me." They decide to take him to some of the places that he remembers having lived in the late 19th century and early 20th Centuries – Kentucky, Alabama, New York, Michigan, and Virginia. They travel in a science fiction-like flying machine, long and cigar-shaped.

His extraordinary air trip in the dream gives him a bird's eye view of the world of 2158. Much of life has become decentralized, with industries scattered across the countryside. Homes look to be rather high-tech with their architecture fashioned of glass. The Norfolk/Virginia Beach area has grown immensely from the time Cayce lived there and is now a huge seaport.

But most dramatic are the destructive changes he sees. New York has been destroyed and is in the process of being rebuilt. It is not clear to him in the dream exactly how this destruction took place. Tremendous flooding has left large portions of Alabama now underwater.

Especially important to the dream was the success of this scientific investigation team. They locate the records of his work as Edgar Cayce in the 20th century. Apparently his readings have proven to be valuable over the generations. The team gathers the evidence about his previous lifetime and they all return to Nebraska.

We can imagine the bewilderment that Cayce no doubt experienced upon awakening from the dream. On that train headed back to Virginia, the recent traumas and discouraging events in Detroit still with him, what would he have interpreted all this to mean? Was this a precognitive dream – a prophetic dream – that had come as a warning? Was it merely the byproduct of his imagination, the fantasy of a mind that was disturbed, worried, and fearful about the future of his clairvoyant work?

Even after returning to Virginia Beach, the dream stayed in his thoughts, still a riddle in need of solution. Finally, it seemed best just to ask for an interpretation in a psychic reading.

On that June morning in 1936, Cayce's own superconscious mind – his own higher wisdom – offered an explanation of the dream. The interpretation was two-fold. First, the reading indicated that the dream was metaphorical. It had come as an experience to leave the dreaming Cayce with a feeling. The dream was to reassure him of the value of his work – "that there might be strength, there might be an understanding that though the moment may appear as dark..." In essence the dream was an indication that his clairvoyant work would have a lasting impact, that it would be remembered for centuries to come. And certainly at this very discouraging point in Cayce's career this would have been a welcome message.

But that day in the psychic reading, a second level of interpretation was also offered. This was a prophetic dream, too. "These changes in the earth will come to pass." This is certainly an extraordinary claim, if for no other reason than the extent of some changes depicted in the dream.

What could Cayce himself or any of us do about such a scary prospect? Near the end of the interpretation offered by this reading is a reminder to stay focused on today. "Do thy duty *today*! *Tomorrow* will care for itself."

Evidence of Cayce's Prophetic Powers

Perhaps Edgar Cayce should not have been too surprised by what came in that reading of 1936. There had been previous prophecy readings that hinted at some of these same themes, although none quite so explicit about what the world two hundred years into the future might look like.

But Cayce's own times were a period of turmoil. The 1930s and early 1940s were especially times of tremendous difficulty and upheaval. And Cayce's precognitive abilities had already been demonstrated in regard to some of those events. For example, he had foreseen the Stock Market crash, trying to help two of his closest supporters Edwin and Morton Blumenthal to protect their economic interests as successful brokers on the Exchange. In April, 1929, a reading given for Edwin had warned "there must surely come a break where it would be panic in the money centers – not only of Wall Street's activity but a closing of the boards in many centers ..." (#137-117). There could hardly have been a more detailed and accurate prediction than that one.

Just as dramatically Cayce predicted World War II. Speaking in a reading in October, 1935 (just a month before the ill-fated trip to Detroit), Cayce offered his vision of the catastrophes to come. Interestingly the prophecy is contained in an otherwise modest and unremarkable reading given to a 29-year-old man who worked as a freight agent and telegrapher (certainly an archaic profession from our early 21st century perspective!). But for whatever reason Cayce may have picked this man's reading to make his spectacular prophecy, it was certainly ominous. "This will make for the taking of sides, as it were, by various groups or countries or governments. This will be indicated by the Austrians, Germans, and later the Japanese joining in their influence.... For these will gradually make for a growing of animosities. And unless there is interference from what may be called by many the supernatural forces and influences that are active in the affairs of nations and peoples, the whole world, as it were, will be set on fire by the militaristic groups and those that are for power and expansion ..." (#416-7).

One noteworthy aspect of this prophecy concerns a theme to which we will return many times in this book. The intervention of higher forces can alter the course of events which otherwise have such a momentum that the results are inevitable. At first the principle sounds like all we can do is stand back and hope that the angels get involved. And perhaps that is one level of meaning to Cayce's statement. But in other readings we find that altering the course of events is within the domain also of *our own* "supernatural forces" – that is, our own co-creative powers that are activated especially by prayer and loving deeds. This is a subject to be explored later in this book. For now, we should note simply that Cayce's prophecy in October, 1935, seems to have very actually described exactly how human history was about to unfold. The man's clairvoyant and precognitive abilities seem undeniable, and all the more reason for us to carefully consider the other prophetic statements he made in the course of his life's work.

The Signs of Change in Our Own Times

It doesn't take a prophet to tell us that we live in the midst of unprecedented change. Just pick up a newspaper or news magazine and you won't have to look far to find yet another piece of evidence. The world is transforming faster than it ever has before.

The disturbing changes are all too familiar to all of us. The erosion of the nuclear family as the foundation of the society. The rise of technology as an ever more powerful force shaping the culture. The disruption of weather patterns and the widespread collapse of the ecosystem in many parts of the world.

Of course, not all the signs are bad. There continues to be an extraordinary expansion of holistic treatments for a wide variety of ailments. The Internet has helped create a kind of global village that more and more links us as one human family.

But perhaps most significant of all is the way in which people are changing inwardly. In spite of the many influences that tend to make us discouraged, confused, or fearful, nevertheless there is a growing audience for the message that Cayce championed in the 20th century and which has many spokespersons today: *We are each responsible for our own lives and we have the power to shape a positive future.*

A vision of my own has served for many years as a framework for how I view changing times. I have shared this dream in several previous workshop presentation and book publications, but it warrants repeating here.

It came to me years ago as a dream – one that was a response from my inner self to deep questioning I had about the world in which I found myself. I was discouraged; having lost the feelings of hope, promise and expectancy that had been mine earlier when I first read about a new millennium being born. In that initial encounter with the idea of an emergent new world, I had felt a sort of "mission" to be a contributor to its creation. And for many months, perhaps several years, I had carried inside me an enthusiasm and hope about a coming new planetary culture which I felt sure was just ahead. But now much of that feeling of promise and expectancy had dissipated. I was certainly still on the spiritual path as an individual, and even trying to help others around me with their growth. But the world in which I lived seemed just as deeply in the old ways and old values as ever before.

Despite the discouraging outward signs, I realized how much I missed the enthusiasm and expectancy I had once had. I began to pray regularly about my concern and asked that I might understand both what was going on in the world and what had been going on inside me. The dream that came soon thereafter has been a powerful image in my thinking ever since. Mine was not a vision of specific geographic changes as Edgar Cayce's 1936 prophetic dream had been. Instead it was a symbolic picture of how we as individuals may experience the changes of a new planetary culture.

In my dream I was aboard a commercial airline flight. Everything seemed to be going quite normally when suddenly there was an announcement over the loudspeaker. The pilot said that we were about to fly higher than a plane had ever flown before. We were asked to be sure our seat belts were pulled tightly. In the dream there was a tremendous amount of enthusiasm and excitement among all of the passengers (the same sort of excitement I had felt years earlier when I first read of Edgar Cayce's prophecies). I was pleased to have a window seat so that I could view what was going to happen. But as I looked out of the window for the next several minutes, it appeared that nothing changed. We seemed to continue to fly about five thousand feet above the ground. My fellow passengers began to mumble and complain, "What was he talking about? We aren't flying any higher than before."

Then, one of the passengers said he thought he knew what was going on: We were flying up the side of a mountain, staying about five thousand feet off the face of the mountain slope. He predicted, "I bet that soon we'll reach the top of the mountain, break free of it, and we'll see how far up we have really come." And sure enough, as I looked out of my window, the top of the mountain suddenly appeared, and I could see that we were *hundreds of thousands of feet* in the air! And then, the plane disappeared. We were flying by ourselves, and there was a tremendous feeling of exhilaration.

At the time I had this dream, it helped me to understand what might be going on in the world. And it has continued to serve as a potent metaphor to help me deal with the ever-present signs that the old world and the old ways of living are still very much with us. To have looked out the window of the plane and to have seen that we were still just five thousand feet off the ground is much the same experience as watching the evening news or reading the newspaper. The signs so strongly appear to be saying that we have not lifted consciousness in our culture in any significant way. The emergence of a new world order seems like a promise that is not going to be fulfilled.

But as in my dream, things are changing. Consciousness is being lifted, but in a way that is not always apparent. The time will likely come when we will suddenly see what inner progress and change has been going on. At that time we will need to become full participants in the changes that have happened. In a spiritual sense we will need to demonstrate our capacity to "fly" – that is, our ability to claim our creative powers and use them wisely.

The Inner Dynamics of Changing Times

It's natural to wonder, "Just how big of a change do these prophecies suggest?" Cayce indicates that the changes will be immense – on the scale, it sounds, of the beginnings of the Renaissance some five hundred years ago. But that change from the Middle Ages to the Renaissance – at least in Europe – was rather gradual, taking one hundred or perhaps even one hundred and fifty years. This time the transition may be in just a couple of generations. In a short time span the culture of the planet is likely to be altered. What an amazing and rather scary prospect.

So what exactly did Cayce foresee as the keys of how a "new age" or a "new millennium culture" would emerge for us? What is the inner dynamic that shapes how things are unfolding right before our eyes here in the first decade of the new millennium? Three characteristics stand out:

- The role played by bumping up against limits.
- The invisibility of much that characterizes the new culture.
- The role played by individuals.

Let's look at the three characteristics, one-by-one.

The first feature is *limits*. Whenever things begin to change, we confront barriers. Meeting new limits is a signpost to announce that change is coming. For example, each of us has encountered this principle (or we will some day) as our bodies grow older. It's dismaying to discover at age thirty that you can't short-change yourself on sleep the way you did in your college years. It's startling to realize upon entering middle age that you really do need to get bifocals. The list of examples related to physical health is nearly endless. And the same phenomenon can be observed in other parts of our lives. When a relationship is about to end or at least change significantly, the feeling is often one of having reached a wall or limit. The old way of relating doesn't seem to be working anymore. Whenever a phase in any part of our personal lives comes near an end, the existence of new barriers and obstacles comes into focus.

The same process happens on a broader scale. In readings given for thousands of people, Cayce described how our society is being challenged to change. And with the dimming of the familiar and traditional ways of our culture, there comes the experience of *limits.*

Here in the first years of the 21st century, we are experiencing the limits of physical consciousness. Like an embryonic chick straining against the confines of the egg's shell, our culture is pressing against the boundaries of the old world ways. To transcend those limits will be a birth into something new for humanity.

In these days of testing and confusing changes, we find ourselves to be time-bound. Our lives are too full of things that have to be done right away. We're often frustrated that we can't give the needed attention to produce the quality results of which we're capable. Our society is also experiencing at a mass level the condition of being energy-bound. For example, America is dependent upon imported petroleum, and once every decade or so an international crisis makes us painfully aware of how hemmed in we are by this situation.

What's more, as we confront the limits of physical consciousness, we find the most significant boundary: feeling power-bound. Frequently people feel powerless to do anything to solve chronic problems – whether it's AIDS, violent crime, the frequency of hurricanes, the threat of inflation, the rising incidence of divorce, or other difficulties facing us.

A second feature of the emerging millennium is that paradoxically *it's invisable and it's already here.* At a deep level, the essential problem of our times is that we are living in a new world with old world rules. Technology has already made us one world. Because of nuclear weapons, global warfare is unthinkable. Because of international trade in the raw materials needed for industry, worldwide cooperation is already a necessity. And because of communications breakthroughs (such as satellite relay stations and the Internet), we can no longer claim ignorance of what's happening for any failure on our part to help our troubled brothers and sisters in other parts of the world. In this sense we can honestly say that a new planetary culture has already arrived.

However, the world is still being run with the same procedures and ideals as in the past hundreds of years. Feelings of national (or even regional) pride and sovereignty are stronger than feelings of global family. And things won't work well this way. We cannot play a new game with old rules. And the new game is already upon us.

This leads to a third feature of the emerging millennium: *the power of individuals to change the world.* Humanity faces a decision now that the calendar has changed over to the 21st century. It is a choice of whether or not to allow *the spirit of oneness* to guide human affairs throughout the globe. Cayce emphatically emphasized time after time that the great decision would be made up of millions of little decisions by everyday people doing everyday tasks and meeting commonplace problems. By what rules will we choose to live in the new planetary culture now emerging? What will be our ideals and intentions toward each other?

The jury is still out on these questions. Much of the stress we call living in times of change is created by this tension. A new kind of world is already here, but it's still not clear what rules for living and relating to each other we are going to choose.

Edgar Cayce's Definitions of a New Age

One principle runs like a thread through the entire body of Cayce's psychic work: It's a great privilege to be alive in these times at the start of the 21st century and a new millennium. As stressful and difficult as changing times invariably will be, this is an extraordinary moment in human history. Collectively we stand on the threshold of a wonderful opportunity. Each of us has a chance to have a significant effect that will profoundly influence the human family and planet Earth for generations, even centuries, to come.

Although Cayce himself used this phrase only infrequently, we have the chance to move into a "new age." The switch to such a new era is at least as great as the transition five hundred years ago as the Middle Ages faded away and the Renaissance began. It's a privilege to live in these years right before and right after the turn of the millennium because it coincides with a possible transformation of planetary culture. And in his thousands of readings to ordinary and extraordinary people, Cayce documented his philosophy for living in a world going through radical transitions.

The term "new age" is a phrase that has taken on a somewhat derogatory connotation in recent years because of a linkage to a flighty, ungrounded attitude toward life. But this is hardly what Cayce meant when he used the term. Instead he envisioned a renewed planetary culture with individuals deeply grounded in a moral and spiritual vision of life on earth.

The most detailed and specific instance in which Cayce defined the coming new world was in 1939 for a forty-one-year-old woman (#1602-3 in the Cayce files). She was a student of ancient mystical traditions and asked Cayce to comment on prophecies of a 17th century German seer named Jacob Boehme (pronounced Ber-ma). Boehme was, among other things, an expert on astrology and felt that significant changes would come in the late 20th century when the sun moved from Pisces to Aquarius in its 24,000 year progression through the signs of the zodiac. One change would be the reappearance of the legendary lost continent of Atlantis.

Among other questions, the woman wondered specifically when we might expect to see Atlantis. Cayce didn't speak directly to her question about Atlantis. Instead, he spoke in general terms of coming changes on a global scale, and he identified 1998 as the key year of transition. (This particular reading was not one in which Cayce offered details about the land masses or the people to be most directly affected by the changes.) On multiple occasions in this prophecy he emphasized that the coming changes would be gradual ones and "not a cataclysmic activity in the experience of the earth in this period."

In two further questions submitted by this woman for the same reading, she asked about the significance of an Age of Aquarius. What would it mean in regard to the physical, mental and spiritual development of humanity? And more specifically, why had one mystic referred to this coming era as the "Age of the Lily"?

There was no simple answer to this kind of question, Cayce began. It would be a growing and unfolding matter. But to understand the kind of awareness that it would bring, we must start by looking back at the previous age – the Piscean era. Near the beginning of that age, Christ came. He demonstrated the capacity of a single individual to live in communication with the Creator and to follow a Higher Will. The promise was that in times to come each of us might begin to exhibit a similar consciousness. By understanding the meaning of Christ's coming 2,000 years ago, we have a clue to the opportunity that now emerges in an Aquarian Age. In essence, human consciousness during the coming age can develop in a way that Cayce described as "the full consciousness of the ability to communicate with or to be aware of the relationships to the Creative Forces and the uses of same in material environs." But a warning comes with this development – or it should be said redevelopment, because in ancient times humans had similar abilities to draw upon the invisible Creative Forces. For example, Cayce states that the prehistoric civilization of Atlantis brought destruction upon itself because those powers were used willfully and selfishly.

Cayce's answer about what it would be like to live in a new world doesn't describe a physical life-style; it defines the kind of consciousness we would have: a full awareness of our ability to communicate with God and with our own higher selves, and the ability to use these higher vibrational expressions of energy in our material lives. We can well imagine the commonplace use of ESP, psychic and spiritual healing, meditation and the like. However, the warning must stay in the backs of our minds. We might just as easily fall prey to the temptations to misuse these heightened powers.

Cayce continued his prophecy about the birth of the new millennium with this crucial pronouncement: Many people will be unaware of what is really going on during this period of transition. Those who understand the meaning of these times will be the people who are willing to accept the idea that there is an invisible spiritual world. These individuals will recognize the reality of Creative Forces – that is, our Divine Creator. They will see how it is possible to make a direct personal connection with those Forces and make use of them purposefully in material life. What's more, a good place for any of us to start making that discovery is to become sensitive to the vibratory influences that subtly exist between one person and another.

Apparently in these times of change there are likely to be many confused people. Only those individuals who are willing to think in terms of the reality of the psychic and spiritual realms will be aware of and understand what is going on in the world around them. In these times of mass confusion and disorientation, they have a great responsibility. Having at least some understanding of the purposes of what is unfolding, they must share this insight in a form that would make sense of these events for other people.

In the final set of prophetic statements made in this reading, Cayce addressed the issue of why this new millennium might be characterized as the "Age of the Lily" and the timing of its arrival. His answer concerning the lily was simple and elegant. The lily is a symbol of purity. That's what it will take for any of us to achieve the consciousness that humanity is destined to attain during the Aquarian Age. Purity of body. Purity of mind and purpose.

In regard to timing, Cayce predicted that we could best understand what was soon to come as a gradual transition. There would be years in which the influences of this coming new planetary culture would begin to affect human affairs, but there would be a lapping over from the previous era into the new one. One key date, however, was proposed: 1998. This will be the year when "we will begin to understand fully."

This set of prophecies given in 1939 beautifully summarizes the Cayce vision of the new millennium. First, it must be a time of greater purity. To be builders of a new world order, we will have to cleanse our bodies as well as our emotional and thinking processes. Most crucially, our purposes will need to be pure. And then, what is required of us is patience. In spite of calendar dates that artificially define a new era to have come, Cayce suggests that there will be a phasing out of the old and a gradual emergence of this new planetary culture. To his prophetic vision, the year 1998 was to be every bit as significant as 2000 or 2001. According to this visionary timetable we were to expect that times of change will extend well into the twenty-first century. What was to particularly characterize the period up to 1998 was the confusion and lack of understanding about these changing times, surely something that, in fact, took place.

When Will the Big Changes Come?

The question of timing is always a problem with predictions. It's not only a matter of *what* will happen but also *when*. Some people have grown tired of waiting for the fulfillment of predictions about major world changes. They got their hopes up, believing that tremendous changes were just around the corner, only to get up morning after morning to the same old world. For them, additional information about prophecies is like the story of "The Boy Who Cried 'Wolf'" They don't want to be tricked yet again. How long *will* it be until we see signs of a new consciousness directing human affairs?

The old systems and the old consciousness won't keep on working indefinitely, simply because they sow too many seeds of their own undoing. Some type of major change must be just ahead, and there are four basic scenarios for how a new age could emerge out of the present state of our world.

The first hypothesis is a grim one. It suggests that things will have to get much worse before people will be willing to work together to build something better. This theory presupposes a sort of Dark Ages that would precede renewal. Books like *1984* and *Brave New World* could be included in this first category of scenarios, with their frightful images of modern, technological ideals carried to their absurd and freedom-destroying ultimate.

A second theory is that a spiritually refocused new age society will emerge relatively soon – at least by the early decades of the 21st century. This scenario is anti-technology and supposes that soon the world will clearly see how a consumer-based culture doesn't work. It predicts that we will turn to a more contemplative alternative which features the individual in harmony with nature and a suspension of scientific development until the spiritual development in humans can catch up.

A third story also imagines that a new age is coming very soon, but this version is pro-technology. It suggests that science is going to discover what religion has been asking us to accept on faith. Through science we will find evidence for life after death, for psychic healing and for the value of meditation. There will be a wedding of science and religion, which will move us into a new world order. This version predicts that the scientific technological establishment will still be running the world in the 21st century, but it will be with new, spiritual values, the rightness of which has been proven.

A fourth theory suggests that it is still hundreds of years away. In this scenario the transition is very gradual. Each generation will make a little more progress. It rests on the assumption that a new age can come only as a reflection of changes in human thinking and ideals, and it points out that humans are slow to change. According to this fourth hypothesis, the seeds are being planted right now, but it will take many generations for these new values to flower in humanity as a whole.

Proponents of each of the theories feel that they can find something in the Cayce prophecies to support their positions. Since Cayce's death in 1945 the majority of those who have studied his predictions feel that the anti-technology theory is most likely. A new age is coming early in this new millennium, and severe earth changes will be the trigger as they undermine our smug overconfidence in human technological prowess. The Earth itself will shake our pride and, forcing us to our knees, will make us look for a better way to live on this planet.

However, the majority interpretation does not always prove to be the one that's true. We shouldn't be too quick to dismiss the idea that a new age may be hundreds of years away – at least in the sense of a new age in which all humanity participates. Individuals or groups could enter a new type of consciousness and life-style even now, and for them it will be as if a new age is here. But more broadly speaking, humanity must eventually travel *together* in spiritual evolution.

For right now the question of timing cannot be answered. Each of us must decide personally how we will take these prophecies. We must develop for ourselves a perspective of how we build a new world. Are we "sprinters" racing now in the 21st century and the start of a new millennium; or are we "long-distance runners" who believe that in this lifetime we may not see the fruits of all we are trying to accomplish? Maybe we can find in the history books certain lessons that show us how humanity passes through major cultural transformation. If we look back at some of the great transition times for humanity, we can see a variety of examples.

One contrast is between the first century A.D. and the

conclusion of the Middle Ages. Will our own times of change be more like the years A.D. 30 to A.D. 90, or will it be more like the years 1490 to 1550? The first is the period of Christ's ministry and the formation of the early Christian Church. The second period was the time of a flowering Renaissance. Looking at the secular history of the world from A.D. 30 to A.D. 90, it appears that nothing of great importance happened. The Romans merely consolidated their hold on all of the known Western world. Seen from this point of view, these sixty years were not particularly times of great transformation and change. However, we can look back on those years from another perspective and see that they really were the beginning of a new age. A relatively small group of people went through a quantum jump in consciousness. However, it took hundreds of years for that experience to be recognized and accepted by the mainstream culture in which they lived.

Is this what is happening in our own time? Perhaps once again a relatively small group of people is going through a different but equally important quantum jump in the evolution of consciousness. This time it may be hundreds of thousands of people, whereas in the first century it was only thousands. But the pattern may be the same: it may take many years for society as a whole to be affected.

However, this isn't the only pattern for changing times. It may be that our lives more closely parallel the lives of those who lived in the years 1490 to 1550. In those years, there were dramatic transformations that in many ways are reminiscent of our times. As Columbus went to America, we are going into space and below the sea. As in the Reformation, spirituality is being transformed as we are finding ways to combine the best of Eastern and Western religions. At the end of that sixty-year period, an entirely new social system was in place in Europe. The Middle Ages were over and the Renaissance was in full swing. Perhaps there will be an equally dramatic shift for us now that we have crossed over into the 21st century.

We are left to decide which of these two historical times of change is the better model for what we feel is happening in the world now in the initial years of the 21st century. We should be keen observers of inner and outer change. Of course, it can be argued that since the soul is eternal, then timing is not that important. Whether a new age comes in twenty years or two hundred does not make that much difference in the cosmic scheme of things. Nevertheless, the building of a new world requires choice and action. *The personal strategy we follow as individuals in making our contribution is largely affected by what we expect,* by the type of changing times in which we believe we live. Reading this book and learning the details of the Cayce prophecies should help you decide what you believe.

CHAPTER TWO

CAYCE'S PROPHECIES
OF EARTH CHANGES

Some would say that Cayce's predictions of earthquakes, volcanoes, and other natural disasters are now – in the early 21st century – largely irrelevant. The year 1998 has come and gone, and the kinds of changes Cayce suggested might happen by 1998 have not come to pass. And yet, when we look closely at the Cayce prophecies, it's evident that he was forecasting likelihoods, probabilities and options, rather than events that were somehow fixed on a certain date or predetermined.

In many ways the readings that Cayce gave on earth changes have done more to popularize his name than any other part of his work. There is without doubt a sensational quality to the idea of California going into the sea or a once dormant volcano reawakening with a fury. It's the kind of sensational material that sells magazine articles and books. It often seems a shame that so many people know of Edgar Cayce in terms of his visions of a possible earth catastrophe, rather than for his quiet, humble work of helping individuals with physical healing or finding deeper purpose in life.

Perhaps because of the dramatic quality of these few readings on earth changes, they have been frequently misstated and misinterpreted. Perhaps it's fear that causes a person (even unconsciously) to alter slightly one of Cayce's prophecies. Or perhaps there are those who are so frustrated with the way our world is run that they take pleasure in misrepresenting Cayce's prophecies, which suggest widespread destruction. A truly outlandish example of such sensationalism took place in December 1994 when the tabloid newspaper *Weekly World News* ran on its cover a picture of Edgar Cayce and the headline "Secret Predictions of America's Greatest Prophet." It went on to claim that in 1945 Cayce recorded in his personal diary a list of never-before-published prophecies. The only problem with this claim is that Cayce ceased giving readings in 1944 and died on January 3, 1945. The bogus list includes ominous statements, completely disconnected from the authentic Cayce prophecies.

Which Cayce Readings Addressed Earth Changes?

In studying the details of the Cayce prophecies, we should keep in mind that the two dozen psychic readings that produced specific earth change predictions are only *two-tenths of one percent* of all the readings he gave in his forty-three-year career! The other readings – more than fourteen thousand of them – were for people with health problems, individuals looking for greater purpose in life, and those seeking spiritual guidance. Even though the vast majority of the Cayce readings don't directly concern earth changes, most of them do *indirectly*. How can this be?

Many of the people getting these readings were starting to feel the strains and ambiguities of a world of accelerating change. Sometimes their health problems were principally stress-induced. Often their confusion about finding meaningful work was the result of a world already beginning to change dramatically. Frequently their spiritual disorientation was due to the same moral dilemmas and ethical challenges that we experience so acutely today.

The more than ninety-nine percent of Cayce's work that some people have dismissed as irrelevant to the Cayce prophecies is, in fact, a part of the whole picture. It contains his world view, and it provides a backdrop against which we can see and understand the more sensational predictions. To look *exclusively* at those two dozen readings that mention earthquakes, volcanoes, and tidal waves would be to miss the grander portrait that Cayce has painted about the transition into a new millennium. When we examine the Cayce teachings as a whole, then we discover the great purposefulness that stands behind the earth changes that may be coming.

The Cayce prophecies can help us shape our beliefs about the future. But for them to be most effective in doing this, we've got to look at the *whole* of what he stated about changing times. Too often there have been *pieces* of predictions published or quoted in lectures. These fragments can easily create a distorted picture, sometimes serving to stimulate fear. Probably no other portion of the Edgar Cayce material has been more misquoted and misunderstood than his statements about the land mass changes that might accompany the beginning of a new millennium. As already noted, when compared to the immense volume of readings he gave, these predictions of earthquakes, volcanoes and tidal waves are almost insignificant in number. And yet, no other readings have had such an impact on the thinking of people who are familiar with his work.

These particular readings are so easily misunderstood because they are often studied improperly and, to make matters worse, are frequently quoted out of context. Rarely does one see a *chronological* examination of what he said on this topic. In the few instances in which timing has been considered, the prophecies are presented in the order in which we can expect to see them materialize; for example, predictions about the year 1936 before predictions about the years 1958 to 1998. However, what if Cayce gave some of his prophecies about 1936 after he gave the ones for 1958 to 1998? If we are really to experience prophecy as an unfolding, dynamic phenomenon, then the best study would be to recreate for ourselves what it would have been like to be with Edgar Cayce between 1926 and 1944 and *to hear these predictions being made and sometimes changing over the years.* I first published this chronological study of the Cayce earth change prophecies in 1981. It's as valuable now as it was then, and it's reprinted here in the section which follows.

The majority of the Cayce prophecies have not yet proved to be right or wrong. The predictions yet to be fulfilled fall into two primary categories: geophysical earth changes and political/economic prophecies. This chapter will consider each prediction of geophysical change. The prophecies concerning social change and the destiny of the nations will be addressed in the fourth chapter, "A New World Order for the 21st Century."

A Chronological Study of the Earth Change Predictions

Our examination of the earth changes readings in the sequence given by Cayce begins with the year 1926. Before this date we find no reference to major geological upheaval. In other words, Cayce had been giving readings for more than twenty years before this topic even came up!

In 1926 a man in his early forties asked Cayce for a series of readings on the topic of long-range weather forecasting. At the end of the second reading (#195-32), Cayce offered some additional information on weather conditions and the effects they would soon have. He noted that there was a close relationship between these climatic conditions and human affairs. Astrological influences would also play a role. There would be a particularly strong sway by Jupiter and Uranus for a six-day period between October 15 and 20. Significant changes could be expected then. These changes would be seen in the minds and the deeds of individuals and on a global level. Some of the changes would be constructive; others, destructive.

But Cayce seemed to envision things that were bound to go beyond just this six-day period: In human affairs unusual conditions would arise. They would be felt in religion, politics, and the social dimension of life – especially in regard to morals and values. Then he cited one example: Prohibition (i.e., regarding the sale of alcoholic beverages) would be overturned in America.

In the final part of this prophecy he turns his attention back to the weather and adds certain geological predictions: Several violent windstorms will be seen soon. And there will be two earthquakes, one in southern California and the other in Japan. Tidal waves will follow the Japanese one, with one especially affecting islands to the south of Japan.

This 1926 prediction about Prohibition was fulfilled. Congress had approved the laws banning alcohol in 1919. Historians point to a date somewhat after 1926 when a ground swell of public opinion began to move against Prohibition. It was 1933 before the laws were repealed, but Cayce had accurately perceived this coming shift in the moral attitude of Americans.

What do the records show about the accuracy of the rest of these predictions? They're not very supportive. This 1926 prophecy must be viewed as essentially one that failed to materialize – or at least the earth changes portions of it. There was no significant earthquake or tidal wave in Japan on those dates. A moderate quake hit California on October 22, 1926 (two days beyond the predicted dates). However, it was hardly of the magnitude that we might have expected, considering the fact that Cayce had gone out of his way to bring it up. Earthquakes of equal intensity were happening about every two months in California; there were quakes of about the same strength on July 25, 1926, and January 1, 1927.

After the 1926 reading, *six years* pass before we again find someone asking Cayce about earth changes. In 1932 a thirty-year-old man questioned him carefully about the details of what might happen if severe geological changes were to take place. Cayce gave him three separate earth change readings in 1932, spaced about four months apart. Among these readings are some interesting predictions about the order in which events are to take place.

First, Cayce indicated certain signs to watch for which would signal the beginning of the times of great earth change activity. One indicator would be the breaking up of lands in the South Pacific. He states that the changes here could include either sinking or rising. This suggests that we should watch either for island areas hit by earthquakes causing permanent inundation or for geological shifts that cause South Pacific land areas to rise even higher above sea level. Another signal event named by Cayce is to take place at a spot almost exactly opposite on the globe, in the Mediterranean Sea, possibly an eruption of Mt. Etna (on the island of Sicily). When asked when to expect such indicators, Cayce answered that seen from one perspective, these signs had already begun. However, it would likely be 1936 when such changes would be clearly apparent.

Then he was asked whether this would trigger earth changes that would affect North America. His answer was a clear warning of the possibility of severe destruction. All over the country there might come minor and major shifts. But directly targeted was the North Atlantic seaboard, with New York and Connecticut specifically named.

The man who received these readings apparently had a strong personal interest in the fate of Alabama because he asked directly about this area. Cayce predicted that there would be changes there, affecting the northwestern and the extreme southwestern parts of the state, but not until after the ones he had previously described. The timetable he suggested was between 1936 and 1938; however, he made it clear that the changes would be gradual rather than sudden.

Finally, the questioner asked about Norfolk, Virginia, and its vicinity (Cayce's own home area). The prophecy was that changes would come to this area, too, but those were much farther away – some twenty years after the ones he foresaw for the North Atlantic seaboard and for Alabama.

We're left to wonder how we should take this set of predictions. Obviously, nothing of the scope he mentioned here in 1932 took place in the period from 1936 to 1938. Has the timing simply been delayed? Does the warning sign related to the South Pacific and Mt. Etna still hold? Most scholars of the Cayce material take the position that Cayce was able to see specific, interconnecting conditions beneath the earth's surface; and even if the timing was wrong, the same series of warning events is still relevant.

In the next important series of predictions, Cayce became even more specific. These readings, from early 1933 through 1936, were given to a man in his late forties who lived in San Francisco. There is a strong sense of the unfolding, dynamic quality of prophecy in these passages. The predictions start to change as the months go by and Cayce is asked repeatedly about the fate of San Francisco.

Cayce began in February 1933 sounding quite sure that in 1936 there would be a major destruction of San Francisco. He couldn't have been more blunt. When asked to compare this coming quake to the famous one in 1906, he said, "This'll be a baby beside what it'll be in '36!" (#270-30).

By mid-1934 he was less inclined to specify dates. The same questioner had come back and wanted more details about 1936 (#270-32). He wondered if the predicted earth changes were so fixed and predetermined that Cayce could clairvoyantly describe the Pacific coastline of America after the earthquakes. Now Cayce seemed to back away from any specific chronology, while still affirming that earthquakes in this area were due and that it was written in the cosmic scheme of things that they would happen at some point.

But even more significant, Cayce stated that what was to transpire depended upon the attitudes of individuals and groups – something so important to Cayce's prophecies about changing times that we'll look at it much more closely later in this book. Of course, this is a radical idea that has no place in mainstream geology.

The notion that human psychology or daily behavior (short of rash acts such as detonating underground nuclear explosions) could affect earthquakes seems like nonsense to the typical earth scientist.

By June 1936, he had backed away from his San Francisco prediction for that year, stating that he no longer saw any great material damage coming to that city for the coming year. However, he went on to predict that there would be some major earthquake activity in areas to the east and to the south of San Francisco, places where there had not been previous damage.

He then went on to give more details about the factors that affect earthquakes. In addition to the obvious geological ingredients (internal movements of the earth) and to the more esoteric influence of people's thoughts and deeds, he added something else: astrological influences. He asserted that earth changes are impelled at least partially by planets and stars in relationship to the earth.

Next came one of his most famous prophecies concerning the West Coast of America, of a warning sign for which people could be alert. Significant eruptions at one of two volcanoes would be the sign – either Mt. Vesuvius on the island of Sicily or Mt. Pelee on the island of Martinique in the West Indies. If either were to take place, then *within three* months severe flooding would be widespread as a result of major earthquakes. The areas specifically mentioned were the southern coast of California plus the areas between Salt Lake and the southern portions of Nevada.

Much has been made of this prediction in the decades since it was given. Stretching the truth of the matter, some people have claimed that Cayce predicted California "falling into the ocean." Various coastline maps purported to be based on the Cayce predictions show the vast amounts of North America gone, with the Pacific coming in to Utah or even farther east.

What's more, there has been considerable misunderstanding about the warning. The reading clearly predicts that the major flooding would occur within three months of the eruption. It does not say, as many have misquoted, that once Mt. Vesuvius or Mt. Pelee erupts in a major way, then California residents have a three-month safety or grace period in which to sell their houses and get out!

Finally, the series of earth change predictions from June 1936 concludes with this prophecy: there will be greater seismic upheavals in the Southern Hemisphere than in the Northern. Earlier predictions indicated that the earth changes would be a *worldwide* phenomenon – not just something confined to America. Because many more specific references to catastrophic changes point to America than to other countries, some people have mistakenly believed that Cayce predicted America would be hardest hit. Others have gone so far as to believe that Cayce implicitly suggested that America is especially deserving of punishment. However, this unambiguous prophecy about the Southern

Hemisphere puts that mistaken notion to rest. In fact, there is a more plausible and very simple reason that the majority of Cayce's predictions concerned changes occurring in America. The people receiving the readings were most often Americans and were naturally more inclined to ask about their own part of the world. People from Alabama worried about what would happen to Alabama; people from San Francisco, about that city. Cayce generally met people at the level of their own concerns, so naturally we have a majority of predictions about earthquakes and flooding in America. But this frequency shouldn't give us a distorted view of his vision of the global scope of these changes.

In fact, the most international of the prophecies was given in 1934 – in one of the so-called world affairs readings. These were readings given about political, economic and sociological factors for the world as a whole. Some of Cayce's most important prophecies are found in this series – both prophecies about earthquakes and predictions about changing human affairs.

In January 1934, Cayce gave the fifteenth reading in this series (#3976-15). Here he made it clear that the coming earth changes would be spread throughout the world. In fact, this set of earth change prophecies has become the most often quoted portion among all his predictions. In this set of visionary statements he was clearly speaking about a forty-year time span between 1958 and 1998 as marking the beginning of the changes he listed. This point has often been missed in articles and books about Cayce's prophecies. The readings do not say that all of the changes will be accomplished by 1998, rather that the forty years ending in 1998 encompass the beginning of major global upheavals. *We might well expect them to continue into the 21st century.* Here are the specific predictions for world changes prophesied to commence in the forty years between 1958 and 1998:

1. There will be a breaking up of the land mass of the western portion of America.
2. The larger part of Japan will go into the sea.
3. There will be certain changes to the northern parts of Europe that will happen so quickly that it might be called "in the twinkling of an eye."
4. Lands will rise up out of the Atlantic Ocean off the east coast of America.

5. Major upheavals will hit the Arctic and Antarctica.
6. Volcanoes will erupt, especially in the tropics.
7. A shifting of the poles will alter climatic conditions. For example, certain frigid and semitropical areas will become tropical.

In that same reading he was asked more specifically to make predictions for world changes that very year – 1934. Although he clearly missed the mark with many of the statements, many scholars of Cayce's work agree with parapsychologists who point out that precognition (or prophecy) is the most difficult form of psychic ability. Predictions require the seer to operate in a dimension of consciousness that is beyond the normal constraints of time and space, but then to articulate his visions in terms of a specific time frame. We'll address later some of the factors that may have come into play when Cayce's prophecies failed to materialize by the date he stated. For now, let's consider these prophecies from reading #5749-15, even though they may not have happened when Cayce said they were most likely to take place.

1. Open waters will appear in the northern portion of Greenland, presumably another effect of climatic alterations.
2. The new lands arising from the Atlantic will more specifically be located in the Caribbean Sea area.
3. South America will be "shaken from the uppermost portion to the end."
4. In the Antarctic region, new land will arise off Tierra del Fuego.

Several of these earth change predictions seem to relate directly to Cayce's vision of a pole shift. This is a frightening notion if it's taken at face value. The destruction that might come from a shift in the rotational axis of the earth would be immense. Of course, some interpreters of the Cayce prophecies have suggested that his visions were in this case symbolic or metaphorical references to worldwide humanity getting a new orientation or set of values. But the fact remains that the pole shift prophecy, given more than once by Cayce, is stated as a literal event to come. And in one prophetic reading he offers a specific time frame that has *not* come to pass because his target dates have come and gone. When asked what changes would happen in 2000 or 2001, he answered, "There is a shifting of the pole. Or a new cycle begins" (#826-8).

Two final readings in our chronological sequence are especially significant. Both were given in the later years of Cayce's work. The first, given in 1939, was mentioned earlier. A woman who had studied the three-hundred-year-old prophecies of Jacob Boehme asked Cayce to comment on what was coming. Cayce's prophetic reading for her contains important statements concerning the intensity of the changes as we move into the 21st century:

1. In 1998 we will find a great deal of activity that has been created by the gradual changes that are coming about.
2. As to the changes, the change between the Piscean and the Aquarian Age is a gradual, not a cataclysmic one.

So this gives a somewhat different angle on the future than some of the other Cayce prophecies may have implied. This set of predictions – *among the last ones given by Cayce* – minimize the likelihood of a cataclysmic future. Instead, these prophecies, offered in 1939, present the image of an earth that will undergo gradual alterations. Rather than an apocalyptic transition from the so-called Piscean age to an Aquarian era, possibilities exist for a more piecemeal change, even though that gradual scenario still includes dramatic events.

The final important earth change predictions came in 1941 to a woman in her mid-sixties. Very detailed descriptions were offered of the future map of America (#1152-11). Here again, Cayce's timing seems to be off, because phrases such as "in the next few years" suggest that at least some of these changes would have happened by now. However, the enumeration of those changes was *preceded* by the words "changes here are gradually coming about," which suggests that these events may take a while to unfold. In summary, here is what Cayce presented in his final prophecy reading about earth changes:

1. Geographic alterations are coming for most of America. They will be experienced especially along the two coasts, but also in the central part of America.

2. New land will appear up out of the Atlantic and the Pacific. Other coastal areas that are currently dry land will become "the bed of the ocean."

3. These inundations won't be limited to America. Some of the battlefields of World War II (going on as this reading was given) will eventually be submerged places.

4. Affected portions of the East Coast will include the New York City area. However, this will not happen as soon as many of these other changes, and will rather be in some other generation.

5. Much sooner than the changes along the northern Atlantic seacoast will be alterations along the south Atlantic. Portions of the Carolinas and Georgia will become permanently submerged.

6. The drainage basin for north central America will be altered so that waters from the Great Lakes will empty into the Mississippi River basin (and into the Gulf of Mexico) rather than via the St. Lawrence River.

7. Severe changes for Los Angeles and San Francisco will happen well before any changes coming for New York.

8. Certain "safety lands" exist – places less vulnerable to the coming changes. Among these safety lands of North America are southeastern Virginia (e.g., Virginia Beach, where Cayce's own readings had instructed him to move in the mid-1920s for reasons more complex than just potential earth changes), portions of Ohio, Indiana, and Illinois, much of the southern and the eastern portions of Canada.

The notion of "safety lands" is a provocative one. It easily captures our imagination because it's natural to want a place of refuge when such global threat is predicted. However, we need to be very careful as we interpret this prophecy from Cayce. He does not say that these are the only places that will be safe.

But what if we could somehow identify all the locations that would be on such a list of "places to be spared." Does that mean that we should all try to move to such a spot? Maybe that's not what Cayce meant. First, let's realize just how inconceivable it really is that any area of America (or any country, for that matter) would be unaffected if the predicted earth changes do occur. Even if that effect isn't geological, it will surely be felt in terms of food, energy, or most importantly, the emotional ties we have with other people.

Most bluntly put: there is no place to go and sit out the changes. Thinking for just a moment about America, this nation has grown to the point where we are one interdependent people. The very resources with which we live our lives have come to us through a complex exchange involving countless other people. If one aspect of the whole is interrupted – by an earthquake or any other catastrophe – it will be felt throughout our nation and beyond. Just imagine, for example, the impact on our food supplies if there are huge earthquakes in California. Or, simply remember the national impact of what happened in New York City and in the Washington D.C. area on September 11, 2001.

And this same principle governs the world, as well. We are a world community. Isolationism is no longer an option for any country. When something occurs that disturbs the balance, then it's usually felt within days throughout the world.

What does this principle of interrelationship tell us about so-called "safety lands"? For one thing, it makes us look very carefully at our definition of the word "safety." What could Cayce have really meant? On the one hand, he may have been trying to identify actual areas of the continent where there would be little or no flooding or shaking. And yet how could any spot be entirely "safe"? Cayce's own oceanfront hometown of Virginia Beach seems particularly vulnerable, even though it was mentioned several times as a safe place. If the prophecies prove to be correct – if, for example, land rises off the east coast of America – logic suggests that these upheavals would at least cause some coastal flooding. It's already happened with sub-hurricane level "nor'easter" storms. Earthquakes and land formation in the Atlantic would almost certainly cause destructive flooding.

All this suggests that we need to look for other meanings to the phrase "safety lands." *To assert that there is any private safety would be inconsistent with Cayce's total philosophy about the millennium.* Authentic safety must fundamentally rest upon being secure spiritually. No soul is "safe" just because it's outside the path of material harm. Real security is an inner state. We are safe when we are right with God and when we are in alignment with the ideals that we've set. For example, in 1942 one person asked if he would be safe in his hometown of New York – that is, safe from bombing or enemy attack. Cayce's answer points to the deeper meaning of safety and security: "Why should he not? If he lives right!" (#257-239).

A new theory is needed for the concept of "safety lands" as we move into the 21st century. It need not contradict the literal interpretation of these words, but it should be complementary and demonstrate how the notion of safety may have multiple levels of meaning.

Here's one possibility: Cities, regions, and even entire states can create by the attitudes and actions of its people a kind of group consciousness. And that collective mind and energy gives a location a particular vibration. In turn, that vibration – if it's resonant to spiritual values – can afford its people a sort of protection. This protection might be from outside threats or even disturbances of the earth. But more importantly, in times of upheaval or severe testing, it affords a protection for the individual *from those parts of the self that would lead to fear and doubt.* That's the real threat – that we might lose faith in our future, our Creator, and ourselves.

Cayce's readings speak in detail about such a concept of vibration for a particular location: "Each state, country, or town makes its own vibrations by or through the activities of those that comprise same" (#262-66). Although it's hard to describe logically, this is something that most of us have intuitively felt. When we visit a new location, we can often sense or feel something intangible about that place. We can perceive its collective spirit. We might verbalize such an impression with words like, "I just really feel at home here!" or, when the vibration doesn't match our own, "I need to get out of here because something about this place keeps me from being myself."

And so, what does all this suggest about Cayce's prophetic statement in 1941? What about that rather limited list of areas that would be safe from earth changes in North America? Perhaps he was identifying those areas of the country that had especially large numbers of people who were creating a vibration or aura of attunement. However, that was 1941. It's reasonable to hope and expect that since that time many more locales in America (and throughout the world) have developed to the status of "safety lands." Even though in the future some of these places may be shaken physically – even though every one of them will feel the effects in some way if the earth changes do take place – they may, nevertheless, be places of special opportunity. These special locations may help people stay psychologically and spiritually safe in times of change, because of the way in which the collective consciousness there brings out the best in individuals in times of crisis.

We don't have to move to one of the existing "safe" locations. We can each work to build that status for the community in which we already live.

PART II

PROPHECIES OF A WORLD IN DISORDER

Nostradamus

IRENE HUGHES

CHAPTER THREE

THE MANY STREAMS
OF PROPHETIC WISDOM

"God's mysteries are incomprehensible and the power to influence events is bound up with the great expanse of natural knowledge, having its nearest most immediate origin in free will..." Nostradamus

This passage from Nostradamus' letter to his son (see below) is an apt theme with which to begin a chapter on the many streams of prophetic wisdom. It is crucial to keep in mind that the deepest wisdom about our future always reminds us that we are co-creators of the future – that free will is our birthright.

Edgar Cayce was not alone in prophesying about the millennium. Psychics and seers of other times and cultures came before him to make similar prophecies, although we have no reason to suspect that the waking Cayce ever knew of them. The correspondences among these independent sources are compelling. It is not enough evidence to claim any sort of "proof," because who can ever prove the future? But it does suggest that we should explore seriously these visions of the future. Many ancient and modern sources echo the same themes about what the millennium will bring. This chapter samples a variety of prophetic traditions and modern-day visionaries, whose predictions are close parallels to the ones given by Cayce. The prophecies mentioned in this chapter come from Nostradamus, Native American people (i.e., Mayans, Aztecs, and Hopis), the visions of near-death experiences, contemporary visionaries, and another respected psychic.

Nostradamus

The psychic most often compared to Cayce was the Frenchman Michel de Notredame — better known by the Latinized form of the name which he adopted upon university graduation, Nostradamus. Born in 1503, Nostradamus, like Edgar Cayce, was deeply committed to compassionate service and healing in his adult career. Whereas Cayce was relatively unschooled and approached healing as a clairvoyant diagnostician, Nostradamus was a trained physician. He gained some notoriety for his skills helping victims of the plague to regain health.

But it was not his medical skill that made him famous throughout Europe. After twenty years of medical practice, in 1550 he published the first of his books that combined useful daily knowledge with predictive insights largely based on astrology. These almanac-like volumes appeared annually for sixteen years. During this second phase of his professional career, he also published a book of home remedies (again, like Cayce, whose own home remedy suggestions have been published in several forms).

By far the most famous of Nostradamus' publications is a collection of visionary poems that first appeared between 1555 and 1558 and have stayed in print continuously for over four hundred years! Entitled *Centuries*, they were published as a series of books, each with one hundred quatrains, hence the title. However, some people have assumed that these collections of prophetic poems were titled so as to imply that they looked centuries into the future. Perhaps Nostradamus intended the ambiguity.

Like Cayce, Nostradamus was sought after in his own times. On two occasions the queen of France requested his predictive advice. Politicians and businessmen from all over Europe knew of his reputation and wrote for counsel before starting new enterprises. It was not merely in retrospect that these two men gained appreciation and notoriety.

In spite of their common reputation as prophets, there are many significant differences between Cayce and Nostradamus, which make it hard to portray accurately the similarities in their visions of the 21st century. Perhaps most notably, the prophecies of Nostradamus are cloaked in astrological imagery, symbolism, and vague references, which may be difficult for a person of our times ever to decipher.

Although Cayce's language is no doubt difficult for most people to get used to, his predictions for the millennium are in many cases straightforward. Consider one example presented earlier: repeatedly Cayce said that the years 1958 to 1998 would be the four decades in which extraordinary planetary transformation would begin. The dates are clear and unambiguous. Not so with the quatrains of Nostradamus. They required interpretation from the time they were given, and that process continued after his death. In 1594, just twenty-eight years after Nostradamus' death, the first published interpretations appeared. Since then dozens of writers have attempted to unravel the meaning behind the enigmatic pronouncements of *Centuries.*

Some of the predictions in his quatrains seem unarguably accurate, particularly some that were fulfilled in his own century. For example, four years before the death of King Henry II in a jousting mishap, Nostradamus' predictive poem foreshadowed the sad event with details that proved to be valid. "The young Lion shall overcome the old one/ In a martial field by a single duel/ In a golden cage he shall put out his eye/ Two wounds from one, then he shall die a cruel death."

But unfortunately very few of the quatrains can be linked so specifically to historical events. Ambiguity and multiple possible meanings for various symbols make it very hard to say exactly what Nostradamus predicted, especially in regard to our times. Critics go so far as to say that trying to make sense of *Centuries* is like a Rorschach inkblot test; they allow interpreters to read into them almost anything they want. These skeptics argue that the imagery and astrological references are often so ambiguous – especially when one has nearly four hundred years of history through which to look for coincidental matches – that any claims of prophetic power beyond the sixteenth century itself are farfetched.Others who analyze the evidence are more generous in their assessment, pointing out that Nostradamus seems to have had an uncanny ability to foresee air warfare and other aspects of modern life that could hardly have been dreamed of four hundred years ago. But there is an unmistakable lack of general agreement among the believers as to exactly what it was that Nostradamus predicted for our own era. Dozens of books in the last twenty years have offered a myriad of interpretations. On one count, however, all seem to agree. Researchers, translators, and scholars of the Nostradamus material all concur that he foresaw cataclysmic changes – even the destruction of the world. But the translations of his poetic imagery into calendar dates range from 1988 to nearly A.D. 3800. *Perhaps the best that can be said of the Nostradamus prophecies when compared to Cayce is that both predicted the likelihood of global destruction and transformation on a scale far beyond anything else in human history.*

One of the most famous remnants of Nostradamus' work is a letter that he wrote to his son Cesar in 1555. The following is that letter, with some parenthetical interpretative comments from serious researchers into his legacy.

The Letter to His Son Cesar

Greetings and happiness to Cesar Nostradamus my son.

Your late arrival, Cesar Nostredame, my son, has made me spend much time in constant nightly reflection so that I could communicate with you by letter and leave you this reminder, after my death, for the benefit of all men, of which the divine spirit has vouchsafed me to know by means of astronomy.

And since it was the Almighty's will that you were not born here in this region [Provence] and I do not want to talk of years to come but of the months during which you will struggle to grasp and understand the work I shall be compelled to leave you after my death: assuming that it will not be possible for me to leave you such [clearer] writing as may be destroyed through the injustice of the age [1555]. The key to the hidden prediction which you will inherit will be locked inside my heart.

Also bear in mind that the events here described have not yet come to pass, and that all is ruled and governed by the power of Almighty God, inspiring us not by bacchic frenzy nor by enchantments but by astronomical assurances: predictions have been made through the inspiration of divine will alone and the spirit of prophecy in particular.

On numerous occasions and over a long period of time I have predicted specific events far in advance, attributing all to the workings of divine power and inspiration, together with other fortunate or unfortunate happenings, foreseen in their full unexpectedness, which have already come to pass in various regions of the earth. Yet I have wished to remain silent and abandon my work because of the injustice not only of the present time [the Inquisition] but also for most of the future. I will not commit to writing.

Since governments, sects and countries will undergo such sweeping changes, diametrically opposed to what now obtains, that were I to relate events to come, those in power now - monarchs, leaders of sects and religions - would find these so different from their own imaginings that they would be led to condemn what later centuries will learn how to see and understand. Bear in mind also Our Saviour's words: Do not give anything holy to the dogs, nor throw pearls in front of the pigs lest they trample them with their feet and turn on you and tear you apart.

For this reason I withdrew my pen from the paper, because I wished to amplify my statement touching the Vulgar Advent, by means of ambiguous and enigmatic comments about future causes, even those closest to us and those I have perceived, so that some human change which may come to pass shall not unduly scandalize delicate sensibilities. The whole work is thus written in a nebulous rather than plainly prophetic form. So much so that,

You have hidden these things from the wise and the circumspect, that is from the mighty and the rulers, and you have purified those things for the small and the poor, and through Almighty God's will, revealed unto those prophets with the power to perceive what is distant and thereby to foretell things to come. For nothing can be accomplished without this faculty, whose power and goodness work so strongly in those to whom it is given that, while they contemplate within themselves, these powers are subject to other influences arising from the force of good. This warmth and strength of prophecy invests us with its influence as the sun's rays affect both animate and inanimate entities.

We human beings cannot through our natural consciousness and intelligence know anything of God the Creator's hidden secrets, for it is not for us to know the times or the instants, etc.

So much so that persons of future times may be seen in present ones, because God Almighty has wished to reveal them by means of images, together with various secrets of the future vouchsafed to orthodox astrology, as was the case in the past, so that a measure of power and divination passed through them, the flame of the spirit inspiring them to pronounce upon inspiration both human and divine.

God may bring into being divine works, which are absolute; there is another level, that of angelic works; and a third way, that of the evildoers.

But my son, I address you here a little too obscurely. As regards the occult prophecies one is vouchsafed through the subtle spirit of fire, which the understanding sometimes stirs through contemplation of the distant stars as if in vigil, likewise by means of pronouncements, one finds oneself surprised at producing writings without fear of being stricken for such impudent loquacity. The reason is that all this proceeds from the divine power of Almighty God from whom all bounty proceeds.

And so once again, my son, if I have eschewed the word prophet, I do not wish to attribute to myself such lofty title at the present time, for whoever is called a prophet now was once called a seer; since a prophet, my son, is properly speaking one who sees distant things through a natural knowledge of all creatures. And it can happen that the prophet bringing about the perfect light of prophecy may make manifest things both human and divine, because this cannot be done otherwise, given that the effects of predicting the future extend far off into time.

God's mysteries are incomprehensible and the power to influence events is bound up with the great expanse of natural knowledge, having its nearest most immediate origin in free will and describing future events which cannot be understood simply through being revealed. Neither can they be grasped through men's interpretations nor through another mode of cognizance or occult power under the firmament, neither in the present nor in the total eternity to come. But bringing about such an indivisible eternity through Herculean efforts, things are revealed by the planetary movements.

I am not saying, my son - mark me well, here - that knowledge of such things cannot be implanted in your deficient mind, or that events in the distant future may not be within the understanding of any reasoning being. Nevertheless, if these things current or distant are brought to the awareness of this reasoning and intelligent being they will be neither too obscure nor too clearly revealed.

Perfect knowledge of such things cannot be acquired without divine inspiration, given that all prophetic inspiration derives its initial origin from God Almighty, then from chance and nature. Since all these portents are produced impartially, prophecy comes to pass partly as predicted. For understanding created by the intellect cannot be acquired by means of the occult, only by the aid of the zodiac, bringing forth that small flame by whose light part of the future may be discerned.

Also, my son, I beseech you not to exercise your mind upon such reveries and vanities as drain the body and incur the soul's perdition, and which trouble our feeble frames. Above all avoid the vanity of that most execrable magic formerly reproved by the Holy Scriptures - only excepting the use of official astrology.

For by the latter, with the help of inspiration and divine revelation, and continual calculations, I have set down my prophecies in writing. Fearing lest this occult philosophy be condemned, I did not therefore wish to make known its dire import; also fearful that several books which had lain hidden for long centuries might be discovered, and of what might become of them, after reading them I presented them to Vulcan. [i.e. burned them]. And while he devoured them, the flame licking the air gave out such an unexpected light, clearer than that of an ordinary flame and resembling fire from some flashing cataclysm, and suddenly illumined the house as if it were caught in a furnace. Which is why I reduced them to ashes then, so that none might be tempted to use occult labours in searching for the perfect transmutation, whether lunar or solar, of incorruptible metals.

But as to that discernment which can be achieved by the aid of planetary scrutiny, I should like to tell you this. Eschewing any fantastic imaginings, you may through good judgment have insight into the future if you keep to the specific names of places that accord with planetary configurations, and with inspiration places and aspects yield up hidden properties, namely that power in whose presence the three times [past, present, and future] are understood as Eternity whose unfolding contains them all: for all things are naked and open.

That is why, my son, you can easily, despite your young brain, understand that events can be foretold naturally by the heavenly bodies and by the spirit of prophecy: I do not wish to ascribe to myself the title and role of prophet, but emphasize inspiration revealed to a mortal man whose perception is no further from heaven than the feet are from the earth. I cannot fail, err or be deceived, although I may be as great a sinner as anyone else upon this earth and subject to all human afflictions.

But after being surprised sometimes by day while in a trance, and having long fallen into the habit of agreeable nocturnal studies, I have composed books of prophecies, each containing one hundred astronomical quatrains, which I want to condense somewhat obscurely. The work comprises prophecies from today to the year 3797.

This may perturb some, when they see such a long timespan, and this will occur and be understood in all the fullness of the Republic; these things will be universally understood upon earth, my son. If you live the normal lifetime of man you will know upon your own soil, under your native sky, how future events are to turn out.

For only Eternal God knows the eternity of His light which proceeds from Him, and I speak frankly to those to whom His immeasurable, immense and incomprehensible greatness has been disposed to grant revelations through long, melancholy inspiration, that with the aid of this hidden element manifested by God, there are two principal factors which make up the prophet's intelligence.

The first is when the supernatural light fills and illuminates the person who predicts by astral science, while the second allows him to prophesy through inspired revelation, which is only a part of the divine eternity, whereby the prophet comes to assess what his divinatory power has given him through the grace of God and by a natural gift, namely, that what is foretold is true and ethereal in origin.

And such a light and small flame is of great efficacy and scope, and nothing less than the clarity of nature itself. The light of human nature makes the philosophers so sure of themselves that with the principles of the first cause they reach the loftiest doctrines and the deepest abysses. But my son, lest I venture too far for your future perception, be aware that men of letters shall make grand and usually boastful claims about the way I interpreted the world, before the worldwide conflagration which is to bring so many catastrophes and such revolutions that scarcely any lands will not be covered by water, and this will last until all has perished save history and geography themselves. This is why, before and after these revolutions in various countries, the rains will be so diminished and such abundance of fire and fiery missiles shall fall from the heavens that nothing shall escape the holocaust. And this will occur before the last conflagration [1999].

For before war ends the [twentieth] century and in its final stages [1975-99] it will hold the century under its sway. Some countries will be in the grip of revolution for several years, and others ruined for a still longer period. And now that we are in a republican era, with Almighty God's aid, and before completing its full cycle, the monarchy will return, then the Golden Age. For according to the celestial signs, the Golden Age shall return, and after all calculations, with the world near to an all-encompassing revolution - from the time of writing 177 years 3 months 11 days - plague, long famine and wars, and still more floods from now until the stated time. Before and after these, humanity shall several times be so severely diminished that scarcely anyone shall be found who wishes to take over the fields, which shall become free where they had previously been tied.

This will be after the visible judgment of heaven, before we reach the millennium which shall complete all. In the firmament of the eighth sphere, a dimension whereon Almighty God will complete the revolution, and where the constellations will resume their motion which will render the earth stable and firm, but only if He will remain unchanged for ever until His will be done.

This is in spite of all the ambiguous opinions surpassing all natural reason, expressed by Mahomet; which is why God the Creator, through the ministry of his fiery agents with their flames, will come to propose to our perceptions as well as our eyes the reasons for future predictions.

Signs of events to come must be manifested to whomever prophesies. For prophecy which stems from exterior illumination is part of that light and seeks to ally with it and bring it into being so that the part which seems to possess the faculty of understanding is not subject to a sickness of the mind.

Reason is only too evident. Everything is predicted by divine afflatus and thanks to an angelic spirit inspiring the one prophesying, consecrating his predictions through divine unction. It also divests him of all fantasies by means of various nocturnal apparitions, while with daily certainty he prophesies through the science of astronomy, with the aid of sacred prophecy, his only consideration being his courage in freedom.

So come, my son, strive to understand what I have found out through my calculations which accord with revealed inspiration, because now the sword of death approaches us, with pestilence and war more horrible than there has ever been - because of three men's work - and famine. And this sword shall smite the earth and return to it often, for the stars confirm this upheaval and it is also written: I shall punish their injustices with iron rods, and shall strike them with blows.

For God's mercy will be poured forth only for a certain time, my son, until the majority of my prophecies are fulfilled and this fulfillment is complete. Then several times in the course of the doleful tempests the Lord shall say: Therefore I shall crush and destroy and show no mercy; and many other circumstances shall result from floods and continual rain of which I have written more fully in my other prophecies, composed at some length, not in a chronological sequence, in prose, limiting the places and times and exact dates so that future generations will see, while experiencing these inevitable events, how I have listed others in clearer language, so that despite their obscurities these things shall be understood: When the time comes for the removal of ignorance, the matter will be clearer still.

So in conclusion, my son, take this gift from your father M. Nostradamus, who hopes you will understand each prophesy in every quatrain herein. May Immortal God grant you a long life of good and prosperous happiness.

Salon, 1 March 1555

Nostradamus and Cayce are not the only psychics who predicted the likelihood of dramatic earth changes. There have been literally dozens of psychics in the years since Cayce's death who have said similar things, often giving greater details and more specific dates than did Cayce or clearer imagery than Nostradamus ever offered. But in many instances those specific earth changes predictions have already proved to be incorrect. It is also hard to say to what degree the post-Cayce psychics were simply mimicking Cayce, whose influence on the profession of prognostication can hardly be overestimated. It is an open question of the extent to which the study of the Cayce earth changes readings is significantly strengthened by psychics who followed him. At the very least, we need to look for additional sources of corroborative evidence, preferably even independent of Cayce. The finest such comparative material predates his own work – material coming from other cultural traditions.

Native American Prophecies

One especially noteworthy source of ancient prophecy about our own times comes from native societies of central and North America. The Mayan civilization is the most ancient in this part of the world, with the earliest archaeological evidence stretching back to 9000 B.C. in what is now coastal Belize. By 2500 B.C. the Mayans had established agricultural settlements.

The key to their success was an elaborate and highly sophisticated set of calendars that allowed for the precise timing of planting and harvesting. These calendars came from many generations of careful observations of the heavens, and they were actually several interlocking measurements of time, each with its own periodicity. The most significant of the Mayan calendars were the solar year of three hundred sixty days (divided into eighteen months of twenty days each) and the sacred almanac with two hundred sixty days (comprised of thirteen months of twenty days each). Once every fifty-two years a remarkable coincidence occurs as the same day comes up simultaneously on both calendars. This cycle was known as the Calendar Round, and formed the basis of some Indian prophecies – not only Mayan, but the other native cultures of Central and North America who were significantly influenced by the Mayans.

Especially significant to a comparison study of Cayce's predictions is the four-hundred-year cycle the Mayans called "baktuns" and the series of thirteen consecutive baktuns called the Great Cycle — fifty-two hundred years. Our current Great Cycle is dated to conclude precisely on December 21, 2012. Mayan prophecy describes events surrounding this date as rather frightful, but mingled with signs of hope and breakthrough. To the generation that lives during that turning point will come "the day of withered fruit"; "the face of the sun will be extinguished because of the great tempest." But finally there will come blessings to renew humanity – "ornaments shall descend in heaps, and there will be good gifts for one and all." Although not exactly matching the dates that Cayce focused on, nevertheless the themes of painful transition and grace-filled conclusion are embedded in both prophetic sources.

By the tenth century A.D. the sophisticated and impressive centers of Mayan culture were abandoned, for reasons that are still relatively mysterious to scholars. Mayan civilization continued, but now at the modest level of village life, and other native civilizations rose in prominence (still highly influenced by many Mayan developments). The Aztecs and Toltecs were two such civilizations. Their culture hero and godlike figure Quetzalcoatl was a source of prophecies about changing times. His name roughly translates as "spirit of light," and he was revered as an ancient teacher of the people in the areas of mathematics, agriculture, theology and the arts.

Legend has it that Quetzalcoatl returned (that is, reincarnated) in a year now calculated to be about A.D. 947. There is considerable controversy concerning a date for his first incarnation, with some scholars of the opinion that there was no previous lifetime that any earlier figure was mythological. Yet other writers and scholars assert that Quetzalcoati was a historic character living sometime before Christ. For example, the renowned esoteric philosopher Manly Palmer Hall writes in *Twelve World Teachers:* "At some remote time a great initiate-king arose among the civilizations of Mexico and Central America. It is impossible at this late date to determine the period during which he lived, but it is safe to say that it was some centuries before the Christian Era." In *Voices of Earth and Sky*, anthropologist Vinson Brown describes the original Quetzalcoatl as the "Great Prophet of the period 200 B.C. to the beginning of A.D."

In this second life with his people, Quetzalcoatl foretold many important events and cycles of change to be experienced in the coming thousand years or so. His prophecies stated that within the ongoing fifth age there would be thirteen cycles, each comprised of fifty-two years. During these six hundred seventy-six years there would be decreasing consciousness and free will. Then would come nine cycles, once again of fifty-two years each, which would be characterized by darkness or hell.

Scholars use the year A.D. 843 as the starting point of all these cycles (that is, at the end of the classical period of Mayan culture). Quetzalcoatl's reincarnation would have come after two of these fifty-two-year cycles had already been accomplished, and some very interesting correspondence can be found to recorded history. If we look six hundred seventy-six years into the period (that is, the full thirteen cycles of diminishing consciousness and free will), we see that Cortez arrived in America in 1519 with his armies. And after a brief struggle he conquered and enslaved the people of this region.

The year 1936 marks the beginning of the final fifty-two-year cycle of darkness and hell. It is interesting to note that this date marks well the time when Hitler began moves to start World War II. The year 1987 – that is, 1935 plus 52 – was to be the final one in this last cycle of darkness. Then was to come the "great purification," reminiscent of Cayce's vision of global changes. This purification sounds dire: the equipoise of nature will be lost, the ocean tides shall obey no more, cities and mountains will collapse, leveled by great earthquakes. Although this kind of destruction did not occur in 1987, we are left to wonder if the timing has been delayed or if human choices may be altering what was once a likely future; indeed, according to a second prophecy, the intensity of suffering accompanying this purification would depend upon mankind's choices.

Despite the intensity of this purification process, the prophecies contain a hopeful view: a new era of cooperation, peace and plenty will be born. Quetzalcoatl promised to return "in the time of the great-great grandchildren of the white conquerors," initiating a new set of cycles, "a golden age of spiritual rebirth, planetary harmony, and for many the awakened consciousness of the Divine Life."

The Hopi Indians of North America provide another ancient tradition of prophecy that is remarkably parallel to the one given by Edgar Cayce. The immediate ancestors of the Hopi were the "Ancient Ones" – the Anasazi cliff dwellers whose history can be traced back to around 100 B.C. By the year A.D. 500 the Hopi had become a peace-loving, agricultural civilization that spread across large portions of what is now the southwest United States. The peak of the Hopi culture was approximately A.D. 1100, and they constructed impressive buildings at places such as modern-day Mesa Verde, Colorado, and Chaco Canyon, New Mexico.

The prophecies of the Hopi are said to have come from Massau'u, their spiritual teacher for the age. Ancient Hopi prophecies were handed down on stone tablets accompanied by an oral tradition of interpretation that was passed on by the elders of the community.

Certain of these prophecies concern events near the end of this current age in the Hopi framework of history. Some seem to have been fulfilled, including the coming of automobiles and telephones – "horseless chariots" that would roll along "black snakes" across the land, and "cobwebs" through which people would speak over great distances.

Among the prophecies is a petroglyph, or rock carving, that

depicts the Hopi Life Plan Prophecy. In part, it shows two horizontal time lines, the top one representing our modern technological, materialistic society and the bottom line depicting the Hopi's own world of attunement to natural forces. Along the materialistic line are the figures of human beings with their heads detached from their bodies, an apt image for contemporary men and women whose intellectual self and feeling self are so often disassociated.

Also shown in this prophetic petroglyph are two vertical lines that connect the horizontal time lines. One of the connecting lines – symbolic of the opportunity for materialistic society to reconnect with the wisdom of the Hopi – is placed chronologically just before a pair of circles, which interpreters decipher to be the two World Wars. The second vertical connector comes after the images for these two great wars, at approximately the point in time in which we now exist. Thus, there is the opportunity, but not the certitude, for technological society to join with the wisdom of the ancient ones. If not, the Hopi Life Plan Prophecy depicts yet another period of great destruction. Beyond that point on the prophetic carving, the time line for materialistic society begins to fade out and disappear. The other horizontal time line, the one that is in harmony with the natural order, continues on.

Many Hopi prophecies have seemingly been fulfilled: trees everywhere will begin dying; people will build a house and throw it into the sky (the American space shuttle or the International space station); and dramatic changes will occur in the weather. With these signs confirmed, the Hopis believe that they can well expect the next stage in the prophecies, events to take place somewhere around the year 2000, even into our own immediate times here in the first decade of the 21st century. The Great Day of Purification will be traumatic, but it will usher in the next age. Certain cataclysms like war, famine and earthquakes are predicted. However, their severity is something to be determined by humanity. The Hopi vision of the future includes the option for these catastrophes to be lessened, if humankind will work together in the proper spirit.

Near-Death Experiencers As Prophets

Another category of visionary is the near-death experiencer. Most research has focused on the remarkable similarities among accounts provided by those who were resuscitated after brief periods of clinical death. Since the publication of Dr. Raymond Moody's best-seller *Life After Life* and several other comparable books, certain common aspects of the near-death experience have become well known to millions: going down a tunnel, confronting a review of one's life, encountering a Being of Light. But what has not been widely reported is that many near-death experiencers also have visions of the future during their brief moments in this extraordinary altered state of consciousness. Apparently, the near-death experience does not focus exclusively on one's own personal transition into the spiritual world. At least for some it also takes on global proportions, as one views current planetary conditions and catches glimpses of what may be ahead for humanity.

One researcher, Dr. Kenneth Ring of the University of Connecticut, collected prophetic visionary accounts from several dozen near-death experiencers, which he reported in his 1984 book *Heading Toward Omega*. Although now somewhat "dated," this work is still very significant to our study of prophetic material. Ring distinguished more common precognitive material – what he calls "personal flashforwards" – from a somewhat rarer kind of experience, the prophetic vision. This latter group concerned predictions with a planetary scope. What's more (and this is what made Ring's research so intriguing) these prophetic visions were highly consistent from person to person. In his systematic assessment of prophetic visions of near-death experiencers, they seemed to be seeing the same sort of world about to emerge.

Before going into the details of these prophetic visions, it's interesting to note another characteristic that Ring discovered. Most of those who received prophetic visions had the clear sense that they had been shown or told far more than they were able to recall upon resuscitation from the near-death experience. Ring notes several factors that seem to stimulate recall in greater detail months or years later:

1. *Temporal proximity.* Some individuals claimed that within a few days of when an event was to occur, the knowledge of its occurrence would resurface.

2. *Spatial proximity.* For some individuals, being in a certain physical location seemed to trigger a more detailed recall of the prophetic visions they had been given during the near-death

experience.

3. *Spontaneous recall.* For some visionary near-death experiencers, details came back to mind several months or years later for no logical reason. Often their own interpretation of such spontaneous recall is that it was simply time for them to have access to the additional knowledge.

What, then, did these prophetic visionaries see in the course of their near-death experiences? Ring described the elements of a model to which almost all of them conform. First, the visionary had a sense of being able to see the entirety of the earth's evolution and history. That is to say, any predictions about specific events were seen in a broader context. In spite of this panoramic view of time, the actual prophetic visions were much more narrow in scope and rarely extended beyond the beginning of the 21st century.

The visionaries shared a view of the world in chaos as we were to move toward the end of the 20th century: massive geophysical changes, huge disturbances in the weather and in food supplies. They saw the economic system collapsing and the distinct possibility of nuclear war or accident. And yet, in spite of these dire images – perhaps even more severe than Cayce's millennium prophecies – the near-death visionaries had a collective sense of these changes being for the best. They were to be merely a very difficult transition into a much more healthy and spiritually enlivened culture in the 21st century.

While Ring's research on the one hand seemed to corroborate the Cayce prophecies, there was obviously a problem, because these things did not happen, at least on the timetable envisioned. Concerning timing, Ring himself stated in his book published in 1984: "While agreeing that the date for these events are not fixed, most individuals feel that they are likely to take place during the 1980s." Most of the visionaries honed in on a date around 1988 or 1989, which surely must be judged now to have been wrong, unless we look at some of the prophecies symbolically and note the sudden and surprising downfall of communism in 1989 and the way that event shook and transformed the world.

Ring's book, written when there was still ample time for these prophecies to come true literally and within the predicted time frame, nevertheless tries to consider the visions from a number of angles. He is quite open to the possibility that the kinds of events described in these prophetic visions will come to pass later. But as a careful researcher and systematic thinker, Ring also notes that at an individual level these prophetic visionaries were enduring bodily pain associated with almost dying before their hospital resuscitation and transformation back to life. Their visions for the world reflect the same themes. Is it merely one's personal trauma being projected onto the grander canvas of international politics and world geology? Or, conversely, does a personal encounter with near death, resuscitation, and transformation make one more sensitive to receive those patterns and possibilities on a global scale?

Also noteworthy in Ring's book is a careful consideration of the workings of prediction and precognition. He looks at various models to explain how prophecy is even possible. Ring himself seems to favor a model that draws upon quantum physics and the idea that subatomic processes exist in terms of probabilities. For example, suppose that three alternatives exist for how a certain event will turn out. Perhaps alternative A is seventy percent likely; alternative B, twenty percent; and alternative C, ten percent. Quantum mechanics suggests that until the event occurs and is observed, each alternative outcome is associated with a wave function. When B is in fact the alternative observed, then the wave functions linked to choice A and C "collapse" just as B becomes a certainty.

However, another theory of reality suggests that A and C don't disappear. The so-called "Many Worlds Interpretation" or the "Theory of Alternative Futures" would say that A and C also "happen," even if we don't observe them from our perspective in the world where alternative B took place. As Ring notes, this notion is at face value rather outlandish and untestable. Nevertheless, it matches stories that Ring has heard from some of his near-death visionaries who have seen multiple lines of trajectory that lead toward the future.

Near the end of *Heading Toward Omega*, Ring makes use of this theory of alternative worlds to interpret the prophetic visions of his near-death studies. He suggests that his group may have connected with just one of a large set of alternative future scenarios. Since they may not have suspected that other scenarios also existed, they had a sense of absolute certitude about what was actually only a probability. Perhaps, along some other trajectory that is not the one that we're on here in the early 21st century, those catastrophic events did play themselves out in an alternative world.

Admittedly it is a fanciful and untestable idea – untestable at least with any methods of investigation we currently understand. But the nature of reality is not limited by our three-dimensional logic. For example, so-called "imaginary numbers" don't "make sense" because they depend on the existence of some number, which is multiplied by itself to make -1. Logic says there is no square root of -1. But what happens when we momentarily suspend that objection and theorize such a number, labeling it "i" for "imaginary"? That somewhat illogical approach ends up allowing us to solve many complex scientific and engineering problems having to do with the physical world. Maybe just as surely the "alternative worlds" theory helps us understand the apparent error in the prophetic visions of these near-death experiencers.

Visions of a Cultural Historian

Recognizing historical trends is one tool of the futurist, who can extrapolate to create a vision of what might happen. This principle can be applied to major cultural transformations in history. Recurrent themes appear in society's experiences of paradigm shift. Not only can we learn from these historical periods, but we can also formulate predictions of what may lie ahead for us.

One especially noteworthy cultural historian who has tried to do this is Dr. William Irvin Thompson, who has taught at MIT, York University and Syracuse University. In 1973 he founded the Lindisfarne Association, a contemplative educational community devoted to the study and realization of a new planetary culture. In a number of his books, particularly *Darkness and Scattered Light*, Thompson examines the alternatives for the future, which he has inferred based on recurrent patterns of major historical change.

A summary of his ideas about these times of change fits nicely in our exploration of prophecies for the 21st century. In many ways his theories closely parallel the concepts in the Cayce readings, although they are often much more explicit and detailed regarding a new millennial life-style. Like the Cayce readings, Thompson saw the latter portion of the 20th century as a period for a paradigm shift at least as great as the Renaissance five hundred years ago. In his words, the change will be from civilization to planetization. Civilization is to be understood as a world order that focuses on material production and consumption. Planetization is a world order whose priorities are contemplation, consciousness and ecological balance. It is not that production and consumption will cease to be relevant issues in a planetized society, but rather we will have new priorities – or in Cayce terminology, new ideals.

The particularly difficult times of change, which Cayce foresaw beginning in the period from 1958 to 1998, are designated by Thompson as an initiation period for the earth. Using the three classic stages of initiation in mystery religions of the past, Thompson provides a framework for viewing both recent current events and predictions about our future. In other words, the ancient concept of spiritual initiation for an individual seeker may be acted out *collectively* by all of humanity. The traditional challenges and difficulties faced by the individual initiate may be analogous to the ones humanity will confront during these times of testing. Briefly, here are the three primary stages and, in Thompson's interpretation, the way in which we collectively may experience each phase:

1. The illumination of one's darkness or shadow side. The individual initiate might expect to face terrifying images from his own unconscious – the destructive, selfish potential within his own mind. Facing this inner demon can be not only frightening but also discouraging. There are likely to arise feelings of doubt and unworthiness in seeing this shadow side of ourselves. This testing is felt most acutely by the initiate's ego.

When this state is applied to humanity as a whole, it is easy to see examples of the illumination of humanity's dark side, such as the wars in Viet Nam, Kuwait, Bosnia, and Iraq, plus the ecological disasters caused by the misuse of technology. In Thompson's theory it is especially the elite of society (that is, the "ego" of a civilization) that experiences the humiliation of this first stage of initiation.

2. Discovery of the edge of one's sanity. For the individual initiate, this is the point at which he realizes that all the old definitions of reality no longer work. The old images of the ego no longer hold together. A breakdown in the sense of oneself and in the sense of reality results.

At a collective level, considerable evidence indicates that our society has entered this second stage of testing. The old systems and approaches – upon which we used to depend – no longer work. Many perplexing national problems seem to have no solution, and so many proposed solutions create even bigger problems while trying to solve the original difficulties. As one editorial in the *Washington Post* observed, no new ideas are around, and the old ones no longer hold things together like they used to.

3. The defeat of the ego. It is at this point in the individual initiation process that the seeker lets go. In that instant of openness and vulnerability, a new self-identity can be born. Our society has not yet reached this point. It may be years or decades away. As long as the leadership of a society convinces its people that the old ideas and identity might still be made to work again, the courage to surrender and let go will be wanting.

These three classic stages of initiation are the archetypes of transformation that historically have been known to only a few. The alchemy of changing consciousness is about to make a quantum leap – from the level of the single person to the level of humanity as a whole. As these three stages are enacted for the masses of the planet, Thompson predicts that they will affect different segments of society at different times. In his view, the changes will be felt first in the spiritual/religious community. This is not the group of religious leaders who hold stubbornly to the old paradigm. Rather, it is those who are genuinely open to a mystical revelation of what is being born in the world. Thompson cites Teilhard de Chardin as a good example.

The second segment is the artistic community. The new spiritual vision is given new life in art. Through art a great portion of humanity can sense the imaginative possibilities seen by the mystic.

For Thompson, the third segment of society to feel the impact of this new vision is science. Whether it is the architecture of people like Buckminster Fuller or mystic physicists like Fiitjof Capra, the original vision of the attuned spiritual community finds expression for the masses in science. In fact, many modern-day physicists sound more like mystics than most ministers and priests of traditional Christianity.

The final segment of society to feel the change is the political faction. In effect, the political process is the last area to reflect transformation. It is the hardest to change, the most likely to depict our past rather than our future. In Thompson's view of change, cultural transformation is nearly complete by the time it reaches mainstream politics.

In Thompson's writings we find a description of various

cultural forces at work to reshape the planet. One force is the emergent sense of world community. Even if we are not yet able to cooperate very effectively with other nations, the inescapable fact remains that our future and well-being are tied to that of other countries. The "planetization of the nations" is being felt first in its uncomfortable aspects – problems in one part of the world almost immediately create problems worldwide. But as a force for cultural change, this development could just as well nurture a sense of world fellowship. The days of a nation choosing isolationism are over. The planetization of the nations is ultimately a force for transformation that requires a choice between cooperation or suffering.

A second force at work upon our world is the decentralization of cities. In other words, there is a trend away from urbanization and a growing new respect for smaller communities as optimal places in which to live. As large urban centers of America (particularly the older cities of northeast America) decay, we shall be faced with hard choices about rebuilding them. Cultural forces at work point toward smaller and more manageable models for living instead of the urban centralization that has characterized the industrial age.

Thompson writes that the miniaturization of technology is a third force for transformation. At first glance it would seem that technology has been a part of the problem in the old paradigm. We might wonder how a product of technology could constitute a push toward developing a new set of assumptions for living. It is indeed ironic that the most remarkable of achievements of the old world order would create an impetus and an aid to a new life-style. However, this is exactly the effect that the miniaturization of technology has. Observe what has been made possible by computers or medical equipment so small they are portable. For example, on his or her laptop on a plane trip a business person can now have an information retrieval system as powerful as one that twenty years ago required a thousand times the space. When the technological tools for living become portable, the decentralization of population centers becomes possible. We no longer have to live in unwieldy urban centers to have access to the technological, medical and communications resources we need. The miniaturization of these tools for living open up new options in life-style.

A final, crucial force at work to change our world is the interiorization of consciousness. With this fourth force as well as the first one (that is, the planetization of nations) we find the most direct parallels between Cayce's and Thompson's prophecies. As humanity begins to look for the source of the good life within rather than without, value systems begin to shift. A contemplative culture can emerge which finds new meaning in meditation, dream study, mythology and the arts.

In Thompson's view these four cultural forces work to create a new model for living, what he calls the meta-industrial village. The prefix "meta" means beyond, so the meta-industrial village is an evolutionary step beyond the life-style models of industrial life. The idea of village life may sound like a retrogressive step; it conjures up images of America in the days of George Washington: semi-rural communities with no electricity, no plumbing, and no modern communications devices. But Thompson goes to great lengths to explain that this is not his vision at all. Although some proponents of "back to nature" would like to see us return to an 18th century way of life, he proposes a return to the village scale, but incorporating the technological breakthroughs of science. Communities of like-minded people – perhaps several hundred residents per village – can become models for new age living. Each such meta-industrial village would include:

1. *Energy self-sufficiency,* using a combination of replenishable energy sources, such as solar, wood and wind power.

2. *Agricultural self-sufficiency,* using organic or biodynamic methods for growing food that respect the delicate ecological balance.

3. *Cottage industries* for the production of salable goods. Such small-scale production could range from handcrafted furniture to farm implements to microcomputers. The sale of products of the village's cottage industries would provide a source of income or a means of bartering items manufactured in other communities.

4. *Education of body, mind and spirit* for village members of all ages. Thompson beautifully describes this ideal in which "the entire village would be a contemplative educational community," with its basic way of life being "the adventure of consciousness.... Everyone living in the community would be involved in an experiential approach to education, from contemplative birth ... to contemplative death."

The concept of the meta-industrial village is the end product of Thompson's theories and visions and an impressive contribution to speculations about the future. It seems to be quite consistent with the ideals and spirit of Cayce's perspective on the 21st century and beyond, but it is far more detailed and specific in its description than is any lifestyle model proposed in the Cayce prophecies. There appears to be no requirement in his vision that everyone live in such a village. We can well imagine that major cities will continue to exist into the 21st century. However, the quality of life and the security to be found in the meta-industrial village would likely attract many people – perhaps a majority – to this new model for living.

Visions of a Modern Mystic

Among the many teachers and psychically sensitive people who have written about a new millennium, David Spangler is a significant contributor. For several years he served as a formulator of educational development for the spiritual community Findhorn, in Scotland. Returning to America, he founded the Lorian Association and has been active in lecturing and writing about the emergent new world order. He describes his own method of receiving information on this theme as an attunement to both a universal consciousness and specific nonphysical beings in other dimensions of reality.

Among Spangler's various books, *Revelation: The Birth of a New Age* beautifully expounds his ideas about these times of transition. An essential feature of that book is the notion that a new millennial consciousness is already here, but its current existence is simultaneous with that of the old world. The idea of two worlds may at first sound confusing, but if we look with sensitivity at what is going on within and without us, we may recognize that this is exactly the state of affairs in these changing times.

In Spangler's view, a new era is born first in the formative etheric energies of the planet – a level of subtle energy not yet a part of the established scientific worldview. A major shift has already occurred ethereally. Nevertheless, the old world's momentum perpetuates its apparent reality and produces a seeming inertia to the change in etheric patterns. For centuries, old world assumptions have guided the creative dimensions of higher realities, which have in turn manifested as the physical world we have known. Even after the creative impulse is removed from these old etheric patterns, they continue to have their effect for some time. But they will necessarily play themselves out. They have within them the seeds of their own demise. An effective yet admittedly distasteful analogy is a chicken whose head has been severed, but who continues lifelike movement for a while.

When we take this concept a step further, it suggests to us a strategy for building a new planetary culture. Our forces should not be in conflict with the old. The old world will fail of itself – primarily, Spangler feels, because the creative input at the etheric level no longer exists. Our job is to be a part of the new world, to be attuned to a new consciousness that already exists and to learn to manifest its reality. Spangler puts it this way: "To know the new, one must be the new. To engage in conflict with the disintegrating patterns is to be at one with them, just as to use violence to stop violence is to defeat one's essential purpose. The old will separate itself naturally..." (*Revelation*, p. 170).

This philosophy about times of change is certainly found in the Cayce prophecies, as well. To those who inquired about how to build a new world, he always responded this way: *focus on the positive.* In other words, both Cayce and Spangler point out that by keeping our attention directed toward whatever is helpful and hopeful, we play the most constructive role possible in allowing a new consciousness to emerge on earth.

Prophecies of a Modern Day Psychic

Irene Hughes is one of the most gifted psychics of our own times. For decades she has been highly regarded for her clairvoyant and precognitive abilities. Although many contemporary psychics seem to merely mimic Cayce in what they have to say about the future, Hughes is clearly her own woman. And, just like Edgar Cayce, she has established her work over many decades. One of her most famous predictions was the Chicago blizzard of 1967, which gained her headlines around the world. Dozens of internationally known personalities have consulted directly with her; and throughout the 1970s and 1980s she was one of just a small number of psychics and intuitives who gained wide acceptance and respect. Much of her notoriety can from her uncanny talent of helping police departments around the country solve or locate key crime evidence. In addition, she has been a longtime newspaper columnist on astrology, and she was the on-air host of a highly regarded radio program for 10 years.

Although she is now semi-retired, Irene was graciously willing to share a few of her prophecies to be included in this book about the Cayce prophecies. Here are some of the things she foresees for us:

- Regarding the weather: All the writings and talk about "global warming" seem to be totally false. Just because it is warmer in some areas of our planet than in others, is no proof. Nor is the melting of bits of icebergs. Scientists should be aware that our sun is weakening in energy, and that massive changes will soon be obvious in the Milky Way, which foretell of some "chilling" endings of our solar system. All the floods, destructive lightening and violent windstorms, indicated by the changing positions of the revolutionary Uranus and Saturn, and even our very cool summer in the normally very warm conditions, indicated by them, warn us of a forthcoming deep freeze. I predict that our summers will continue to be cooler, and our winters much colder, with lots of ice and snow.

- Due to foreign countries, especially Saudi Arabia, Japan, and others, dumping American-bought stocks and investments, we will be in a more massive Depression, beginning July 17, 2005, than we have had in 40 years.

- Wall Street will "close its doors," no later than the end of 2006, and trading on the floor will end; stocks biddings will be done through new technologies and the computer.

- These events will force the United States to create a totally new financial/economic system, not using "American currency." I first published this prediction in the late 1970s, and have repeated it several times since. My prediction indicated that I "psychically" saw a card (like a credit card) that would be used for our automobile license, our address, and other important information on it, that we would use that card for all purchases, for every form of monetary payment, and this would lead to extreme banking changes.

- I have published a prediction in the 1990s that God put Pluto, the "great exposer" planet, in the sign of religion (Sagittarius), to expose all of the evils of all religions; that this planet rules the sex organs of men and women, and therefore the exposure of pedophiles and other non-Christian activities would lead to the end of all religions by 2012. And with that prediction (repeated in 2003), I wrote that God has also put the "great awakener" Uranus in the spiritual sign of Pisces, to awaken all mankind to greater spiritual ways of life, at the same time all organized religions are dying. And that we would have a more beautiful, moral, caring people, and the "thousand years of peace" would begin at the end of 2012.

- Medical miracles will be very obvious in 2005, with the use of "chips" inserted in the eye, to help the blind see; and that other chips put into bananas that humans eat will reveal any problems with internal organs, when that person stands before an incredible television.

- One day, unusual X-rays will show "pictures" of the thought the brain is producing, and it will be amazing that the pictures are like a "movie."

These fascinating images and visions from Irene Hughes may, in some case, stretch us to consider what may at first seem impossible. The same was true in Edgar Cayce's own era as people who heard his readings had to rethink what sort of future might lie ahead.

Conclusions

One of the strongest and most reliable methods of investigation is to search for parallel statements and principles. Corroborative evidence is often the most dependable way to recognize reliable information. In this chapter we have examined half a dozen independent sources of prophetic wisdom, some dating back many centuries and some from creative thinkers and visionaries of our own times. Although certain differences are to be found among these sources and the Cayce prophecies, the large number of parallels is strikingly significant. This comparative approach makes even stronger the conclusion that the Cayce prophecies are worthy of serious consideration.

But what is perhaps most impressive from this kind of parallel study is the sense that each of us who is living in these dramatic times of change has an important role to play. To a large measure the future is still being shaped, and we have a say in making the new millennium what it will be. Especially in Part III of this book – A Primer for Living in the 21st Century That Cayce Envisioned – we will explore how we can go about co-creating a positive 21st century.

Edgar Cayce

Born: **March 18, 1877** **3:03 p.m.**
Died: **January 03, 1945** **7:15 p.m.**

CHAPTER FOUR

A NEW WORLD ORDER
FOR THE 21ST CENTURY

Humanity is ready for a fundament change. It's not a fine-tuning of what has come before. It's a radical transformation of how we live. That is the basic assumption of a set of prophetic readings that Cayce gave about the political and social dimensions of our modern world. The first century of the new millennium will see a whole new way of living on earth – a change even more drastic than the one five hundred years ago when the Middle Ages ended and the Renaissance began. A new consciousness in humanity will arise in the 21st century – something that is so completely different that Cayce called it a "new root race." It will profoundly affect political, social, economic, and scientific aspects of our society.

The expression "root race" is found in several metaphysical systems of thought, and it is not a reference to racial differences as we typically think of them. Instead, it refers to a new order of human being. The Cayce prophecies for the 21st century and beyond challenge us to imagine that we are on the verge of a dramatic new beginning, a new root race. One critical aspect of the consciousness of this new root race concerns an understanding of material versus nonmaterial life. In this new millennium we can expect a revolutionary change: the universal acceptance of the fact that we survive physical death. The continuity of life will be accepted, not just as a statement of religious faith, but as a mainstream scientific reality. Of course, the early signs of this widespread understanding are all around us, led by research into out-of-body experiences and near-death experiences. These findings are dramatic – some would say nearly incontrovertible – for anyone who looks objectively at the research data. Truly we live in times when a remarkable convergence is taking place on this age-old question of survival. Religion and science are coming to the same conclusion.

Nevertheless, strong cultural forces work against this new agreement. Certain elements of our society would just as soon we dismiss or forget such an important fact as our own timeless existence as spiritual beings. Much of our impatient, consumer-driven culture depends on the emotions of fear and desire – the very feelings that so easily melt away when we accept the continuity of life. And so, there is still considerable work to be done if the consciousness of a new root race is really to take hold and guide the world.

How might this Cayce prediction about overcoming the fear of death actually unfold? The development of a certain form of psychic perception may play a great role in such a change of consciousness. (We'll look more broadly at the topic of psychic awareness later in this chapter.) If large numbers of the human family evolve clairvoyant abilities, imagine what might be the result. Perhaps people would begin to "see" and communicate with those who have passed on. Using the same type of expanded sight that allows someone to see auras, people in this new century and thereafter might perceive the spiritual world bodies of friends and loved ones.

Such a development would have tremendous impact on the values and awareness of humanity. So much of human behavior has long been motivated by a fear of death, by uncertainty about our long-term future as individual beings. Competition and aggression stem largely from the drive to survive and strengthen our sense of power and permanence. If it was a common *experience* to know that death is merely a transition to a new way of living, we can guess that efforts for peace and cooperation in the world would be enhanced.

This speculation dovetails nicely with a biblical prophecy about times of change. Certain verses from the Bible seem to predict that the reappearance of the Christ is to be associated with a period in which the dead will be resurrected. But how probable is it, we might wonder, that corpses will crawl out of the graves? Another interpretation is that *experientially* it will be *as if* the dead have been resurrected. In other words, to those of us still alive in flesh bodies, it will be as if the dead have come back to life – because we will sense them and communicate with them in their astral or etheric forms. Perhaps the biblical prophecy means that the reappearance of Christ will come at a time in history when humanity has developed its spiritual sensitivity to the point where other dimensions of life can be readily sensed and experienced.

Humanity has flirted with this breakthrough principle in the past, according to Cayce. The new root race will possess an awareness similar in many ways to one that was present on the earth long ago. In ancient times, he said, there were societies based on an understanding of the inherent oneness of all energy and the continuity of soul-life. The opportunities for humanity in the 21st century and beyond are not merely a return to something we had many millennia ago; but, one task of the new root race is to go back and reclaim certain elements of the human legacy that have been ignored or forgotten.

The trigger for this collective recall is to be an astounding archaeological discovery. According to the Cayce prophecies, this event is a strong possibility for the years right at the turn of the 21st century. In several places on the globe, records can be found of an extraordinary human civilization, which predates by many thousands of years the earliest known advanced civilization. That culture had developed many sophisticated scientific ideas, including the harnessing of solar energy via specialized crystals, plus advanced energy medicine techniques. What's more, that civilization possessed a knowledge base that connected their religious understanding with their scientific principles, just as we are on the verge of doing here in the initial years of our own new millennium.

If the traces of such a civilization – victim of its own mistakes, internal discord about purpose, and ultimate self-destruction – could be found now, it might be one of the most important breakthroughs in recent history. The Cayce prophecies suggest it could be just around the corner. Those records are to be found in any of three spots:

1. Beneath the sands in front of the Sphinx. A small, pyramid like Hall of Records is buried there, according to Cayce, and just waiting to be unearthed. Among the three possibilities, this is the location about which Cayce was most *specific*; he saw an underground passageway coming from the paw of the Sphinx that would lead archaeologists to the tremendous find. In recent years, research teams have been actively investigating Cayce's hypothesis. They have used noninvasive technologies such as underground mapping radar to discover intriguing anomalies (e.g., unexpected spaces or cavern like areas) for which the Egyptian government may eventually permit limited drilling or excavation.

2. Somewhere on the Yucatan peninsula. Here Cayce was not as specific, but he suggests that remnants of that same ancient

civilization left records nearly identical to the ones buried in the other two spots. The best clue about exact location indicates that the archaeological find could come from investigating an area near or beneath an existent, ancient temple: "where the temple there is overshadowing same" (#2012-1).

3. Somewhere near the island of Bimini in the Bahamas. The Cayce prophecies offer some tantalizing clues about exact underwater spots to investigate, and limited investigations for the legendary Atlantis have been going on for several years to test Cayce's theory. (We'll explore, too, in a later chapter the possibility that Cayce's story of Atlantis may have been precognitive rather than retrocognitive – that is, prophetic and warning us about our own future, instead of a clairvoyant peek into an unrecorded history.)

What might be the impact if one or more of these areas yield evidence of an advanced civilization that was based on sophisticated understanding of the oneness of all energy and the direct experience by its people of the soul's survival? Skeptics might argue that it would have little or no influence on a modern world whose attention span for news gets shorter every year, whose inhabitants aren't even interested in history.

But a counterargument can be made that if such an archaeological find coincides with times of turmoil and stress (perhaps even daunting earth change events), it could well trigger a whole new way for modern society to see itself. Consider what might happen if we stretch our sense of roots back thousands of years earlier and realize that some of the fruits of civilization we're most proud of were actually accomplished long ago. It might humble us. It might awaken us to the possibility that our own culture is fragile and that in our vulnerability we could suffer a similar fate and practically vanish.

With these background ideas in mind about a new root race – a new kind of humanity for this planet – let's consider some further prophecies and visions of Cayce. Each prophecy is a piece of a grand mosaic. That big picture is ultimately a hopeful and exciting one about the new kind of awareness that is about to emerge. The prophecies of change documented in the remainder of this chapter will cover five areas:

1. International politics and the destiny of nations;
2. A transformation of medical science;
3. The convergence of metaphysics and science, especially in

regard to the journey of the soul and an understanding of our origins;

4. Expanded human mental capacities, especially via intuition;
5. A new philosophy of material resources and the Law of Supply.

Through these prophecies Cayce tried to help us catch a picture of what it might be like to live in the world that stretches into the new millennium, what it might be like as members of this new root race.

The World Affairs Prophecies

Cayce made many surprising, bold statements about the nations of the Earth and their destinies. The so-called "world affairs readings" most often focused on questions of Cayce's own day: the Depression and the tensions that eventually led to World War II. However, occasional prophecies looked beyond the war and predicted the course nations would take well into the 21st century.

The essential ingredient in these predictions is the need Cayce saw for a "leveling" in the world. In calling for equality he was not associating himself with any particular political system. Rather, his political philosophy, as well as his vision of the direction in which the world must head, focused on *the oneness of humanity*. That "leveling," as the readings called it, is a process that pertains to judgment as well as resources. All persons must be seen as equals in the way they are measured or judged. And all persons must have an equal opportunity to share in the resources that sustain life. This means not only food, shelter, clothing and energy, but also knowledge, appreciation and love, which sustain the mind and soul.

A single reading (#3976-18) given just fourteen months before the outbreak of World War II in Europe best outlines Cayce's visionary ideas about a world in flux: A new order of conditions is eventually to emerge. It will be accompanied by a cleansing at all strata of the society, from the richest to the poorest. Central to the transition will be the principle that each soul is its brother's and sister's keeper. In many elements of society – political, economic, and social – the understanding will emerge that a "leveling" is required.

But Cayce's prophecy goes on to say that these changes won't happen instantaneously or magically. Individuals, groups, and organizations that espouse this ideal of oneness and equality will need to work hard, to practice and apply what they believe in. The transition may not be easy because it will require a new way of thinking and behaving in society: "There cannot be one measuring stick for the laborer in the field and the man behind the counter, and another for the man behind the money changers. All are equal – not only under the material law, but under the spiritual."

The prophecy continues with a warning of great stresses ahead. Family members will find themselves on opposing sides in this struggle. Groups will clash, as will races. But this transition is a part of human destiny. "The leveling must come." Our only real protection comes from a single source, according to the way this prophecy ends: by personally setting a high spiritual ideal and then diligently living it in relationship to the people around us.

In one passage the readings made clear that this task of leveling was not a call for communism, even in the pure sense of the word, thus stated, "Not that all would be had in common as in the communistic idea, save as to keep that balance, to keep that oneness" (#3976-19). On the other hand, the Cayce prophecies spoke even more strongly against the notion of survival of the fittest (or of the greatest and most powerful), which has characterized pure capitalism. It will not do for us to sit back and say that those people who are exploited are simply not motivated enough. Nor will it do to slip into a distorted notion of reincarnation and soul-level responsibility, claiming that the disadvantaged of the world are merely meeting their own karma. Cayce's visionary image of international affairs was that peace can come only when the ideal of "I am my brother's and sister's keeper" has been adopted.

How will that come about? What changes will we have to see in specific nations if that purpose and ideal is ever to be achieved? The analysis given by Cayce was that the problem lies in a particular tendency of all nations to "set some standard of some activity of man as its idea" (#3976-29). In other words, nations have different concepts about:

1. How human life should be evaluated,
2. What constitutes the good life,
3. What constitutes justice, and
4. What scope of authority a government should have over individuals.

And the efforts of nations to impose their own standards on other nations create international tensions and wars. For each major nation Cayce saw a work or a change to be done.

In the case of Russia, Cayce foresaw a tremendous transition. He warned that there would never be peace in that country until there was freedom of speech. He predicted a reawakened religious spirit in Russia, which if developed would be the hope of the world. He also clearly predicted a major role in world leadership for Russia.

When asked to comment in 1938 about the prospects for Russia, he predicted that a new understanding would come to a troubled people. Oppression and self-indulgence had produced the excesses of communism, and until there was authentic freedom – of speech and worship – turmoil would persist.

The theme of religious freedom had actually been part of a Cayce prophecy six years earlier in reading #3976-10. In his vision of the world of a new millennium, Cayce saw Russia's religious development as pivotal. He said, "On Russia's religious development will come the greater hope of the world." These words indicate that spiritual transformations among Russians will trigger changes in people and nations worldwide. What's more, we can expect that religious progress in Russia will so ease international tension that it will make room for hopeful, new conditions to arise.

Years later, in 1944, yet another Cayce prophecy used the theme of hope in relation to the Russians. The key to Russia fulfilling its potential will be freedom and the ideal of service ("that each man will live for his fellow man").

What sort of timing can we expect for such planetary leadership, and in what form? The Cayce prophecies made clear that such a potential can be fulfilled only by Russia joining in cooperative efforts with the United States. As to timing, he stated that "the principle has been born" (#3976-29). What could he have meant by this? In 1944, when this reading was given, a group of souls had recently incarnated into Russia with a purpose to turn that nation around-to make it a champion for peace and permit a religious rebirth within its borders. It took years for this possibility to crystallize. Those souls born in 1940 or thereabouts were unable to assume positions to exert much influence on the decision-making process of the government until they were at least fifty years old. Throughout the Cold War era aged leadership characterized that nation. The timing seems about right that in 1989 extraordinary changes began to take place in Russia. Certainly the Gorbachev-led changes were just a beginning, a start toward what Cayce predicted. But the transformation is about more than just one man's political efforts. The group of souls that Cayce envisioned still has considerable work left to do. They must remember the purpose for which they came and not get caught up in the ways of the old system.

What about prophecies concerning the United States? In the case of America, Cayce had some strong words of warning, but words of promise as well. Again the principle of leveling came up. There is a warning that unless creative, loving steps are taken to insure greater equality within this nation, there will come a revolution, a physical, armed struggle, because this is the means that some people will resort to when they feel helpless to effect change in any other way. Cayce did not give an endorsement of such methods – only a warning that they may be just ahead for us.

The prophecies regarding America emphasize freedom and the leadership role that America is to play on the world stage – leadership both with responsible expressions of freedom and the deepening of spirituality. Although America is destined to have the opportunity for spiritual leadership as we move into the new millennium, it is by no means certain that we will collectively claim that special role. The outcome rests with our use of the freedoms we possess.

The ideal of freedom is one to be admired, but Cayce questioned just how honestly America lives that ideal. In a prophecy given in 1944 – some two decades before the civil rights movement – he observed that our nation was being run in such a fashion that the hearts and minds of many people were "bound." This surely refers in large part to minorities, such as the African-American citizens of the country. He identified three aspects of life where this constriction affected many people: speech, worship, and the basic physical needs of life. It could be persuasively argued that progress has been made in the sixty years since that warning, but no doubt we still have considerable room for improvement.

Another prophetic reading identified the great fear of Americans: servitude in any form. We are afraid of losing our freedom, and yet we may have distorted what that very word means. We have made the quality of obedience a sign of weakness and in so doing have undermined our spirituality. *Our actions cannot fulfill the challenge and opportunity of spiritual leadership in the world if we have a self-serving definition of freedom.* Authentic freedom comes from the desire and ability to be obedient – not to another nation but to God. And in our obedience to God we will be called to loving, responsible service. This means national actions that place a high priority on the well-being of others. Although it seems paradoxical, Cayce states that the nation that would be greatest – and most free must be a servant to all.

Cayce clearly articulated this principle as the guiding definition for national greatness in the 21st century. It's a hard principle for our nation, or for any nation, to understand and to live. Misunderstanding it, we slip into what Cayce called the great sin of America: pride. This quality could stand between America and its spiritual destiny to provide leadership for the world. *Pride, not just on the part of the government, but in the people as individuals, needs to be overcome.* Our tendency to boast separates us from other nations and people of this world; it puts up barriers between Americans and the citizens of other countries.

Once Cayce was asked very directly about American spiritual destiny. He answered that every nation has a specific spiritual destiny- that each one is led by forces from the heavens. America can fulfill her destiny only by adopting greater brotherhood and love of others. Otherwise the leadership of the world will once again move westward: "...Each and every nation, is led-even as in heaven. If there is not the acceptance in America of the closer brotherhood of man, the love of the neighbor as self, civilization must wend its way westward. . ." (#3976-15). From other Cayce prophecies we can ascertain that that westward movement would be to eastern Asia.

The key to whether or not leadership eventually moves is this question: What will individuals do with the spiritual knowledge they have? It is not so much the choices of government officials or the legislative bills passed by Congress that determine whether or not we will fulfill our national challenge. Instead, it's what each of us does as an individual that will collectively create our future.

Perhaps the beneficiary of a movement of civilization westward would be China. This mysterious nation has only in the past few years made efforts to become part of the world community once again. Its resources and people are vast. Its spiritual legacy from several thousand years is matched by no other major nation except India. It is exciting to imagine what good could be done by these people if their national ideal and purpose became unity and spirituality. It was just such a vision that Cayce put forth in the world affairs prophecies. China will eventually be the "cradle of Christianity, as applied in the lives of men" (#3976-29). However, no time frame accompanies this prediction beyond the caution that "it is far off as man counts time."

Are we then to expect that someday there will be widespread Christianity in the world's most populous nation? A few decades ago that seemed nearly impossible. During the 1960s what churches were there had to be closed and religious activity was forbidden. But now there are signs of change, and maybe Cayce's prophecy will yet come true. Recent newspaper accounts tell an amazing story. The World Council of Churches reports that Christianity is growing in China "at breathtaking speed." A council delegation returned from an eleven-day trip to China in the spring of 1996 and made a "conservative estimate" of baptized Christians: ten million and growing fast.

But maybe the proliferation of Christian churches isn't exactly what the Cayce prophecy meant. The key word in the prediction is Christianity as applied in human lives. Perhaps it is in this country that *the way of living with each other* that Jesus proposed shall find a willing climate. Whether or not the Chinese accept Jesus is secondary to this prophecy. Here is a people, in Cayce's estimation, who may be especially ripe for the application of Christ's teachings. In doing so, they would surely assume the spiritual leadership of civilization on this planet. But, as the prophecy says, this may be many years away. We have our own work to do closer to home right now, toward that same ideal.

Finally, it should be noted that amongst all the world affairs predictions of revolution, turmoil, changes of government and so forth, there is still a message of profound encouragement. It is so easy for us to be discouraged by current events and to dwell upon the great confusion among nations. However, Cayce may have been able to look at the world from a broader perspective. In that remarkable state from which he gave his prophetic readings, he may have been able to see the unfolding of history in terms of ages and not just the decades and centuries we see. And from this vantage point, he said that *there is hope.* For our own times, just past the turn of the millennium, Cayce foresaw a tremendous seeking in our world. Remarkable numbers of people would desire oneness with God and an understanding of God's

purposes. The seeking would be greater than it had been for a
And it will continue to increase each year, giving us good reason to
hopeful.

Prophecies of Health and Healing
in the 21st Century

Cayce made many hopeful predictions about healing in the new
millennium. In fact, there is considerable evidence of his skill at
predicting trends in medical science. For example, in 1927 he boldly
asserted that the day would come when a person's overall physical
condition could be completely diagnosed from a single drop of blood.
At that time it seemed fanciful, but the day is fast approaching when
medical technology can do exactly that.

His prophetic statements about finding a remedy to cancer are
also noteworthy. In the 1920s and 1930s, Cayce spoke on repeated
occasions of a different orientation to the prevention and cure of many
(if not all) cancers, one of strengthening the immune system. This ran
counter to the prevailing wisdom about cancer in Cayce's own era. It
wasn't until the early 1960s that a failure in the immune system was
even seriously considered by mainstream medicine as linked to some
cancers.

In a few of his psychic readings on cancer, Cayce spoke of
culturing the blood – that is, removing a small portion, mixing it with
prescribed solutions, and then re-infusing this cultured blood,
apparently to stimulate the white blood cells. This procedure, although
never carried out for any of the cancer patients Cayce diagnosed,
closely resembles an experimental method of modern cancer research.
In the 21st century we may well see that Cayce was far ahead of his
time in associating cancer with the immune system.

But such novel techniques are simply fascinating details of a
much bigger picture. Cayce envisioned for the new millennium a
profoundly different kind of human understanding about how the body
stays healthy and how it reestablishes health when something goes
wrong. Those prophecies are based on the emergence of a
fundamental conception of the human being, which is holistic. In fact,
Cayce was characterized as the "father of holistic medicine" by an
article in the *Journal of the American Medical Association.*

that in the 21st century we would begin to
'e human being is a set of interpenetrating energy
...iotional, mental, and spiritual. The concept of
...ilness (already widely accepted as an explanation for
...ments) will have greatly expanded. Not only will we
...ciate the authenticity of psychosomatic health, but our approach
to healing will also appreciate the deep, spiritual undertones to many
illnesses and maladies.

To encapsulate Cayce's vision of medicine in the new
millennium, it will be energy medicine. Patterns in the flesh, in our
emotional outlook, in our attitudes, and in our deepest sense of purpose
will all be understood as expressions of energy. Although modern
medical science is only begrudgingly beginning to consider the subtle
forms of energy that mystics like Cayce describe, the day may be soon
ahead when they will be widely recognized.

As noted earlier, Cayce even predicted that in the centuries just
ahead humanity will understand that religion and science must merge.
A starting point is the discovery that electricity is one way for us to
understand the creative force that is God. That is to say, electrical
forces are the key to the elusive "vital force" healers and
metaphysicians have sought for ages.

That is not to say that Cayce advocates giving up our worship
of God as the imparter of high ideals and moral principles. Cayce's
innovative concept of electricity is not an invitation to worship
electrical batteries or the products of the electronics industry. Instead,
it's a recognition that there is *one fundamental life force,* which is
creative and healing in its nature. That divine force expresses itself in
the three-dimensional material world as positive and negative charges:
electricity. As one Cayce passage put it: "For materiality is – or matter
is – that demonstration and manifestation of the units of positive and
negative energy, or electricity, or God" (#412-9).

The potential consequences of such a breakthrough
understanding by humanity is astounding. For example, an energy
medicine of the 21st century will begin to show us how new forms of
electrical therapy can stimulate healing and even regeneration.
Experimentation in the late 20th century began to show in some animal
studies that electrical impulses can promote the re-growth of limbs. *In
the 21st century and beyond, electricity will be seen as the fundamental
building block of everything we experience in material life, including*

our bodies.

So what might be possible in the decades and centuries to come? One exciting possibility is the sustenance of human life to age 120 or even 150, as noted in the Introduction to this book. This is a lifespan that Cayce suggested is within our reach and would even be normal if we began to practice health care appropriately. He even went so far as to say that a human being really ought to be able to regenerate himself and live as long as he desires, if he is ready to "pay the price" in terms of the sacrifices and commitments required for a holistically balanced life- style.

Several basic features make up Cayce's health care approach, and he predicted they will form the foundation of our health and healing practice in the new millennium. In his book *Keys to Health* which summarizes the essence of Cayce's visionary health philosophy, Eric Mein, M.D., identifies several key points about what is possible for a health science of the future. Each of these points concerns our own attitudes and approaches to health and wellness:

1. *The interconnections of the body.* Cayce tried to show, well before most medical experts were willing to listen, that the systems of the body are deeply interlinked. Slowly evidence is mounting of the wisdom of this idea. For example, as the new medical science of psychoneuroimmunology has begun to demonstrate, the mind, the nervous system, and the immune system are all connected. Even though this link might make sense to the layman, it was not until recently that scientific research had any evidence that these three human systems directly affect each other.

2. *Self-responsibility.* We'll certainly still have physicians throughout the 21st century, but we will come to see health and healing as processes that require our own participation first.

3. *No magic bullet.* Modern medical research has provided us with so many impressive medications that it's easy to slip into expecting a magic pill for any ailment. But in spite of the wonderful progress in pharmacology, the fact remains that for many (if not most) human maladies it's the body itself that creates the healing, not a magic medicine. Dr. Mein writes that by some estimates as many as seventy-five percent of the patients who visit their doctors have illnesses that will get better on their own, if they are going to get better at all.

In the 21st century medicine that Cayce envisions, there will be formulas, pills, and drugs. But we will have learned more about the marvelous self-healing forces that can be elicited from within ourselves. This potential is beautifully illustrated by the way that most current prescription drugs work within our bodies: they mimic what the body has the potential to do for itself. For example, morphine can eliminate pain because the chemical structure of its molecules attach to specific receptors that exist on cell membranes. But morphine molecules can block pain only because human cellular chemistry already provides receptors for certain molecules to do so. That chemical possibility existed in the human body for thousands and thousands of years before poppies were ever refined to make the drug morphine. And, in fact, in the 1970s medical researchers discovered why. The body has a drug of its own – endorphins – that blocks pain naturally. In the medicine of a new millennium we will discover many more ways in which drugs are only a temporary, stopgap measure until the patient can learn for himself how to elicit his body's own healing forces.

The Cayce prophecies include several specific breakthroughs in medical understanding that might be just ahead for us. Each one is related to the innovative holistic philosophy he pioneered, among them these promising areas for discovery:

1.   The majority of people in mental hospitals will show measurable improvement from properly administered osteopathic adjustments to the spinal vertebrae.

2.   The mysterious skin disorder psoriasis will be completely curable using a specialized diet, specific herbal teas, and osteopathic adjustments.

3.   Many cases of asthma will be treated as a disorder of the nerve reflexes, using osteopathic adjustments, along with a specialized diet and improved eliminations.

4.   Although slow acting in its healing effect – requiring three to seven years to cure – a new therapy for multiple sclerosis will emerge, one that stimulates the body's ability to absorb the trace mineral gold, plus the use of therapeutic massage along the spine and the extremities.

5.   Many who suffer from epilepsy will be significantly helped by a new form of treatment that recognizes the role played by spinal lesions and a portion of the intestinal tract called the lacteal duct.

External castor oil packs on the lower abdomen, along with osteopathic adjustments of particular vertebrae will be key elements of this new therapy.

6.   A diet made up of eighty percent alkaline-producing foods (most fruits and vegetables) and twenty percent acid-producing (most meats, grains, and starches) will be identified as the nutritional balance most likely to sustain health.

These are just a few of the revolutionary methods Cayce proposes for 21st century energy medicine. If even a few of them result in positive findings by medical researchers, they may prove to be among his most important prophecies.

A New Understanding of Our Origins

In the 21st century there can be a meeting of "evolution theory" and "involution theory." Charles Darwin is, of course, the most famous proponent of evolution as the way to understand our human origins. Cayce, on the other hand, seems to advocate another approach that sees spiritual beings "getting involved with" materiality.

One doesn't usually speak of Charles Darwin and Edgar Cayce in the same breath. These two pivotal figures, both born in the 19th century, seem to have worked creatively in different spheres – one as a pioneer of natural science; the other as an explorer of the inner places of mind and spirit. In fact, it might be easy to assume that their research and teachings contradict each other – one focused on the physical realities of biology and natural selection; the other emphasizing the primacy of the invisible world that stands behind any material reality.

However, a personal adventure made me rethink just how far apart or how compatible Darwin and Cayce really are. By traveling to a far off place that was pivotal to the development of Darwin's theories, I was stimulated to look for ways in which these two men could be seen at least as *complements* in creating a bigger picture of how life works.

In many ways the "New Age" of which Cayce and others spoke is largely a matter of science and spirituality finding a common ground. For example, one cutting edge of our times is to see explorations of the inner world and explorations of the outer world as essentially two sides of the same coin. Those who resist this synthesis will be like the leaders of the Church in the Renaissance era, who stubbornly held to the medieval world-view and rejected the new knowledge of scientists such as Copernicus and Galileo. And now, at the start of the 21st century – a period that looks to be the century of biological and life sciences — those of us deeply interested in spirituality should be looking for ways to bridge the teachings of pioneer figures such as Darwin and Cayce.

For me, the stimulus to this kind of thinking was a recent trip to the Galapagos Islands. Not long after the publication of our A.R.E. Press book *Twelve Positive Habits of Spiritually Centered People*, my daughter Sarah and I were invited to Ecuador for a series of lectures and workshop presentations in the two major cities of this beautiful country that straddles the equator. Then we traveled some 600 miles west out into the Pacific to the Galapagos Islands for four days to see firsthand the spots that Darwin had visited in the 1830s as he continued to work on developing his theories of evolution and natural selection.

The Galapagos Islands are volcanic in origin – somewhat like the Hawaiian Islands – and they have been called an archipelago of unrivaled beauty, mystery and amazing creatures. They lie exactly along the equator at zero degrees latitude, and also at 90 degrees west longitude, half way between the International Dateline and the Greenwich Line in England. Occupying this auspicious geographic spot, these ten major islands and many other smaller ones have amazing variations. To the traveler's eye, this is a little world unto itself. The islands have a wide variety of topographical appearances and vegetation, not to mention the famous varieties of animal life, such as land tortoises, iguanas, and albatross, just to name a few. But as we will see later, there was something very special about these islands that made it possible for Darwin to collect some of the most important evidence to support his developing theories.

It seems like a far off and inhospitable place, however, for a young genius to have come. And who was this man who has gone down in history as one of the most revolutionary figures in science? At age sixteen, Darwin left home to study medicine at Edinburgh University. But the sight of surgery performed without anesthesia repelled him, and he eventually went to Cambridge University to prepare to become a clergyman. After receiving his degree, Darwin continued to develop his passion for studying nature, and he accepted an invitation to serve as an unpaid naturalist on the *H.M.S. Beagle*, which departed in late 1831 on a five-year scientific expedition to lands of the Pacific Ocean.

Darwin's research resulting from this voyage formed the basis of his famous book, *On the Origin of Species by Means of Natural Selection*. Published in 1859 – some 18 years still before Edgar Cayce was born – the book was highly controversial. In this groundbreaking publication, Darwin outlined his theory of evolution, challenging the contemporary beliefs about the creation of life on earth. Darwin continued to write and publish his works on biology throughout his life, and he lived with his wife and family just outside of London. There are indications that in the latter part of his life he suffered from panic disorder, as well as from a rare disease contracted during his travels in South America. Darwin was plagued with fatigue and intestinal sickness for the rest of his life, and he died in 1882.

As we will all remember from high school biology class, Darwin's observations, theories and publications flew in the face of biological science of his times. In fact, it served to undermine the entire worldview of his era including the notion that God had carefully and purposefully created the world and each type of creature and plant, exactly as we find them in modern times. In that era most people thought that the world they lived in was the same as that created by God thousands of years ago, as described in Genesis. Darwin's most controversial point of all was the notion that became popularized as "humans descended from monkeys," which of course is not precisely the point of his theory but still captures *the essence of the principle: human beings are really not so special; we are just yet another species that has developed by the process of evolution.*

At first glance it would seem that Cayce's teachings several decades later refute Darwin, at least when it comes to the origins of humanity. As Cayce once put it: "Man DID NOT descend from the monkey, but man has evolved, resuscitation, you see, from time to time, time to time, here a little, there a little, line upon line and line and line upon line." (#3744-5) But how are we to take this statement, especially in light of the nearly irrefutable scientific evidence that our own bodies as Homo sapiens contain such extensive DNA similarity to other primates? We must be careful here. We become like the stubborn leaders of the Church 500 years ago if we ignore the inescapable fact that our bodies belong to the animal kingdom and they are the product of millennia of biological evolution.

In fact there are 123 of Cayce's readings that refer to "evolution," so it was not a principle he disputed. *Rather it was a matter of defining "what" evolves and how the invisible, non-material world of spirit is ALSO involved in the process.*

Cayce's story of creation and the emergence of life forms on the earth is certainly a complex and fascinating account. Some find it inspiring; others are left with the impression that it is a fantastic tale, devoid of supportive evidence. But lest we get caught up in the sensationalistic sides of his account – spiritual consciousness rebelliously projecting into animals and plants; mixed breeds of animals; humans with tails and feathers – let's focus on the essence of his story of our creation.

Cayce's emphasis was upon "involution" rather than "evolution." Involution is the process of "becoming involved with or entangled within." And so, in Cayce's spiritual philosophy, man's origin is a spiritual creation first and foremost. In this sense, "man did not evolve from apes" because each of us was initially a being of the spiritual world. But the divine plan was for us to grow beyond what we were at the beginning – in this sense, to "evolve" in consciousness. The plan was for us to know our oneness with God *and* to know fully our own individuality. ("...as soul-entities, might know ourselves to be ourselves, and yet one with Him...#3003-1) That plan required involution – the coming of spiritual beings into the three-dimensional, material world. *Through involution we were given the opportunity to experience ourselves in a focused, individual way.* A new kind of awareness at least was being made possible.

But in Cayce's elaborate account, things got off track. Souls began to use their free will in a rebellious way. Experiences became not so much a matter of bringing spiritual awareness *into* material reality, but instead self-gratification and self-diversion. Materiality began to serve not as a proving ground for a new kind of conscious awareness but instead as a prison and entrapment. The potential of involution was being lost.

To redeem the possibilities of involution, evolution needed to play a role. *But it was not the purely materialistic evolution, the sort that was all Darwin could envision.* From the spiritual world, a very special kind of body was created for souls. The human form was created first as a spiritual creation. That body made of subtle energy had the pattern for a highly sensitive nervous system and the spiritual centers (or "chakras") that would make possible a new kind of individual consciousness.

But that pattern of the subtle energy – that spiritual body – needed to take on a physical presence, and now the physical process of evolution came into play also. Through intervention from the spiritual world, a species of primates came under the influence of that bodily pattern which had been created in the invisible realm. And over many millennia – *following the physical laws of mutation and natural selection* – a new species slowly evolved as Homo sapiens. In the "Philosophy" chapter of Cayce's biography *There Is A River*, Thomas Sugrue describes it this way: "Souls descended on these apes – hovering above and about them rather than inhabiting them – and influenced them to move toward a different goal from the simple one they had been pursuing." Into those physical bodies souls could projection or "incarnate" and now human history began – yet still with that original intent that had been previously distorted and lost: that souls would become conscious co-creative companions with God, knowing themselves to be themselves and yet still one with the Whole.

So what *facilitated* Cayce's vision of how involution and evolution were both players in our history? *What was the laboratory* that allowed Cayce, the spiritual scientist, to capture these images weaving together involution and evolution? What was the equivalent for Cayce of what Darwin found on the Galapagos Islands?

To answer those questions, consider what made the Galapagos such an extraordinary laboratory for Darwin. He was able to isolate variables. He was able to see what happens over time when an organism is left on its own to change. The best examples were the finches – thirteen different species on the different islands, each of which had a different sort of beak, designed exactly to match the kind of food that was available on a particular island. The same type of evidence was there to inspire Darwin as he examined different species of iguanas. The different islands have different features, and so the iguanas had evolved to best survive on their particular island – for example, black marine iguanas on some islands and the light brown land iguanas on other islands.

But Cayce's laboratory wasn't quite the same. For him the "lab" was the room from which he did his clairvoyant readings. And it was the physical health readings that gave him some 9,000 spiritually scientific observations over a 43-year period. In each of these thousands of case histories, he was able to isolate the variables and see how they interact. His medical clairvoyance and his spiritual vision allowed him to see in a new light the purposefulness of the human body.

In fact, the significance of the physical readings is often overlooked. They contain far more than a set of holistic, natural medicine health recommendations. They are a highly sophisticated philosophy of how body, mind and spirit interact. Those 9,000 medical readings are the heart and soul of Cayce's legacy. Some would argue that he gave exclusively physical readings for the first twenty-three years of his clairvoyant work because he was still refining and developing his gift for the others kinds of readings that would be possible in the final twenty years. That line of reasoning makes the life readings or dream interpretation readings or mental-spiritual readings somehow more important than mere physical readings.

It contrast it could be argued that what makes Cayce such an important figure in human history is his revolutionary view of the human body. He shows us a way to understand the body as a vehicle of spiritual work. He presents the human body not as an obstacle to soul growth but rather the instrument through which soul growth is enhanced.

And all of this is possible in Cayce's holistic philosophy because of the skillful way that he was able to synthesize the principles of involution and evolution. He *added to* the brilliant observations Darwin made on the Galapagos Islands. Cayce takes the facts of materialistic biological science and supplements them with his clairvoyant perceptions of how the energies of body, mind and spirit interplay. In this marriage of evolution theory and involution theory, Cayce offers us such an important model for the decades ahead. No doubt both traditional sciences and explorations of spirituality will continue to unfold in the 21st century. Our challenge is to find ways to understand these two steams as complementary – pursuits that ultimately lead us to the same truth.

Intuition and Psychic Ability in the Millennium

Another quality of the "new root race" as envisioned by Cayce is psychic sensitivity. In the minds of many people, extrasensory perception and the new millennium seem to go hand in hand. This is probably because psychically gifted individuals have been widely publicized for their descriptions of what may be in store for us in the 21st century and beyond. However, this linkage is not necessarily the proper one. Just because psychics claim to see the future does not mean that most people who live in that future will be psychic themselves. However, Cayce's prophecies about ESP becoming commonplace make sense as a natural outgrowth of something else he predicted: attunement. If we imagine a world in which most people are consciously making efforts to align the body and the mind with the spirit, then we have a society ripe for psychic development.

As Cayce put it, psychic experience is *"of the soul."* It is an expression of the spiritual forces manifesting in the material world. When people meditate regularly, watch their dreams carefully and sincerely try to be of service to each other, then the stage is perfectly set for the flowering of clairvoyance, telepathy, and precognition.

However, with the blossoming of these latent abilities come challenges and potential difficulties. One needs only to read the biographies of many modern-day psychics to notice that the development of psychic perception usually creates problems. The predicament in which they found themselves was not due exclusively to the skeptical society in which they lived. These gifted psychics had to wrestle with tough questions that came with being telepathic, clairvoyant or precognitive: For what purposes should such abilities be used? How should intuitive, non-rational sources of information be combined with logical common sense? If coming generations are to be more psychically tuned-in, we might expect that these kinds of questions will be as frequent in one hundred years as are questions today about inflation or global warming.

Cayce's fundamental explanation of how psychic perception works is extremely insightful. It places ESP in a balanced, helpful context. The first principle – as already stated in the phrase "psychic is of the soul" – is that psychic experience can be fully understood only in the framework of a physical, mental and spiritual human nature. Add to this a significant second premise: Psychic awareness is a normal and natural response of the mind to the desire to be of service to others. One Cayce reading referred to this orientation as the "love intent," acting as a catalyst upon the unconscious mind. That intention to serve and love opens awareness to the ever-present connection between all souls.

Both of these fundamental principles are rather metaphysical in nature. They depend upon our willingness to think in terms of nonmaterial reality. However, at the same time, Cayce suggested that ESP should be a practical, down-to-earth tool for daily living. It is of little value unless we can find ways to use it productively in materiality – for example, healing baffling diseases (as demonstrated in Cayce's own work) or making insightful leadership decisions that benefit many people. But whatever form it takes, psychic sensitivity needs to be applicable, in a three-dimensional, physical sense.

This brings us to a distinct challenge for how we will respond to awakening psychic abilities within ourselves. What do we do with impressions we receive about others, impressions that we suspect may be accurate extrasensory information? What is the next step if we are praying for someone and unexpectedly get a strong feeling for what that person should do? It is rather disconcerting to imagine that in the new millennium we will have everyone walking around giving unsolicited psychic readings for each other. We must have a balanced way of sharing this information without seeming pushy or invading the privacy of others. If, in fact, psychic experience is to become commonplace in the decades and centuries to come, then it is crucial that we find acceptable approaches for sharing intuitive impressions.

A part of the answer may lie in a willingness to communicate impressions "without forcing the issue," as Cayce put it. In other words, we can relate our inner experiences while simultaneously admitting that they might not be telepathic or clairvoyant at all. A dream or meditation experience can be told in such a way that the listener can comfortably refuse to see it as a psychic impression about him or her.

For example, suppose you have a dream in which your next-door neighbor is trying to put out a smoldering fire in his bedroom. You suspect this may be a telepathic dream about his emotional conflicts related to his marriage because several years earlier – during a period when you were having marriage difficulties of your own – you had dreams about trying to put out a bedroom blaze. You now suspect that the dream about your neighbor is telepathic sensitivity to an unspoken problem. Cayce would encourage you to share the dream with him, but in a way that makes it easy for him to respond that your dream must surely be only about yourself. However, in telling the dream, the possibility always exists that it may actually be psychic in nature and may be received gratefully by your neighbor, allowing him to open up and talk with a sympathetic friend or to admit that he needs a counselor's help.

Related to the same issue is how we treat information that seems to be precognitive in nature. This is tricky, and we can subtly mislead ourselves if we're not careful. What do you do with impressions that appear to be "guidance"? Sometimes that information comes in response to prayers asking for direction in a decision. Other times it may come without your particularly seeking it. In either case, a delicate balance is needed between obedience to the inner reality and plain common sense. God wants you to use your logical, intellectual mind – but not *exclusively* that level of mind. To do so is to become rigid and uninspired. On the other hand, soul growth does not come from blind obedience to every subjective impression that comes into awareness.

In a number of readings, Cayce recommended a specific exercise for developing one's psychic perception in making practical life decisions. We can well imagine that in the 21st century a technique such as this one will frequently be employed. In Chapter 8, "A 21st Century Approach to Guidance and Decision-Making," the details of how to do it will be spelled out.

A New Consciousness About the Law of Supply

We've already seen that in the world affairs readings Cayce made a number of prophetic statements about the destiny of the nations, including some economic prophecies. Chief among them was the likelihood of an armed revolution unless humanity found a way to "level" the playing field, in regard to all the physical necessities of life. His prophecies also addressed the question of personal finances. That is, Cayce envisioned a way that people would one day live in relationship to a universal Law of Supply – or, as he called it, the Law of Abundance.

Many people are convinced primarily because of financial pressures that these really are times of change. The challenge comes as a test to make do with less. Unfortunately others who could potentially get by with a more modest way of living won't do it. Instead, their frequent response is to go deeper in debt, borrowing against the future. But when a person has borrowed against the future, oftentimes tomorrow looks more and more like something to be avoided. Hope, expectancy and optimism fade because the future toward which they are headed is ever more debt-ridden.

In whatever way we personally experience these times of change in regard to finances, the opportunity of the 21st century is to rediscover that God is the source of all supply and that by our own consciousness we create the degree of our access to it. In personal advice given to many individuals who came to Cayce because of economic woes, he said that the financial challenge at hand was an opportunity to understand this link between God, one's own consciousness, and material resources.

Ideally we would live in a world guided by the principle that God is the source of all physical supply. It would be a world whose people were fed, sheltered and cared for medically. The personal and physical needs of every individual would be secure. Such a condition is part of Cayce's vision for our future, but we still have considerable work to do in achieving such a consciousness. Until the day comes when all humanity is prepared to adopt this type of awareness, we can only work as individuals to manifest the law.

To understand Cayce's vision of the Law of Supply and how economic healing works, we must begin with a definition of "supply." Think of it as physical resources for living, which include food, shelter, money or anything else of the material world we need. The Bible, the Edgar Cayce readings and so many other teachings all instruct us that God is the source of all supply. In other words, the physical plane of existence is a creation of the Infinite and is sustained by it. The energy that is in food is a projection into matter of God's creative forces. The mineral kingdom – be it oil, gold or whatever – is a manifestation of divine energies of a higher dimension. Even money itself, which symbolizes a kind of earthly power or influence, is only a lesser-dimensional projection of God's power. This idea of power is reminiscent of Jesus' statement to Pilate that he had no power except that which God had allowed him to have.

Note that we have said, "God is the source of supply," not "God is the distributor of supply"; it is a subtle but highly significant distinction. Many people hear the words of the first phrase but understand them as those in the second phrase. This kind of thinking supposes God to be the dispenser of material goods and money. It suggests that if you are on good terms with God, then He will put material rewards in the pipeline for you. And you do not need to have an anthropomorphic notion of God to think in this fashion. Even if you have a more abstract idea of God such as Universal Mind or Creative Forces or Cosmic Love, this sort of outlook can still control your thinking.

But this is not what is meant by God as the source of supply. *God IS supply.* The energies and consciousness of the Divine are infinite, yet they manifest in the three-dimensional physical world. Those manifestations are everything we think of as the resources for material living. It is in this sense that God is the source of all supply; but we do not have to coerce Him into a willingness to give us our share. God is not the boss at work who must be convinced that we deserve a raise.

Instead it is by our own consciousness that we create our access to supply. We are the dispensers and distributors of the Infinite Energies as they manifest in materiality. By the patterns of our thinking, feeling and acting, we determine as individuals the amount of physical resources to which we have access and responsibility. That means money, food, energy, shelter, clothing, free time, and much more. Contrary to what many still believe, there is not a limited supply which can accommodate only a select few. Certainly there may appear to be current shortages in some specific forms of supply. But the resources of physical living are obtainable for every person of planet Earth if our consciousness is properly attuned – as individuals and collectively.

However, sometimes our experience seems to contradict this fundamental principle. Sometimes it doesn't seem that by our consciousness we create our access to supply. We all know of people who seem to have a highly attuned, loving spirit, and yet they still experience material shortages. Some of us may be good examples of this ourselves. To understand what is going on, we may have to look more deeply than the conscious patterns of thinking. The matter of economic healing and supply is the concern of the soul and necessarily involves unconscious levels of the mind, especially memory patterns from the present lifetime and past lifetimes. Simply put: We often must be patient in achieving economic healing just as we would with physical healing. We might prefer a quick metaphysical trick to make us rich. We might be tempted by simplistic positive thinking that promises instant riches, in the same way we might like a pill to take care of illness instead of having to make deep changes of body, mind and spirit.

Many souls have chosen to meet in this lifetime certain karmic patterns from the past which express themselves as the challenges and tests of privation. Certainly a good first step toward healing those conditions (especially the inner conditions of the soul) is a positive conscious outlook, even the expectation of better times. If material levels of supply do not alter instantaneously, it is not because the spiritual principle is wrong. Instead it might be that unconscious distortions of mind and emotion change slowly.

Keeping in mind this need for patience, let us consider some of the ways in which we create our access to supply. God is the source not just of supply, but abundant supply. By the way in which we understand and respond to this divine characteristic of abundance, we are creating a key aspect of our consciousness toward material supply. The Bible beautifully illustrates God's intent to express Himself abundantly. The story of the loaves and fishes is an excellent example. Not only did Jesus manifest enough food to feed everyone who was there that day, but there was such an abundance of food that tremendous quantities of leftovers were collected.

Yet what does abundance have to do with painful shortages that we may now be experiencing? By a twist of irony, the spiritual law is that our access to supply today is at least in part created by what we have done with abundant conditions in the past. In other words, we may be facing difficult challenges of material shortages to help us grow and change our previous tendencies to misuse abundance.

Observe two circumstances in which we have a problem with supply. One is when there is not enough; and we experience discomfort, pain or frustration. Of course, when there is just exactly enough – when supply perfectly matches need – then none of these problems exist and everything is fine. But a second challenging circumstance exists when there is more than enough. It is an often-overlooked difficulty, which is created when the amount available exceeds the need. What do we do with what is left over? How do we deal with such abundant conditions? The degree to which we deal responsibly and lovingly with the extra amount may clearly depict our real ideal toward material supply.

To understand how this process may have been working in your life, consider some of the categories of supply and some questions about how abundance might affect each one of them. Some of the most important categories are not ones we immediately think of when we consider material resources, but which are still significant aspects of physical life and the gifts granted by God to a soul in its incarnation.

1. *Money.* What do you do when you have a little extra money? How is it used? What desires is it used to fulfill?
2. *Free time.* What do you do with your extra time in the day? Do you waste it or use it creatively?
3. *Energy.* How responsible are you with energy when you are not paying the utility bill? For example, when you stay in a hotel, where you seem to have all the heat, lighting, and hot water you want at no extra expense, how conservation minded are you?
4. *Food.* How careful and responsible are you in taking only the food you genuinely need – or will even be able to eat — when you visit an "all-you-can-eat" restaurant?
5. *Talent and skill.* What do you do when the job you have to perform requires of you less talent or skill than you already have? Do you do just the minimum acceptable standard or do you fully use the abundance you have and produce a better-than-expected result?

The answers to these and similar questions will help you get a sense of how you deal with abundance. It may give you a clue as to what kind of consciousness and access to supply you are creating for the future. In observing this process you should realize that effects can be produced *across categories.* In other words, misuse of abundance in one area of life can create the need for lessons of shortage in another category. Fortunately, the principle also works in a more positive way, too. Responsible use of abundance in one area of life can produce proper supply in another area.

Cayce envisioned that roughly the last four decades of the 20th century would be a time of testing to prepare us for the challenges of living in the new millennium. Many of those tests had to do directly with material resources and the Law of Supply. Collectively the American people seem to have experienced the working of this law as a nation between 1958 and 1998, the decades of testing that Cayce identified. Americans were blessed with an abundance of natural resources and yet have not been ecologically responsible in stewardship. Twenty-first century problems such as pollution are, in turn, creating difficulties in maintaining the previous levels of energy, clean water and safe air. The same process can be at work for an individual soul. The waste or misuse of resources may have developed in this lifetime or a past one. In either case, it is a pattern of behavior that runs counter to the evolutionary flow of the soul, and it is the soul itself that chooses and creates shortages to stimulate the learning process.

That learning can be straightforward and efficient if the individual chooses to try a new attitudinal and behavioral approach. Or it can be protracted and painful if the shortage is blamed on others and violently resisted. This is not meant to be a call for passivity in the face of poverty. There are social injustices in our world that foster poverty. But for any individual soul the work to change such conditions of shortage must begin with personal responsibility and motivation. It can be done and has been done by specific individuals; and largely by their courageous efforts and example will the acute material shortages of great segments of humankind be transformed in the 21st century and beyond. It did not come overnight with the year 2001, nor will it arrive magically *anytime* in this century. But Cayce's visions of the future were hopeful and state that we will some day understand and live purposefully with the Law of Abundance.

A Conclusion About the Cayce Prophecies

Throughout this chapter and the previous ones, we've examined Cayce's visionary statements about the future. Some sound rather frightening, while others quickly inspire hope and enthusiasm for the future. But how are we to understand these predictions about earth changes, geopolitical shifts, and an emerging new life-style, even a new order of human being? How do we cope with the measure of uncertainty and anxiety they are likely to instill in almost anyone who hears these prophecies? The best answer probably lies in a careful look at the one central theme of the prophecies.

The very *essence* of Cayce's prophecies was not earthquakes or tidal waves or volcanic eruptions – not cities destroyed or the changing coastlines of the earth's continents. Nor is the essence of his prophecies a change in the balance of power, a new way of doing medicine or science, or a new relationship to the Law of Abundance. Instead, *the heart of the Cayce prophecies is a new world about to be born.* It is a world that is so different than what has been experienced for a long time on this planet that some kind of a transitional experience is required. The old patterns of living, the old ways of thinking, are so contrary to what the new must be that a big step for humanity is just ahead. There needs to be some rite of passage.

However, there are various ways to get from where we have been to where we need to be. All that a psychic or prophet can do is to read the momentum of the present day. In effect, all that Cayce could do was to describe the trends and identify the likeliest among the possible pathways humanity could choose. And in 1932, 1936 and 1941 Cayce kept seeing the same scenario. The momentum of our choices seemed to be taking us on a pathway leading to tremendous earth changes and painful socioeconomic alterations.

Have we stayed on that course since Cayce stopped giving readings? We can only look at our world and guess. The signs do not look very promising. Humanity continues to pollute the earth and to start destructive wars. Surely these are the kinds of activities that alienate us from the earth – from the mother aspect of God. A symbolic way of viewing earth changes, if they literally do happen, is that the earth will shake us to our senses. We will be forced into a new humility and a respect for the forces of nature. We will have to reexamine what we have been doing to the earth and, by consequence, what we have been doing to each other.

However, all of that is only one pathway. Remember the vision. Remember what the prophecy really is: a spiritual rebirth on this planet. A global family. An era of peace and cooperation. And there are many paths to get there. Some of those ways are more catastrophic than earth changes would ever be, such as nuclear war. Others are more "graceful" (that is, full of God's grace). Not that they would be without their pain, because certain things must be surrendered, and there is always discomfort and pain in letting go of old possessions and self-images.

The choice is still with us to select a transitional scenario full of grace. Our primary concern about times of change should be to find such a pathway. We should not be as concerned about whether people believe the Cayce prophecies of earth changes as we are with how people can begin to live with a new consciousness. If sufficient numbers of us will live now the vision of what the world and humanity are to become, then it is quite likely that our collective rite of passage can be survived by most all of humanity. Many of the remaining chapters in this book concern such a hopeful point of view and way of living.

CHAPTER FIVE

◆———————————————————◆

VISIONS OF ATLANTIS,
WEATHER CHANGES,
AND THE SECOND COMING

The 21st century and beyond is about many changes, according to the Cayce prophecies – geological, social, political, economic, and spiritual. In this chapter we will explore three primary areas of prophecy that were not significantly addressed in previous chapters. First is the possibility that many of Cayce's hundreds of statements about ancient Atlantis may, in fact, have been prophetic visions of the centuries *ahead*. Second, we will examine that possibility that the "real earth changes" are dramatic alterations in the weather patterns of the earth – something we have seen powerful hints of in the past few years, even the extraordinary occurrence of repeated hurricane catastrophes in the Caribbean and Florida. And finally, this chapter will examine some of the most controversial and hopeful of all Cayce's prophecies: the Second Coming.

Was Atlantis Our Past or Our Future?

The story of ancient Atlantis is one of the centerpieces of Cayce's view of human history – even the history of the Earth itself. In many hundreds of readings, Cayce tells an extraordinary story of an ancient civilization that spanned tens of thousands of years. Covering an area of the present-day North Atlantic Ocean, Atlantis struggled with many of the same problems that we deal with in the modern world, including the proper use of technology, the polarization of people into two philosophical camps, and dealing with the changing forces of nature.

When a reader first encounters Cayce's Atlantis story, it may seem a bit overwhelming. It fits into no historical context that we learned in school. Conventional wisdom teaches that 50,000 years ago human beings were living on the Earth at a subsistence level. In contrast, Cayce describes flying machines, sophisticated social structures, and advanced knowledge about a wide range of topics. It is virtually impossible to take mainstream timelines of human development and insert the Cayce saga of Atlantis. One or the other is surely wrong.

However, maybe there is a way to respect the findings of modern archaeology and at the same time find value in Cayce's Atlantis story. The answer could lie in the possibility that Cayce's visions of Atlantis were a look *forward rather than back*. That is to say, he may have misunderstood or misinterpreted what he saw. Rather than descriptions of ancient history, this may be material that is precognitive. At least in a thematic way – if not a literal fashion – Atlantis may be telling us something about life in the 21st century and beyond.

To some people such a hypothesis is not very attractive. Advocates of Cayce's psychic powers might be hard pressed to accept such a possibility. They would be concerned and ask, "How could he have been wrong so often?" Admittedly there are numerous references to Atlantis, and one might assume that the entranced Cayce would have at least occasionally come to the realization that he was describing patterns for the future rather than the past. And yet, psychic information is closely attuned to the unconscious mind, which is notoriously "out-of-time," and the human unconscious works primarily with symbols. The unconscious – the mind of the soul – works with patterns, themes and intentions, and it is much less focused on the details of pragmatic life, as compared to the conscious, rational mind. The conscious mind wants predictions and prophecies that are specific: what is going to happen and when it is going to happen. But we cannot always get that kind of material from the unconscious mind, which is more attuned to the deep connections of past, present and future. From the soul mind comes pictures in which timing can be blurred or not even a relevant factor. It's not surprising that Cayce might have communicated visions that sound like they are about the distant past when they are actually more relevant to the future.

Cayce's Psychic Images of Atlantis

In *The Mysteries of Atlantis Revisited,* Edgar Evans Cayce (the younger son of Edgar Cayce) and his co-writers point out that there is considerable "internal consistency of the information [about Atlantis]. There were readings given as much as twenty years apart, for different individuals, which agree in minute detail... Names for over 400 different people were given in the Atlantis readings, with no confusion."

They go on to define the three primary epochs of Atlantean history, as told in the Cayce readings. First is an extraordinarily lengthy period from ten million years ago up until a series of destructive events that happened around 50,000 B.C. As Edgar Evans Cayce describes it, "The first destruction of a portion of Atlantis appears to have been accidental; or to have been caused by explosives that got out of control and triggered volcanic action."

A second epoch runs from just after those initial destructions to about 28,000 B.C., when another series of destructions took place. With this series of catastrophic events, what had remained of Atlantis after the first destruction was now broken up into merely a set of islands – three principal islands and a few smaller ones. Political struggles between two factions led to a misuse of technology and the resultant second destruction.

The final destruction, again precipitated by political struggles and technology, occurred about 10,000 B.C., when the last islands were submerged. Some would argue that this was the sinking of Atlantis referred to by Plato.

As mentioned, the details of Cayce's story of Atlantis are remarkable for their specificity and their internal consistency. And for those readers who would like to explore the saga in greater detail, there are numerous books on the subject – none finer than *The Mysteries of Atlantis Revisited* by Edgar Evans Cayce, Gail Cayce Schwartzer, and Douglas Richards. But for purposes of this book and our examination of possible Cayce prophecies for the 21st century and beyond, we'll turn our attention to statements about Atlantis that might actually be about the *future* of humanity.

Keep in mind that Cayce's descriptions of Atlantis often make it sound a lot like our own times at the end of the 20th century and the beginnings of the 21st. Because of the lack of corroborative archaeological evidence, it's not inconceivable that Cayce's apparent retrocognition was really precognition. Edgar Evans Cayce and his colleague offer this summary which sounds strikingly like our own times: "Some people [in Atlantis] were said to have worked with machinery, electrical and chemical forces, radiation and heating, and mechanical appliances. Others were said to have worked in art and decorative work, or as ambassadors and diplomats. Still others worked with 'crystals' that sound like modern lasers. Many readings imply the existence of atomic power plants and the ability to transmit power without wires."

Here then are just a few of the topics and subjects about Atlantis that suggest something about our own future.

Longevity. Cayce proposed that Atlanteans were long-lived, perhaps as long as several hundred years. Could it be that our own future is to have life expectancy far beyond the norm of today? We have already explored this idea in the Introduction to this book.

Social imbalance. A recurrent theme in Cayce's Atlantis story is the inability of the people to achieve a stable social order – a nearly impossible task throughout human history. In the Atlantean saga, the social tensions revolved around two groups: 1) those who understood and advocated the essential unity of life (the Law of One) and 2) those who viewed life primarily in a materialistic and selfish way (sons of Belial). Clearly this is a "good guys" versus "bad guys" model, and it's tempting to draw parallels to our own times, placing ourselves in the role of "good guy." It's a more mature position, however, to see how each of us has *both* influences within ourselves. Nevertheless, much of our modern struggle to find social harmony seems to be a lot like the stories that Cayce tells about these two groups quarreling and trying to gain the upper hand. The warning is actually quite explicit in the Cayce prophecies: destruction will happen if we allow this kind of discord to characterize our own times.

Ecosystem destruction. Cayce suggests that there were numerous instances of Atlanteans making choices that led to severe – even catastrophic – destruction of the environment. The first series of destructions, which broke Atlantis into separate islands, was from explosions that got out of control and triggered volcanic disturbances.

In a later era, the Earth was overrun by some type of beast ("forces of the animal world and kingdom that made men and men's life miserable," as Cayce once described it). But as often happens in today's world, the "cure" was worse than the "illness"; and as one portion of the Atlantean population attempted to use their technology to eradicate those animal enemies, wide scale destructions were caused. As Cayce told one person, "the sons of Belial brought about destructive forces in the attempts to destroy the animal life that in other lands overran same." (1378-1)

Advanced technology, but the temptation to misuse it. Destruction of the beasts is but one example of a broader pattern identified in Cayce's readings on Atlantis. The consciousness of the people was essentially not mature enough to make responsible use of the power coming from technological achievement. Some aspects of the technology sound like they were used for general well-being of the people, especially sophisticated medical procedures for ridding individuals of atavistic, animal appendages. Although it sounds like the stuff of myths and legends, Cayce's story of Atlantis claims that humans of that era sometimes had features resembling other animal forms, and that their medical technology was used to assist people to attain a more purified physical form.

Another technological achievement – the so called "firestone" or "Tuaoi stone" – had fascinating potential to link science and spirituality. Cayce indicates, as we see at the beginning and the very end of the following quotation, that originally crystal stone was used to make some sort of connection to the invisible realm of mind and spirit. Then its use apparently got lost in material advancement alone, and this crystal stone played a central role in one destruction of Atlantis. It should give us pause about how those same temptations arise for us in the 21ˢᵗ century.

> [The Tuaoi stone] was in the form of a six-sided figure, in which the light appeared as the means of communication between the infinity and the finite... It was in those periods when there was the directing of aeroplanes, or means of travel; though these in that time would travel in the air, or on the water, or under the water, just the same. Yet the force from which these

were directed was in this central power station, or Tuaoi stone; which was as the beam on which it acted. In the beginning it was the source from which there was the spiritual and mental contact. #2072-10

Other related aspects of their technology also sound like they were quite vulnerable to misuse. One application of their skilled use of crystals sounds much like our own modern-day lasers. Cayce even speaks of a "death ray" which became part of the Atlantean arsenal. "And this was administered much in the same way and manner as if there were sent out from various central plants that which is termed in the present the death ray or super-cosmic ray, that will be found in the next 25 years." (262-39, in February, 1933) Although it has taken more than 25 years, this sounds eerily like some of our current high-tech military equipment.

Although *The Mysteries of Atlantis Revisited* concludes that Atlantis needs to be seriously considered as historic fact, an equally fascinating possibility is that Cayce's statements about Atlantis are best understood as prophecies for the decades and centuries after his death. In other words, his stories about the misuse of technology in Atlantis and how it led to catastrophic destructions could be taken as a prophetic warning for our own era.

Extremism. Nowhere is this prophetic warning more exact than in terms of the Atlantean tendency to experience extremes, our final Atlantean feature to consider. In fact, a prophecy about the dangerous instability of extremes is especially relevant to our own times in which sharp polarization characterizes almost every element of society – political, religious, economic and philosophical. Humanity stands in deep danger when it divides itself into competitive (even antagonist) extremes, such as we see today. Surely Cayce may well have been describing our own times in the 21st century, rather than a civilization from tens of thousands of years ago. If so, then the hundreds of readings he gave about Atlantis are actually his *most* extensive set of prophecies!

Weather Upheavals: The Real Earth Changes?

The weather. "Everybody complains about it but nobody does anything about it." So goes the old joke. But could it be that extraordinary climate change is what Cayce really meant when he articulated vivid images of mass inundations and reformulated coastlines? Maybe he used the imagery of volcanoes and earthquakes to describe something that will actually be effected by climatic change. Lacking a science of ecology and environmentalism in the 1920s and 1930s, when he gave the bulk of his prophetic material, it may well be that the language of geology is what he was forced to draw upon. And so, his earth change prophecies might well be metaphors for the profound changes that were really to come via weather and climate transformation.

There is actually some hint of this in the earth change readings we have from Cayce. On occasion he describes a coming change in terms of the alterations that could be expected in the weather. His very first earth change prophecy was about the weather. As we saw in Chapter 2, it all started in 1926 with a man who wanted information on long-range weather forecasting. At the end of the second reading (#195-32), Cayce offered some additional information on weather conditions and the effects they would soon have. He noted that there was a close relationship between these climatic conditions and human affairs.

But some of the most dramatic earth change prophecies themselves make striking statements about extraordinary weather changes. Perhaps the best example is a prophecy in 1934 that certain frigid and semitropical areas will become tropical. That, of course, was in relationship to a predicted shift of the rotational axis of the Earth; but even if something as unprecedented as a rotational axis shift does *not* take place, nevertheless, severe climate change *could* still make this Cayce prophecy come true.

Anyone paying attention to scientific reports in the last 20 years knows very well that catastrophic changes for the Earth are quite possible, as a result of the pollution of the oceans, the destruction of the atmosphere, and apparent global warming. One case in point: the threat is very real that places like New York or Los Angeles could be destroyed by rising ocean levels. It may well be that Cayce accurately foresaw these possibilities in his prophetic visions, but he mistakenly used the language of geology rather than climatology to interpret and communicate them.

The United Nations' Intergovernmental Panel on Climate Change (representing 99 countries) issued a dire warning in 2001 – a prophecy every bit as scary as any given by Cayce. The *National Geographic News* (February 6, 2001) summarizes the panel's report, plus the commentary of scientist Will Burns, of California's Institute for Studies in Development, Environment, and Security. National

Geographic states:

> Long- and short-term effects of global warming will worsen as greenhouse gases are added to the atmosphere could have "horrific implications." The IPCC report predicts that warming will cause rising sea levels, increased precipitation, glacial melting, and greater extremes in El Niño weather events such as droughts and floods. Each of these meteorological effects has the potential to dramatically affect life on Earth. The loss of plant and animal species, "is one of the core long-term aspects of climate change," said Burns.
>
> Marine species will be threatened by changing ocean temperatures, he said, resulting in a "catastrophic cascade in the food chain." Land-dwelling animals, he added, will also be threatened, and may not be able to migrate fast enough to escape weather changes.
>
> Humans, named as the primary cause of global warming, are not immune to its effects. Burns said rising sea levels may result in the loss of small islands and "tremendous displacement of people in other coastal areas."

This is a very sobering report, just as are the Cayce prophecies about earth changes. And unfortunately they may be talking about the same patterns of likelihood for the planet, with Cayce simply not having chosen the exact form in which to accurately frame his warnings.

Prophecies of Christ's Return

In Cayce's prophetic visions, a spiritual transformation is central. The millennium brings a spiritual renewal; and ultimately, according to his predictions, the millennium is about the return of the Christ Spirit directly into human affairs. In fact, he suggests that this is to be widely experienced and recognized sometime around the beginning of the 21st century, with certain signs earlier, for those who can recognize them. Among the indicators Cayce foresaw would be a new movement for cooperation and respect among the world's religions – something that arguably started to take place in the latter part of the 20th century. But even greater changes lie just ahead.

The Cayce millennium prophecies unequivocally state that we are on the threshold of a milestone just as spiritually significant as Christ's physical appearance two thousand years ago, an event that is predestined and was known even to the spiritual initiates who constructed the Great Pyramid thousands of years ago. This Second Coming will not be a physical birth, as it was with Jesus of Nazareth, but instead an event of more global proportions in which people of every faith may find a place. It is the drawing of the universal Christ Spirit in direct relationship with anyone who sincerely seeks it. According to the Cayce prophecies, the early signs of this new beginning shall be experienced by a growing number of people as we move from the 20th century to the 21st.

In fact, no vision of a new age is more dramatic than the possibility of a direct, physical interaction of Christ in human affairs – an intervention that would be perceived by all humanity. Nothing better expresses our hope that a new age would include a spiritual renewal for the human family. It is not presented as a certainty in the Cayce readings, nor are there specific details as to timing or appearance. Rather it is a possibility – perhaps even a likelihood.

In the Cayce material on a Second Coming, several principles are especially noteworthy. He clearly thought of Christ as both a universal spirit that could be seen in all world religions and as the soul we call Jesus. However, the Christ-like nature of Jesus was attained over many lifetimes of soul development, culminating in Jesus who became one with the Christ Consciousness. In his teachings about the reappearance of Christ, Cayce indicates that any return will involve this same soul that we call Jesus.

When Cayce was asked in 1932 about the Second Coming, he flatly stated that no date could be given. It would not occur until "His enemies and the earth are wholly in subjection to His will, His powers" (#5749-2). That surely sounds like a very high standard for us to meet. Some might even say it's an almost unrealistic expectation for humanity to be anywhere near that state in the foreseeable future. So it's not surprising that the questioner then backed off slightly and asked if this was now a preparation period for Christ's return. Cayce responded that it was better understood as a "testing period."

In another instance, Cayce was asked by a small group of seekers in 1933 to interpret the biblical passage that "the day of the Lord is near at hand." Although his answer was filled with biblical images and poetic phrases, he nevertheless seemed to confirm strongly that the return of Christ is quite possible for our own era: "That as has been promised through the prophets and the sages of old, the time – and half time – has been and is being fulfilled in this day and generation, and that soon there will again appear in the earth that one through whom many will be called to meet those that are preparing the way for His day in the earth. The Lord, then, will come, 'even as ye have seen him go.'" (#262-49)

When the group followed up with a request for a time estimate concerning such an event, they were told that it could happen only when those people who are Christ's devoted followers make the way passable and clear for Him to come. In other words, there is preparatory work to be done from the human side.

The need for efforts to make the way passable is not the result of some inadequacy on the part of Christ. It is not a matter of an inability of Christ to appear in materiality without our help. Instead we might think of it this way: Unless a sufficient portion of humanity lifts itself into a new awareness, then a reappearance of Christ would confuse us or be easily misunderstood by us. Christ will come again only when such an intervention will be truly helpful in the spiritual evolution of which we are a part. It is out of the most profound kind of love that any wide scale, directly physical appearance of Christ is delayed.

Perhaps the most remarkable question and answer exchange about Christ's return took place in 1933. A group of people who were seeking to understand more about the Christ Consciousness inquired about the present location of this spiritual being. They even wondered if He might already be on earth in a physical body but unrecognized.

Cayce's answer was that Christ was not currently in a body in the earth dimension. What's more, if a person needed to have a "location" for Him, it was best to understand it to be "in the individual entity," as spirit that can be contacted by anyone who sincerely desires it and who is willing to act in love to make it possible. In other words, if we feel the need to know a "place" where Christ currently resides, it's in a place of spirit that can be contacted as we each go within ourselves.

Finally, Cayce made it clear that he envisioned an actual return. "For, He shall come as ye have seen Him go, in the body He occupied in Galilee. The body that He formed, that was crucified on the cross, that rose from the tomb, that walked by the sea, that appeared to Simon, that appeared to Philip" (#5749-4). This is a very straightforward reference to the resurrected body of Christ reappearing in our own times.

Another group of Cayce prophecies provides a fascinating aspect of his predictions about Christ's return. These predictions are based on Cayce's perception that hidden prophecies are built into the geometric architecture of the Great Pyramid. To decipher them, Cayce stated that the central passageway of the Great Pyramid is like a timeline. This timeline corresponds to the Ascending Passageway and the Grand Gallery passageway, leading up to the King's Chamber. Among the pyramid prophecies is the indication of Christ's return at the turn of the new millennium. What point in history corresponds precisely to moving into the special room of spiritual initiation, the King's Chamber? According to the Cayce prophecies, it was the period from 1938 to 1958.

What was to be found in the King's Chamber itself? Only an empty sarcophagus. Cayce's interpretation of the empty sarcophagus was that humanity would discover that death is not what we've thought it was. In other words, we would awaken to our connections with the spiritual world, and the continuity of life would become an established fact. "The interpretation of death will be made plain" (#5748-6). One can't help but consider how near-death experience research, started in the 1960s and continuing to expand here in the 21st century, has radically altered our sense of survival.

Interpreting Cayce's Prophecies of a Second Coming

We may well wonder what kind of an expression of Christ we are to expect. What scenario seems most likely? These readings predict that it will not come in the birth of a baby, as Jesus did two thousand years ago. The pattern of incarnation by birth has already been established and doesn't need to be repeated. Instead He will manifest in the very body that He resurrected long ago. Having so purified the flesh body and attuned it to the mind and spirit, Jesus the Christ can manifest that body in any plane or dimension at will.

There are at least three scenarios for His return. One is the spectacular, mass appearance – the Christ seen by millions of people in all His glory. In this scenario the populace of the world is quickly humbled, and the Christ reigns in a spiritual and political sense. Many branches of fundamentalism in Christianity expect some version of this scenario, often coupled with cataclysm and punishments to befall the earth just prior to the reappearance.

A second hypothesis is that Christ will reappear in much the same manner He did just after the first Easter. This scenario involves the direct physical experience of His Presence by individuals and small groups. Recall the way in which Jesus ate fish with the disciples in Galilee just after His resurrection. In this case and in others, He clearly was perceived in a physical way in the outer world.

A third possibility is that a return of Christ will be at nonphysical inner levels of awareness. Already there are individuals who claim to have had such a direct experience, and perhaps the Second Coming implies a dramatic increase in the number of people who experience this. The inner contact (via meditation, prayer, dreams, etc.) could well be with the resurrected body, mind and spirit of Jesus who became the Christ. Such a personal contact by millions of people would have a dramatic and uplifting effect on the attitudes and life-styles of people worldwide.

Cayce's contemporary, the Austrian philosopher and spiritual scientist Dr. Rudolf Steiner, predicted a return of Christ that is much like the third scenario. Steiner believed that it was Christ manifesting His purified etheric body that we could expect in our own times. To personally meet the etheric Christ, one would have to make sincere efforts to purify and attune his or her consciousness – that is, to become more spiritually sensitive. In fact, Steiner even offered a date, predicting that these personal encounters with the etheric Christ would start to happen more and more often, beginning in 1930 (not far from the 1936 date that came up several times in Cayce prophecies).

There is evidence to suggest that such personal encounters with Christ are on the rise. Although they take many forms, some seem to fit the description hinted at by Cayce and explicitly described by Steiner as a kind of extended perception into the spiritual world. For example, in research I conducted with Dr. G. Scott Sparrow for a book he later wrote, *Witness to His Return,* each of us spoke with dozens of individuals for whom the return of Christ was already here – not something still to be awaited.

For example, one man shared with me an extraordinary story of his wife's direct experience with Christ just before her death. It seemed that her consciousness had begun to extend into the spiritual world as her physical body neared death. One day, when a friend came over to visit, she suddenly began to talk to people whom her husband and the friend couldn't see. It was as if she was having a party and greeting her guests, but they were invisible to the others in the room. For some twenty minutes she conversed, speaking and then pausing as if listening to the responses. Finally she began saying good night to her guests, thanking them for having come by to visit.

As his wife's invisible party came to an end, she announced to her husband and to the friend there in the room: "Oh, yes, *He* was here. He told me I was going to die tomorrow. Isn't that wonderful?" The man knew without a doubt that the reference was to Christ, who had come in this vision to tell her of her imminent passing into the spiritual world. In fact, she passed away at 2:00 the next morning.

Edgar Cayce himself from time to time had visionary experiences of Christ, which fit the third scenario of how Christ's return might manifest. Here is but one example, recounted by Cayce in a letter to a friend:

"Often I have felt, seen and heard the Master at hand. Just a few days ago I had an experience, which I have not even told the folk here. As you say, they are too scary to tell, and we wonder at ourselves when we attempt to put them into words, whether we are to believe our own ears, or if others feel we are exaggerating or drawing on our imagination; but to us indeed they are often that which we feel if we hadn't experienced we could not have gone on.

"The past week I have been quite 'out of the running,' but Wednesday afternoon when going into my little office or den for the 4:45 meditation, as I knelt by my couch I had the following experience: First a light gradually filled the room with a golden glow, that seemed to be very exhilarating, putting me in a buoyant state. I felt as if I were being given a healing. Then, as I was about to give the credit to members of our own [prayer] group who meet at this hour for meditation (as I felt each and every one of them were praying for and with me), HE came. He stood before me for a few minutes in all the glory that He must have appeared in to the three on the Mount. Like yourself I heard the voice of my Jesus say, 'Come unto me and rest.'" (supplement to #281-13)

Whichever scenario or interpretation of the Second Coming seems most likely to you, an important factor to keep in mind is the necessity for being open to the new. We must avoid repeating what happened in Jesus' time. Christ will come again only in the spirit of that which is propelling humanity's evolution forward, and hence will appear as something unexpected and new. In *Revelation: The Birth of a New Age,* philosopher David Spangler states this beautifully. It is a principle worth keeping in mind as we work to make the way passable for the coming again of the Christ into the physical plane. Spangler asks us to remember that Jesus faced rejection from many of his contemporaries, largely because he didn't fit their expectations of what a messiah ought to be. Those who spurned him couldn't see the depth and enormity of what he brought to humanity. With this in mind, Spangler warns that "the Christ manifestation for this new age could go unrecognized and rejected by many who are thinking of a Second Coming as a repetition and reinforcement of the past. We are in a new age."

The Christ Spirit in These Times of Change

Our ideas of a Second Coming usually focus on dramatic scenarios in which this high spiritual being Cayce called "Jesus who became the Christ" returns in such a way that believers and nonbelievers alike can directly encounter Him. But perhaps there are other manifestations of a Second Coming – not necessarily ones that replace this kind of direct contact but still broaden the possibilities for how these prophecies will be fulfilled.

In fact, we can look at the trends and events around us right now and find among them many hopeful signs. Although it's certainly more fashionable to focus on the negative and disturbing side of current events, we can just as readily find indicators that something very good is afoot.

Let's consider just a few such movements on the modern scene. In each one we can find key elements of the universal consciousness –

as Cayce's spiritual philosophy defines it – coming to life in extraordinary new ways. Could these be the first signs of the worldwide spiritual revitalization that Cayce's prophecies suggest? Like the first crocuses of March, might these trends be the harbingers of a new sort of planetary culture? If so, then they are every bit as much a part of the Second Coming as any rematerialization of Jesus. Why? Simply because a return of Christ must this time be to stimulate a fuller expression of the Christ-like ways in human affairs. In Cayce's estimation, there's no need for a so-called Second Coming just to bring mankind additional information or teachings. We already received the Gospel – the good news about a whole new way of understanding spiritual growth and the redemption of the soul – two thousand years ago. Now the cutting edge of any fresh involvement of Christ with humanity must be in the arena of application.

The movements described below are simply two examples. Each of us can probably think of other modern events and initiatives that are equally illustrative of the Christ Spirit coming into bold new ways of expression.

Christ as Mediator. One great image of Christ is the force or impulse that "stands between." Cayce put it this way, referring to the role of Christ: "...He who stands between those influences of good and evil, the crossroads of choice, that every one and every soul each day must cross..." (#683-2). Theology has for centuries seen Christ as the redemptive middle ground between the spiritual and the physical, between God and humankind. Cayce echoes that principle with his assertion that "Only in Christ do the extremes meet."

But all that seems rather far off and abstract when we're confronted by a chaotic and contentious world. Perhaps we sense the need for spiritual redemption, but too many other problems get in the way, particularly struggles with other people. What does "Christ as Mediator" have to do with a landlord-tenant dispute, two state governments bickering over water rights, or a messy child custody battle between divorcing parents? That's the stuff of which daily life is made.

Remarkably there is, indeed, a social movement growing very rapidly to bring this consciousness of "mediator" into human affairs, especially problem solving. It rarely carries with it any kind of religious language and few (if any) of its practitioners probably think directly of the Christ Consciousness as they carry out their challenging work. But if we look carefully at the spirit and the purposes of this movement, we can immediately recognize a new model for human relations – one in which problems are resolved not by force, but instead with mutual respect and the search for common ground. And if we broaden our vision of what a Second Coming might really mean – if we look at our times with the eyes that the Cayce prophecies encourage us to use – then we're likely to see this mediation movement as a direct expression of the Christ Spirit, especially in the sense of Christ as a middle way between extreme positions.

In this process, parties meet with a trained mediator who assists them in reaching fair, informed decisions to resolve the issues before them. The mediator is not the judge of the conflict. He or she has received extensive training in ways to be an effective bridge and clarifier. The consciousness of the mediator serves as a point where the divergent attitudes and needs can meet and where the parties can explore options in a non-threatening way. Truly such a person is playing a redemptive role – not as cosmic as the theological one of Christ as redeemer and middle ground between God and humanity, but nevertheless a powerful expression of how the Christ Spirit comes to life in everyday human events.

What does this modern mediation movement have to offer our society? Besides being less costly than litigation or warfare, mediation offers participants a great deal of flexibility in reaching agreements that are tailored to their special circumstances. In addition, mediation can be concluded much more quickly than litigation or armed confrontation, and the parties can avoid the usual hostilities that accompany adversarial court proceedings or international brinkmanship.

For family or community relations' problems, mediation sessions are usually designed to be informal, private and voluntary. Unlike litigation in which the sole objective is to "win," mediation emphasizes different goals: communication, understanding and problem solving. The participants meet with this neutral third party to explore the issues and problems that are important to them. The participants, not the mediator, make the ultimate decisions that will affect their lives. The mediator's role is to skillfully assist the parties in identifying significant issues and needs. Then the mediator leads the parties to a resolution of the conflict by brain-storming options, assessing the implications of each option and finalizing an agreement.

Through the mediation process, participants have the opportunity to create custom-made agreements with provisions that are tailored to meet each individual's needs. It is no surprise that mediated agreements are statistically much more likely to be observed and followed than are court-imposed orders. Moreover, through the mediation process, parties have the added benefit of learning how to communicate constructively with one another, so that their future and ongoing relationship may be less stressful and more productive.

Almost any conflict can be mediated, and it's reasonable to hope that in a 21st century culture guided by the Christ Spirit, mediation will become the norm for problem solving in human relations – at personal, community, and international levels.

Christ in Interfaith Dialogue. Cayce's prophecies have a deeply inclusive spirit. Although many of his predictions seem to carry a certain theological slant – after all, he speaks of a return of Christ, not Buddha, Krishna, or Mohammed – the deeper import of his prophecies is fundamentally bigger than any single religion. We must recall that he was making these prophetic statements to people who were themselves rooted in a single religious tradition. For the most part that was a rather conservative, Protestant Christianity of the early 20th century in the South. Cayce started from that point, then challenged his listeners (and us, today) to a broader vision of what's just ahead.

The return of the Christ Consciousness directly into human affairs will require an inclusive vision of faith and spirituality. Here are but two examples of Cayce's vision of a planetary spirituality that is not limited by the terminology or doctrines of one religion.

First, we can look back at an incident in Edgar Cayce's own life. His work as a professional clairvoyant was not always very success, at least from a financial standpoint. He depended upon membership dues from individuals who joined his organization in order to get a reading, but there were periods in which requests for readings were meager. At one point in the spring of 1935 Cayce's supporters asked for a special reading specifically on the question of fund-raising.

A key concern was how to reach their potential audience. How should Cayce's work be described? In the very first question they posed for this special reading, they asked if Cayce's work should be portrayed as direct pronouncements from Christ. Admittedly, for many of us who now look back at that question seventy years later, it seems bold – even a bit presumptuous. However, it was a sincere inquiry on the part of some of Cayce's most ardent followers. They not only felt that Christ was the source of his inspiration, but that it was crucial to label the readings exactly that way.

The answer given that day was a reflection of a more universal spirit: Don't set up limitations. Try to be all things to all people; meet seekers where they are. To get focused exclusively on a name behind these teachings means to limit interested people who might have personal difficulties with certain terminology. Focus instead on the universality of the Creator. "Be ye all things to all men; thereby ye may save the more. For he that declares as a name, in a name, save in the universality of the Father, limits the ability of the seeker..." (#254-85). In other words, Cayce encouraged finding a common ground from which seekers of all persuasions could meet.

A second illustration of Cayce's interfaith ideal is found in the sort of advice he often gave individuals who had adopted too narrow a picture of spirituality. To emphasize the fundamental oneness of humanity's spiritual quest, Cayce tried to bring his hearers back to basics. There is only one God, no matter what name or label is used. For example, one young woman, a student from Sarah Lawrence College, was reminded, "For whether they be Greek, Parthenon [Parthian], Jew or Gentile-whether they be of Mohammed, Confucius, or even Shinto or On or Mu – the Lord, the God, is ONE!" (#1494-1).

Of course, Cayce is only one of many 20th century philosophers, theologians, and creative thinkers who have seen the importance of the ecumenical spirit. Surely, the interfaith dialogue that we see in our midst in the 21st century is a sign of something extraordinary in human history – perhaps even part of the blossoming of the universal Christ Consciousness.

No less a figure than the renowned British historian Arnold Toynbee observed the significance of pluralistic vision. Speculating about what might be seen five hundred years from now as *the* most important event of the century we just concluded, he did not select as the hallmark of the 20th century the splitting of the atom or the human gene, or any war or technological achievement. Rather, he predicted historians of the distant future would recognize as the most significant development of the 20th century a spiritual movement: the meeting of the wisdom traditions of Buddhism and the East with Western Judeo-Christian faith. We need not wait 500 years for the fruits of that work. We can see them even now in our own new century.

The Parliament of World Religions, held in Chicago in 1993, is surely a sign of this movement. At that meeting, more than sixty- five hundred participants from virtually every religious tradition on the planet gathered to look for common bonds. It was a coming together of East and West; of North and South.

One of their central tasks was the shaping of a set of ethical standards that could unite humanity. Not looking for a common set of religious beliefs or devotional practices, they instead focused on the possibility for a mutually acceptable set of behavioral standards in which all men and women could participate for the good of humanity and the earth itself. The declaration of this parliament has been published as *A Global Ethic.* In its preamble, this description of the process was offered: "As was only to be expected, this declaration provoked vigorous discussion during the parliament. However, the welcome thing is that at a time when so many religions are entangled in political conflicts, indeed bloody wars, representatives of very different religions, great and small, endorsed this declaration with their signatures on behalf of countless believers on this earth."

A Personal Reflection on Christ's Return

As stated earlier, we don't need further teachings; Jesus doesn't have to come back to tell us more than we already have recorded in the Bible. The spiritual principles are already available to us. What's missing is the motivation, intention and will to put those teachings into action. We need to find a way to actually *live* the message of the New Testament. And so, surely any new involvement by the Christ with us would have something to do with *application.*

This point was made vivid to me in a profound personal experience many years ago. It came just as I had finished my college education and was contemplating making a commitment to spend my professional career working directly with the Cayce material. It had already touched me deeply with its vision of these special times in which we live, especially in regard to the return of Christ in my own lifetime. I first published an account of this experience fifteen years ago, but it's highly relevant to this exploration of Cayce prophecies and warrants reprinting here now:

In 1972, I joined forty-nine other members of the organization that Edgar Cayce had founded many years before his death – the Association for Research and Enlightenment – for a month-long tour of places of spiritual significance throughout Europe and the Middle East.

One place that I especially looked forward to visiting was the Great Pyramid. I had carefully read the Cayce material about Jesus and pondered the idea that He had traveled to Egypt for schooling in the esoteric traditions before He began His three-year ministry. Cayce describes it as a process of spiritual initiation and indicates that Jesus experienced a kind of final initiation in the King's Chamber of the Great Pyramid. And so, in my twenty-two-year-old youthful enthusiasm, I was ready to be an initiate, too. I was prepared to go to this same spot and hopefully have some sort of a transformative experience.

Egypt was not the first stop on our tour, so I had plenty of time for the anticipation to build as we traveled. Finally we arrived in Cairo, and on our second day there, we took the bus out to the Giza Plateau just beyond the city.

After that forty-five minute ride, we arrived at the Great Pyramid. To stand beside it for the first time is an awe-inspiring experience. Although it is not as tall as other familiar landmarks, such as the Washington Monument, its sheer size and volume is staggering. And the thought that it was built with human labor and archaic tools thousands of years ago defies imagination.

The leader of our group gave the official at the entrance a little extra money, which would provide our group with some private time in the King's Chamber. The fifty of us went in single file. As mentioned earlier, much of the climb inside is along an Ascending Passageway, which slants upward and is so low that you can move through it only in a crouched position. Finally, the structure opens up into the Grand Gallery, still relatively narrow but with a very high ceiling. The ascent through the Grand Gallery leads into the King's Chamber, a room just the right size for the fifty of us to line the perimeter of the stone room. We all sat down and leaned back against the cool, hard surface.

After a short period of discussion from our leader to remind us of the significance of this spot, we had a lengthy group meditation. This was what I had come for. I was hoping for a powerful experience – something mystical perhaps. I knew I wasn't alone in my desires. Most of the group shared my feelings.

Unfortunately, I was so excited that I couldn't get still and quiet, and so my meditation time didn't seem very successful. My enthusiasm ironically had become an obstacle. When the twenty minutes of silence ended, I was disappointed but nevertheless profoundly impressed by this extraordinary place.

We retraced our steps in departing. Finally, back out in the bright Egyptian sunlight, our guide announced that we had about two hours of free time. Among our options were a short walk to the nearby Sphinx or an equally short walk over to one of the two other pyramids nearby. Although I was certainly eager to see the Sphinx, I decided to wait and finish some other business first. I had the sense that I had not yet received what I had come to Giza to experience at the Great Pyramid. So while my companions scattered, I walked around to the back side of the Great Pyramid and began to climb its exterior. When it was originally constructed, a smooth, limestone sheathing covered the huge stones, which layer-upon-layer create its immense size. But long ago those finishing stones were stripped away, and all that remains are large construction stones that create a step-like appearance when seen up close. It was easy to climb, and within a couple of minutes I was seventy-five feet up the side. I found a nice shelf about two feet by three feet and sat down cross-legged to meditate some more.

Rarely in my meditation times had I ever experienced something remarkable. In fact, my special inner experiences had usually been – and continue to be – in my dreams, especially dreams that came immediately upon falling back asleep after a meditation at three or four o'clock in the morning. However, this day, sitting in meditation on the side of the Great Pyramid, "something happened."

Suddenly, as I sat in silence with my eyes closed, trying to keep my attention one-pointed, I saw a scene. It was as if I were looking at something that opened up in my forehead. However, it wasn't mystical or transcendent. I saw myself sitting in a business meeting! At the time of this experience I was only twenty-two and didn't have a job with any organization – but I did have hopes of someday working for the Cayce organization in Virginia Beach. In this meditation experience I saw myself in a roundtable business discussion at that very headquarters center, and I "knew" my identity was a staff member.

I listened intently as I watched this meeting unfold. I had a strong sense that everyone in the room had the same ideal, but I quickly heard that each person had a different idea about how to get some particular task accomplished. There was argument and some spirited tension. I felt myself being drawn in, and I was about to speak up and lobby for my own point of view.

Then, unexpectedly, I heard a voice in my mind that made me stop and surrender all intentions to get caught up in the argument. The voice began, "Be still." I felt my emotions become free from the entanglements of the business meeting. Then this voice of wisdom went on. "The real work of this organization – as it plays its part in this new millennium and the coming again of Christ – is not so much that conferences would be held, books written or lectures given, as important as those things may be. The real work and purpose is simply this: *That a new way of being, with each other, would be born into the earth.*" And with those words I suddenly came back to normal consciousness sitting on the side of the Great Pyramid.

Undoubtedly those images and the accompanying words were especially for me, and they've stayed vividly etched in my mind and ideals. Each of us has his or her own way of understanding what the Christ Spirit is all about in these times, and this was my way of catching the vision for myself. But maybe it speaks to others as well.

Since that day in 1972, my own career has unfolded in such a way that public speaking and book writing *have* been central ingredients of my work. Perhaps this inner wisdom – this meditative voice – recognized well in advance that I would have tendencies to overemphasize them from time to time. The form of Christ's work today (be it lectures, books, or anything else) should never blind us from the authentic spirit. And in today's changing world of the early 21st century, that spirit is perhaps best described as a new "social art," a new way of being present and involved with each other. That, more than any other characteristic, may be the way we recognize the return of Christ.

PART III

A PRIMER FOR LIVING IN THE 21ST CENTURY THAT CAYCE ENVISIONED

CHAPTER SIX

UNDERSTANDING THE INNER SHIFT OF THE 21ST CENTURY

Have you ever dreamed of being in an earthquake? Or maybe you've had a nightmare of exploding volcanoes or violent tidal waves. When these kinds of images appear in your dreams, they might be prophetic statements of impending natural disasters. But just as likely, they mean that you're going through your own inner upheavals. In fact, during times of personal stress, these kinds of images can be expected from the unconscious mind.

For most people an inner millennium shift is in full swing. Earthquakes and other physical changes may or may not be following Cayce's prophetic timetable. But there's no disputing one fact: the inner shift is moving ahead. The personal testing is happening.

Take a look at your own life. Some of your inner shift challenges may be immediately obvious: health crises, career failures, stressful relationships. But inner changes are not always traumatic or catastrophic. In more subtle ways they can seep into our lives and in small, unobtrusive ways succeed in stretching us to our limits. Sometimes these inner changes are happening, but we're only marginally conscious of their importance; we occasionally go through a very significant personal test without being fully aware of what it's all about. But even when this inner shift for the 21st century comes subtly in its expression, it almost always has a potent impact.

Of course, many of these kinds of problems have been going on throughout human history. What makes the times in which we live any different or special? Cayce's prophecy was that the late 20th century and early 21st would be remarkable for the pace of demanding change and for its pervasive quality. Coupled with these two factors would be a simultaneous transformation of cultural values and crucial support systems. Just consider what happens when all these factors collide.

For example, it's one thing to go through a career failure, but at the same time still know what you believe in and where your values lie. People have been going through that sort of personal crisis for centuries. But it's quite another sort of challenge to lose your job and also live in a society that seems to have lost its rudder and forgotten what it believes in.

In a similar way, people throughout history have had painful, debilitating health problems, especially in old age. But usually there were community support systems to help. In our modern world, illness often brings with it a sense of alienation. For example, as the elderly become sick, they're often removed from familiar society and placed in isolated living conditions.

Other characteristics of the inner shift are worth considering. As we see more and more of the features of these challenges, we're more likely to recognize these inner tests for what they are. Being able to name them and recognize their meaning is powerful medicine. Let's look carefully at a few of them.

A sense of frustration is one aspect of the inner shift for the 21st century with which many people are struggling. Often that feeling is linked to a failure to connect with any sense of purpose in life. Nowadays vast numbers of people feel a lack of purpose. Virtually no one is immune. Even the person with a strong spiritual philosophy can nevertheless find himself in this situation. In fact, it's often the person who intellectually understands what these changing times are all about who still ends up feeling a frustrating lack of purpose and direction. In part this is because intellectual knowledge isn't enough. The changes happening in this millennium shift engage and challenge us at every aspect of ourselves: physical, emotional, intellectual, and spiritual.

In an effort to document how people of today are experiencing inner earth changes, I invited more than two hundred students of the Cayce material to submit written summaries of how the times of change were being experienced personally. Many of the accounts I received put an emphasis on the pace of life. For example, one woman's report said: "How am I currently experiencing the times of change? Very fast! Everything seems or feels very fast. A problem comes up fast, and the solution comes up fast, too. Communications, relationships, health – I don't know how to put this into words!"

This person went on to describe that the critical role played by balance in moving from one unexpected spot to another. Properly approached, this movement takes on the quality of a joyful dance:

"Everything about these changing times for me is like walking, taking steps, always poised and flexible enough to put my next step down in a different place than I expected. The challenge is to stay in balance when a stepping stone is moved after I've already started to take the next step. Or perhaps the challenge is to be ready to jump to a different stone. It's not uncomfortable now, as it was at first.... It feels more like doing a dance and enjoying it."

For other people the essence of these times of change has been a test of desire and will. Most notably, our failures and disappointments force us to surrender our familiar sense of what's best. Inner earth changes often mean giving up willfulness. As one woman put it: "My world in these times of change has been completely shaken up over a period of a few years. It has been just like gigantic thunderstorms in most areas of my life. I have been going through a process of learning how to withdraw, lose, and give up the things I desire, whether I want to or not. Emotionally, it has not been easy. To adapt with sanity, I have to continue to flow through it and learn to trust in a higher power." Another person focused his analysis on the need to be fluid and refrain from unnecessary battles – especially battles against inevitable change: "I experience tremendous changes in the workplace, economy, and society. It has been difficult to adjust initially, but now I am letting go and trying to flow with it. I am admitting that old structures, both in the workplace and in personal life, are not worth supporting in battle. In fact, the change will, as I accept it, help me to grow. It's an adjustment. But I know that to fight it is to lose."

Simply having knowledge doesn't make us immune from confusion. Possession of book learning doesn't necessarily mean that the ideas have been fully internalized. Yet, in spite of knowledge about the prophecies, any of us can nevertheless slip into a frustrating lack of purpose. With a part of our minds we can be very objective and "on top of things," but with another side of ourselves we can directly experience pain and disorientation as the old ways die.

Each one of us must go through this death and rebirth process, for, to varying degrees, each one of us has "bought into" the traditional, mainstream world that is going through such difficult changes. And therefore, that aspect of ourselves invariably must experience the transition. This, in essence, is what inner millennium shift is all about. When we have overwhelming feelings of fatigue or a despairing lack of any sense of direction, it's all very natural; we are just passing through the test of transformation. We don't need to feel guilty for those days when we're caught up in our personal, inner shift.

Not only do many of us feel a lack of energy as old patterns are dying, but frequently also a lack of enthusiasm. We may go through periods when the desire is just not there to do what we have long thought was good for us. This may surface as a dry spell in our prayer or meditation life. It may be a period of having no commitment to the nutrition that we know is best for us, or it may be a general lack of caring and enthusiasm for working on a problem relationship.

For other people a nagging sort of anxiety sets in when the inner millennium shift begins. In a society that is changing as fast as ours, what can we depend on? Not interest rates, not prices. Not our political leaders nor our physical environment. Next week there may be an earthquake in our backyards, or we may discover that our community's water supply is polluted with industrial waste. We can fall into worrying. "What will come next?" We can become numbed by all the changes. We can become frustrated to see the many people, institutions and conditions that were once so stable now appear so unreliable. In the midst of this, who can really plan for the future? And without a future to work toward, how can one have a sense of purposefulness in life?

That's a dismal way of thinking, but lots of people follow that line of reasoning. The sense of pessimism is strong. It's a widely held belief that the lives of our children will not be as good as our own have been, at least in terms of a material standard of living. And that reflects a radical shift in the attitudes and spirit of the American people over the last generation. One way of interpreting such an alteration is to look at it in terms of the inner shift. Those changes are undermining the morale of the nation – and it's probably not just in America. People in great numbers are anxious, pessimistic and unenthusiastic about their own lives and about the future.

But there are certainly options available to us. There are other ways of responding to this inner shift for the 21st century. Admittedly the challenge sometimes seems daunting. Events and conditions appear to shift so rapidly that it's hard to find any steady points of reference. Confusion, fatigue, and anxiety are natural – sometimes even the norm. Virtually no one is going to be immune from these symptoms. They come from living in a world that is being fundamentally altered.

However, feelings of despair and pessimism need not become a way of life or a permanent state of consciousness. Cayce's prophetic visions contain a purposeful, hopeful impression of the outcome of these changes. The "testing" really does have a reason. Of course, the word "test" has negative connotations for most of us. Even if you did well in school, there's bound to be a measure of anxiety or resentment attached to the word. Perhaps we can find a new feeling to associate with it – one that reminds us of strength and accomplishment that can come with meeting a trial and successfully proving oneself.

Cayce suggested that each of us is being tested by the Creative Forces of the universe. This has always gone on; human life has always contained challenges through which the depths and beauty of the human spirit can emerge. Something is special, though, about these times in which we live right now. The test is one with higher stakes – not so much for us personally, but for humanity as a whole and for the planet itself. And in this case, the "testing" is not so much like an exam that we might fail and then be expelled from school. Instead, it's a kind of testing that comes for our own benefit – to push us into being something better. It will force us to make changes in ourselves, changes that are likely to make us more capable of living in a different sort of social world and even physical world.

Cayce's visions of the future describe a very different kind of world than the one we're familiar with. The distinctions aren't simply the positions of coastlines or mountain ranges. We're passing through a period of personal and collective testing because it's preparing us to live in a planetary culture that operates by a new set of rules and assumptions. We can see the first hints of this fact already. We're discovering that we truly are a world community. The ancient concept of national boundaries is becoming very elusive. Examples quickly come to mind. We're inseparably linked economically. We share an atmosphere and a set of interconnected oceans. We're linked electronically around the globe with a kind of technological nervous system for the human family. The evidence continues on and on, leading to one inescapable conclusion: We live in times when the world is being turned upside down. It really is a whole new ball game, and we'd better be ready to play by a new set of rules, assumptions and principles.

Cayce's contemporary Carl Jung had a similar notion. (The two were born just two years apart, though they did their work without direct knowledge of each other.) Jung coined the term "modern man" to refer to just the sort of woman or man who was prepared to move beyond the traditional world. Such an individual was ready to be a citizen of just the sort of world that we are now thrust into – whether we are ready for it or not. Writing in the 1930s, Jung describes in his book *Modern Man in Search of a Soul* such a courageous step. But it's one that he sees as more or less optional, chosen by relatively few. Here at the start of the 21st century, it now seems that all of us must be ready for what Jung envisioned decades ago:

> Only the man who is modern in our meaning of the term really lives in the present; he alone has a present-day consciousness, and he alone finds that the ways of life which correspond to earlier levels pall upon him. The values and strivings of those past worlds no longer interest him.... Thus he has ... estranged himself from the mass of men who live entirely within the bounds of tradition. Indeed, he is completely modern only when he has come to the very edge of the world, leaving behind him all that has been discarded and outgrown, and acknowledging that he stands before a void out of which all things may grow.

With this inner shift for the 21st century, we're each being challenged to become just such "modern women and men." Cayce's vision about the very times in which we are now living emphasizes one basic principle: For each of us there already is – or soon will be – a test that gives us the opportunity to prepare ourselves for the millennium, for the new root race (as it was described in Chapter 4). "You expect a new root race. What are you doing to prepare for it?" (#470-35).

For many of us that preparatory challenge is found in some part of our lives where we are especially being made to feel uncomfortable, to feel pinched. It may be in a particular kind of interpersonal relationship. For some it may lie in finances. For others, it will be a desire pattern of body or mind that needs to be transformed.

But whatever it is, we have one thing in common during this test to prepare us for living creatively here in the 21st century. Pressure is being put on something we have directly placed between ourselves and God. The test is a challenging opportunity to change our relationship to God by altering something in ourselves – be it a worry, desire, attachment, fear or anything else.

In many cases the requirement of the preparatory test is merely to move something, not necessarily remove it, from our lives. For example, if our test is in terms of a preoccupation about money, then the challenge is to assign money a lower priority in our lives and put God first. Having passed through the test, we might still use money in our daily affairs, but its importance in our lives would have changed.

In another case, the test might be in a relationship with a person to whom we are overly attached. Perhaps what is required is a change of priorities, not necessarily removing that person totally from our presence. Again, the test is to discover how to put God first in our lives. If we can do that, then we are much more likely to be psychologically and spiritually comfortable with the values of an emerging new world that Cayce foresaw. However, the work that is required of us in order to pass through such a test – the alterations we have to make – will indeed feel like upheavals and earth changes inside of us.

The Dynamic Quality of God

In order to cope with and understand the inner shift for the 21st century, we need a clearer notion of how God works in the material realm. So many spiritual teachers and writers of sacred literature have spoken of the timeless, eternal, unchanging quality of God. In these times when outer conditions change so rapidly, they might counsel us to put our trust in the one thing that never changes: God's perfect spirit and love for us.

Undoubtedly, great comfort may be found in experiencing first-hand this characteristic of the Divine. However, if our knowledge of God never grows beyond that experience, it implies that the world of change around us has nothing to do with God. Simply understanding God to be the steady point of reference in the midst of whirlwind change actually misses the full picture of our Creator.

The nature of God is paradoxical. From the reference point of human consciousness, God is best understood as a two-sided coin or as the two poles of a bar magnet. Certainly, God is a steady, reliable consciousness of love that never wavers. However, God is also the god of unfoldment and of evolution. God is creativity and hence the change that accompanies any creation.

Dealing with this paradox is a crucial challenge for our times. As with most polarities or paradoxes, we might be tempted to embrace one side of the truth and exclude the other side. A good example of this is in religious fundamentalism (not just Christian fundamentalism). It's no secret that religious fundamentalism has been on the rise in recent decades

Fundamentalists have a strict notion of God's nature; it's basically a static one. Of course, they do admit that God may cause some changes now and then; for example, in the Old Testament we find stories of how God causes the destruction of cities and people because spiritual laws are not being obeyed. But for the fundamentalist of any religious persuasion, God is to be worshipped mainly because of one reason: the unchanging, timeless reality of divine existence and spiritual laws.

It's just as possible to embrace the other side of the coin. But inherent problems exist if we exclusively adopt the opposite end of the scale and claim that God is only the God of creation and evolution. Now things get slippery and vague. What happens if we say that each generation must discover its own spiritual realities? It eliminates any sense of continuity, and we can fall into the mire of relativism. Suddenly we have no point of reference. Everyone is doing his or her own thing. We can easily muddle the distinction between genuinely creative acts and self-indulgent habits. Claiming that everything is always changing leaves us with no awareness of where we are going – simply because there is nothing against which we can measure ourselves.

No, the answer lies at neither end of the polarity. Like all other polar tensions, the answer is the middle way – the midpoint of the continuum. Like all paradoxes, we're forced to find a third truth, one that can include both of the other two.

This leads us to one of Cayce's most important prophecies. In the years just ahead we will come to a new understanding of God and the Creative Forces that shape the universe. What will this new understanding look like? On the one hand, Cayce predicts that we will come to see more clearly than ever that God's influence is dynamic and transformative. When we feel tests and pressures to change, it's the work of our Creator that we experience. But at the same time we'll come to a deep understanding of how God brings influences that are constant, reliable points of reference.

It's to be a balancing trick for us. We need to be guided by the unchanging truth of spiritual law and simultaneously accept the divine nudges to evolve and grow into something more than we have been.

Higher Dimensional Life

For those who find abstract analogies or models to be helpful tools for understanding, here is one that may be especially useful. It illustrates what's going on when we're "stretched" by the force of change in our lives. The essence of this analogy was proposed by a Tibetan Buddhist teacher, Lama Anagarika Govinda, in his book *Creative Meditation and Multi-Dimensional Consciousness.* And even if such abstractions "aren't your cup of tea," give this one a try. You may still find that these images stimulate an intuition about how the times of testing are potentially expanding our consciousness.

Let's playfully create a picture of what the inner millennium shift may do to human consciousness. Imagine that your self-awareness is two-dimensional. Suppose, for example, that it's just the surface area of a square drawn on a tabletop. You have length and width – but not height, because you are just a surface

Now, take the analogy one step further as you imagine being this square living on a tabletop. Suppose you are entering times of change. You are experiencing challenges that test you and try to push you to grow into a higher dimensional being.

In fact, that's just what living in modern times feels like. We're being nudged into a higher dimensional awareness. In Lama Govinda's analogy we, as two-dimensional squares, are being pushed to become something more: three-dimensional cubes.

What do we experience as we're pushed through this transitional point between the old and the new? We feel like we're being stretched, and it comes quite naturally for us to be afraid. But afraid of what? Basically it's the fear of our own destruction. The square worries that in becoming a three-dimensional cube its original "squareness" will be destroyed. In other words, we worry that in these times of change – inner and outer – our old identities will be destroyed.

Fear is a big topic for our times, so let's look at it more carefully here in the analogy. The fear is reasonable under only one condition: the impact of forces of change in the familiar dimensions we already inhabit. In Govinda's imaginative analogy, the square should be afraid only of the forces that try to alter its length and width. For example, certain forces might try to change it into a triangle, pentagon or some other two-dimensional figure.

But certain other forces of change do not threaten the square's identity. The forces of change that challenge the square to be transformed into a cube aren't threatening in the same way. Those forces that want to stretch the square into a three-dimensional cube aren't concerned with altering the "squareness." They want to build upon what's already there! In exactly the same way, Cayce's millennium prophecies invite us to see the new world that must be built upon what is already here. That's just as surely true of the new self in each one of us that is trying to be born. It's to be a lifting and transformation of what we already are.

So what kinds of forces are we dealing with most often in these times of change? The first type or the second? The ones that try to undermine who we know ourselves to be or the ones who try to stretch us by building on what we already are? The inner millennium shift is most often about the second kind. The familiar, traditional ways of life exist in the two dimensions of our "squareness." Those forces are usually content to keep going on in just the ways they have been. The forces of change come from a higher dimension, trying to transform us into a richer awareness of life. And therefore, more often than not, our fears about self-destruction in these challenging times are based on a misunderstanding of what's going on.

The analogy demonstrates beautifully why fear is unfounded. Who we've known ourselves to be isn't on the verge of destruction. Rather it's something to be built upon. The square is not eliminated as the cube is created. Look carefully at the cube in the illustration and see that the original square is still there. But what has happened to it?

Its relative importance has been redefined. Previously it was the "whole show," and now it has become only a part of a greater whole. This is what we can expect as the inner millennium shift does its work on us. Our current identity isn't to be destroyed, but instead put into a new perspective. We are being tested to become more than what we are now. The old will be given a new place. Many of our current likes and dislikes, many of our current habit patterns of living, must be seen in a new perspective. Their relative importance in our lives must be redefined.

A Model for Understanding Inner Changes

One way to better understand the inner shift for the 21st century is to borrow a concept from gestalt psychology, a type of perceptual psychology formulated in Germany about 100 years ago. In essence it addresses the question of how we perceive the world. In fact, consciousness itself is largely a perceptual matter. Your awareness is determined mainly by what you "see," both in an outward physical way and in your subjective impressions of the inner world. When these pieces of outer and inner experience are put together, they create the "gestalt" that is functional for you in the moment.

Gestalt psychology questions the mechanism within us that makes certain objects or patterns in an overall field of view stand out, whereas other objects or patterns remain as background. The synthesis of these elements – some foreground and some background – creates the overall perception or experience we have. The classic example is the visual paradox which most of us have encountered:

What do you see? A white goblet or two darkened faces? Probably you see both, but not at the same time. In any specific moment of perception, certain items stand out as foreground and others recede as background. The "gestalt" under which we operate in our perceptions is merely a control system that selects certain things to perceive while others are generally ignored. If your gestalt defined white space to be insignificant in the drawing above, then you would see the two faces. However, another gestalt would also have been possible for you, one that would cause you to see the goblet.

Gestalts become ways of thinking or states of consciousness. Suppose as a teenager you were frequently lonely and never had dates, even though you wished you could. With the consciousness you had at that age, what kind of gestalt controlled your perceptions of life around you? For example, walking through a shopping center on a Saturday afternoon, what did you see? What emerged as foreground perceptions most likely were members of the opposite sex about your own age. Most else was not of interest to you and was little noticed. But suppose you are now forty years old, married with three children, and it is the Saturday afternoon before Christmas. You are in a shopping center trying to get last minute shopping done. What do you notice? What does your current consciousness – your present gestalt – select as foreground perceptions? Perhaps bargain-priced toys in store windows. Perhaps the clothes that other children you pass are wearing. You are a different person than you were as a teenager. Your consciousness has changed and, therefore, so have your patterns of perception.

This principle of a gestalt leads us to a related concept, which will give us a key to inner shift. That concept is the "paradigm." Simply stated, a paradigm is a set of assumptions that creates a mind-set for perceiving the outer world, or even for seeing oneself. It's much like a gestalt, although the term "paradigm" is used more frequently, in many disciplines.

Usually a paradigm refers to an agreed-upon set of assumptions, which a group of scholars or even a whole society has adopted. However, this "agreement" is often passed on in an automatic or unconscious way. Within a given academic discipline, new students learn the old paradigm from their teachers and then years later teach it to additional new students.

For example, there is a paradigm within the domain of Egyptology. Those assumptions include a time frame that does not permit much in the way of civilization to have occurred in Egypt before 3,000 B.C. With that mind-set each new archaeological discovery is viewed and categorized within the agreed-upon assumptions. The paradigm of modern Egyptology is made up of a handful of key assumptions. Rarely are those assumptions questioned. Anyone trained in this field professionally "joins the club" by ascribing to the mind-set of his or her colleagues.

Some latitude may be permitted within the group that shares a paradigm. There is occasionally room for creativity. But that creativity is to be directed toward the discovery of further assumptions that can be added on to the existing paradigm. However, within some groups – such as religious orders with their assumptions about God and the proper way to live – there may be no room at all for truly creative thinkers. The assumptions have been set; there is no room for more. The only "creative" work to be done within such groups is to discover new ways to match up the assumptions, to find new correlations. In other words, groups or fields of study with rigid paradigms are interested only in finding new ways to "prove" what they have already assumed is true.

Admittedly, a study of paradigms can become rather confusing. There are so many different varieties of paradigms, how does one know which are relevant to one's personal journey toward understanding? The problem is complex because our modern world is comprised of so many different fields of study. It was far easier in earlier times. There might have been only the religious and the political paradigms of the day. With only two – which rarely got in each other's way – life was more straightforward. The local priest would tell you about the religious assumptions concerning God and the afterlife. The king or his local representative would tell you about the political assumptions – who were the good guys and who were the bad guys, and whose orders to follow. Areas of study such as agriculture and science had to fall in line with religious and political paradigms of the day. People like Galileo rudely discovered this fact when they tried to assert new assumptions for science that contradicted the established norms.

But in our times just after the turn of the millennium, things are a bit more hazy. It's hard to identify very clearly the prevailing mind-set for areas like religion and politics. And the set of assumptions for certain scientific disciplines, such as physics, has been changing quite rapidly. Nevertheless, there seems to be a common ground to the mind-sets of the various groups, disciplines and organizations of the mainstream culture. There are points of overlap and a few basic assumptions that the majority of people in Western culture hold in common. We can call this the "old world paradigm" to contrast it to a "new world paradigm" which characterizes Cayce's visions of the 21st century and beyond.

Before attempting to identify the specific items of the "old world paradigm," we should make it clear that not every person in Western culture ascribes to these assumptions. Some people already live fully under the "new world paradigm." Others of us shift back and forth. We have days or moments in which consciousness moves and we suddenly see life and ourselves through the eyeglasses of the new assumptions. But then we find ourselves slipping back into the familiar, old worldview.

What, then, does this "old world" view of life look like? What are its assumptions? The list might well include assumptions like those below. They are certainly not what Cayce's prophecies indicated for the 21st century mind-set. But these ways of seeing life still hold powerful sway today:

1. Humans aren't really part of nature. Even though we may have descended from apelike ancestors, we are now apart from the natural world. It's not necessary to try to be one with the planet Earth because it is basically dead. We do things to the Earth and nature – not in cooperation with them.
2. Supply is limited. There is only so much energy and so much food. The universe is running down. Entropy controls not just the cosmos, but our own little microcosms as well. There is simply not enough for everybody.
3. People are generally selfish or evil. The essence of the human spirit is to get what you want. People cooperate only when it is likely to lead to some reward.
4. Bigger is better. Quantity determines value. The more people who buy a book or see a movie, the better it is. The more money a person or a company makes, the more successful they are.

5. Things are real only if they can be physically measured. Concepts such as thought energy, ESP, and healing vibrations are all merely delusions.
6. There is only one truth, and once we think we have it, it is our obligation to make sure others adopt it and the world is run by it.

These six assumptions aren't the only ones that might be on the list, but they're an effective sampling of the worldview that is familiar to us. They create a mind-set for perceiving the outer world and ourselves. The assumptions create an interlocking matrix which is very resistant to being tampered with. However, it's just this very paradigm that is under siege in today's world.

And where is the paradigm? It isn't locked in a bank vault somewhere to keep it safe. It's within human minds, within human consciousness. And the old world paradigm is being challenged by an emergent new set of assumptions – directly contradicting not just one or two of these six, but all of them. Because the old world paradigm is within us, we feel the strains of it being challenged. Our own minds are the battleground. And this is one meaning of the inner millennium shift. The foundations of the old worldview of life are being shaken, and we feel it.

Alternatives for Handling Paradigm Shifts

History shows us that occasionally the assumptions by which humans view life can shift dramatically. As noted earlier, the change from the Middle Ages to the Renaissance is a good example. During this transition period, which spanned more than one hundred years, some of the cornerstones of medieval thought were shaken. A world that was universally understood to be flat was discovered to be spherical. The Earth, believed to be at the center of the Solar System, was found to be only one of many planets traveling around the Sun. The Protestant Reformation transformed Christianity. There was a clear paradigm shift in Western culture.

Since the beginning of the Renaissance, there have certainly been major changes in our world and in human assumptions about reality. Breakthroughs in science and in the technology of warfare in particular have altered our life-styles and thoughts about the world in which we live. However, the transition in human awareness which Cayce and others foresee in the coming generation is the most dramatic paradigm shift since the 15th century. Once again, there is a possibility that nearly all the assumptions held by the vast majority of a society will be challenged and replaced.

It's not easy to live through a paradigm shift. An ancient Chinese curse is noteworthy. It is translated by some, "May you live in times of change," and by others as, "May you live in interesting times." Either way it resonates in our own era. It's difficult to live under such conditions because there are so many ways that people respond to changing assumptions and perceptions. Everyone seems to react differently to the uncertainty, and it's hard to know where people stand. Common understanding and belief make life simpler, and their lack can be frustrating. For example, someone living in 1500 might not have known if a new acquaintance was a "flat Earth man" or a "round Earth man." Or someone living in 1550 might have worried whether his neighbor was joining the new Reformation movement or remaining loyal to the traditional church. In our times we wonder how the person sitting next to us on the airplane will react if we talk about meditation or ecology. Or we hope that our relatives will understand if we quit a lucrative but demoralizing job in order to take work that creates personal joy.

The sense of community among people is easily threatened in times of paradigm shift. And added to this is the personal stress we feel – the inner millennium shift – as the old ways in us begin to die. This extraordinary mix of factors is what Cayce foresaw decades ago as he envisioned the turn of the millennium. It all produces an exciting, troublesome, anxious age.

And so, how are we to respond to times like these? There are two alternatives. We can try to hold on to the old paradigm, or we can embrace a new set of assumptions which is being born. Let's look first at some of the elaborate schemes that people sometimes use in trying to hold on to the old ways.

Holding On to the Old Paradigm. This option is the equivalent of "Let's go down with the ship." Some people are so determined to stay with what's familiar that they even contribute indirectly to their own demise. Of course, it probably doesn't look that way to them. For those who persist with the old mind-set, the adversity is merely a challenging test of their loyalty to the truth.

And so the people of our times who want to retain the six assumptions previously listed have a case to argue. They are defenders of a worldview that has, in many ways, served us well. Those half dozen assumptions – that familiar paradigm – has been a worldview that has produced many fruits. Look at the progress of humanity in the past two centuries, they point out. They argue that there's no reason to believe that the same worldview cannot continue to produce results. In fact, one definition of political conservatism is "applying the worldview and methods that have solved problems in the past to the new problems that face us today."

However, the difficulty with a conservative approach comes if there's an unwillingness to look at facts. The old world mind-set operates with a gestalt that makes anomalies (events or conditions that contradict one of the assumptions) seem like background, at best. They don't see what others see.

For those of us who have experienced contradictions of one or more of the old assumptions, it's very frustrating. Old paradigm thinkers refuse to see or admit what we know to be true. However, it may not be lying or conspiracy or deceit on the part of the people trying to hold on to the old assumptions. Perhaps they really cannot recognize something because for them it's only a part of the back ground. For them it's as if those anomalies don't exist.

Let's look at two modern examples. There are many instances in which a group of people seems to refuse to look at the evidence. Consider psychic ability. Although a majority of people may say that they believe there's something to ESP, this isn't the case among key decision makers, scholars, scientists and others in positions of intellectual authority. For this influential group, it's as if the strong scientific evidence for ESP doesn't exist. Generally, they either refuse to admit that the reports of parapsychologists are true, or they refuse to make the effort to look into these matters. Naturally it's frustrating for backers of parapsychology. More than forty years of carefully controlled scientific research has been meticulously documented in The Journal of Parapsychology and The Journal of the American Society for Psychical Research. These researchers and their advocates believe that an understanding of ESP might help change people's attitudes about the human family. What's more, psychic sensitivity is a skill that Cayce foresaw as widespread in the 21st century.

However, we might wonder why so many intelligent individuals in our society so resistantly hang on to the old world assumption that there's nothing to telepathy (mind-to-mind communication) or psychokinesis (mind over matter). But consider how threatening such a shift in belief would be to some of the leading thinkers of our world. For example, most all of the previous findings of psychological research would become suspect, because telepathy (conscious or unconscious) might possibly have influenced the experimental subjects to do or say what the experimenter hoped. Decades of very expensive research would suddenly lose much or all of its validity. Just think, too, what would happen to research methods in physics or chemistry if one had to account for the possible effects of psychokinesis. Here is a phenomenon that, if true, is so elusive that it cannot easily be shielded or measured. For many people, too much is at stake to readily shift assumptions and take an open-minded look at the findings of parapsychology.

Ecology provides us with a second good example of how some people try to resist a new way of looking at life, especially when that new way seems to threaten their own professional or personal investments. In recent decades there's been considerable progress with the environment. And to a growing number of people there is clear evidence that we have polluted the oceans and air, perhaps to a point beyond repair. Furthermore, it seems increasingly clear that humans are very much a part of an ecological whole – when we do something to affect nature, then we've got to expect to get something of equal quality back in return. And yet that sort of assumption runs contrary to the mind-set that has created a heavily industrial world. It threatens a life-style based largely on plastic and mass-produced, interchangeable goods. The leaders of such industries, and the people who have become dependent upon them, are inclined not to see the anomaly. Their gestalt places in perceptual background the disturbing new evidence of what we are doing to our planet. They tenaciously hold on to the old paradigm.

Refusing to consider the evidence that might require a shift is the most simplistic response, but this is only one method by which people try to hold on to the old set of assumptions when the world is changing. A more subtle technique is trying to patch up the old system. It looks like an open-minded willingness to change, but in essence is not that at all. The steps for this approach go as follows: First, identify the assumption that seems to be disproved by an anomaly. Refuse to consider that this one shaky assumption is a sign that all the major assumptions should be seriously questioned. Instead, maintain one's strong emotional ties to the familiar package of beliefs. Next, try to arrive at a rewritten assumption for the one under attack. Perhaps an added footnote will account for this disturbing new evidence. Or, at worst, the problematic assumption will have to be rewritten, but in a form (no matter how awkward) that will let one hang on to all the rest of the old paradigm.

For example, what do we do when statistics show the rising incidence of cancer in our society? Do we question the entire package of assumptions – the stress created by "bigger is better" thinking, the sense of animosity created by a competitive economic system, the horrendous things we do to nature to extract the resources we demand? Here is a blatant anomaly that announces that something is not right with our style of living on planet Earth. A strong tendency exists to hang on to the old worldview and merely make some patchwork. So what happens? Medical science selects a few scapegoats; it finds several dozen substances that are carcinogenic. Then it announces that you can still be safe and healthy within the old paradigm if you just pay attention to the new footnote which warns, "Don't let yourself come in contact with any of these known cancer-causing substances."

By way of analogy, it's like a man with a leaking roof on his old house. He springs a leak in March and patches it up. But another one occurs in April and two in May. He keeps up this patchwork process, never considering that the time has come for a new roof. He can conceivably keep this up, but the day will come when his entire roof will be an awkward-looking array that is totally patchwork. The sum of his time and dollar expense in all that patchwork will be greater than if he had gotten a new roof.

Sometimes the patchwork looks ludicrous. Like the emperor with no clothes, the situation almost begs for someone to demand courageously, "How could that be?" But the stakes are high. If people are determined to hang on to the old mind-set, then the old assumptions with their new footnotes will do just fine, no matter how awkward it looks. In fact such people would even proudly point to such alterations as proof of their open-mindedness and willingness to change with the times.

Let's look at an example of this technique for handling changing times. The old theory that the Sun and planets travel around the Earth was a major assumption in the medieval paradigm.

However, there were anomalies that should have alerted people to the fact that their view of reality was inadequate. For example, anyone who watched the planet Mars night after night would observe a strange phenomenon. It would seem to move gradually across the background of the fixed stars. Over the course of weeks and months, it would seem to be traveling through the various constellations of the sky. This progression was very much expected because people were sure that Mars was circling the Earth.

But occasionally Mars would do a curious thing – it would reverse its course and for several weeks seem to move backward. (A modern-day astronomer or astrologer would call this a planet "going retrograde.") The observation, which could readily be made by anyone, seemed to cast doubt upon the assumption that the planets, the Sun, and the Moon were all revolving around the Earth. For many centuries after this retrograde motion was noticed, people were not willing to part with the assumptions of their paradigm. It was difficult to ignore the evidence of an anomaly; therefore, the next best technique was employed. They patched up the old assumption, and the theory was changed. According to the revised notion, the Earth was still the center of the Solar System, but some of the planets did not traverse a circular, or even elliptical, orbit around the Earth; rather, planets like Mars traveled with a periodic loop-de-loop in their paths! In the first illustration above we see first the pathway Mars would appear to take as one watched it over the weeks move against the background of the fixed stars. The second illustration shows the "patched-up" assumption – the belief adopted by those who weren't willing to create a new paradigm.

The idea of such an orbital pathway seems ludicrous to us with our modern knowledge of astronomy. But what else could the people of that day do? Their worldview and mind-set were too precious for them to seriously consider new assumptions. It was not until the Renaissance that a sensible idea of the Solar System was generally accepted and the retrograde motion of the planets was easily explained.

The relative difference in speed between the Earth's movement around the Sun and that of another planet like Mars would create the occasional appearance of backward movement.

We can laugh at the people six hundred years ago in their naiveté and stubbornness. But isn't it possible that six hundred years from now our descendants will view some of our patched-up assumptions as equally amusing? To what degree do we now try to modify old assumptions to avoid having to develop an entirely different worldview? Or, in what ways do we take something that is of the new world and distort it so that it looks like part of the old world?

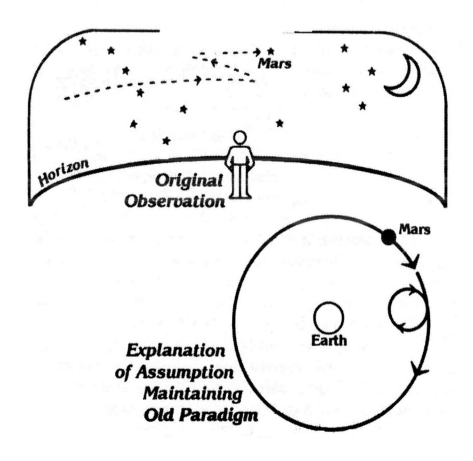

When the world is changing in the way ours is now, such methods can only temporarily slow the movement. People who would hang on to the old assumptions may still be in the majority, but the evolution of consciousness on this planet doesn't depend on majority vote. If it did, then things would never really move forward. Human fears and desires would keep us stuck. But here is the key point: Paradigm shifts on the scale of the Renaissance happen in spite of the majority.

Those who insist on trying various methods to maintain the old set of assumptions will find the coming decades to be especially troublesome. They are likely to feel the inner millennium shift most acutely. The temporizing, patching up, denying techniques won't work for long. They, like all of us, will have to face the new world being born around them, and more importantly being born within themselves.

Joining the Emergent Paradigm. In response to inner and outer shifts of the 21st century, we can choose to work cooperatively with a new set of values and assumptions. Cayce predicted that some individuals would be pioneers of a new planetary consciousness. Who are those people and how can we recognize them in today's world?

They are the ones who sense that the old ways are dying and can perceive a fresh orientation for humanity and planet Earth. They are people who are generally patient and not driven by fears. They trust that there is a plan to what is going on in the world, that there is a spirit of the times that is in keeping with God's plan. They know themselves to be co-creators with God in the transformation to a new worldview, but they humbly recognize that their work is to respond to the divine initiative which will be revealed to them.

What are the characteristics of such a person? In fact, such an individual is within each of us. All of us have the potential to be among those who make this kind of response to the inner millennium shift. All of us have the capability of being receptive in these times, which is a first characteristic of this sort of person. This isn't passivity, because the builders of 21st century culture need to be active and involved. Rather it's a matter of listening before acting. By way of an analogy, it's like being a swimmer in open waters and taking the time to become aware of the position and direction of a current. Once that perception is made, one can then actively swim in the current and be carried along by it. It's a matter of being able to sense the true spirit of these times. Such listening must reach beneath the surface of current events in the outer world.

The true spirit of these times isn't the fear of being down-sized, social unrest, or even earth changes. There will be many symptoms of what is going on, but we need to look deeper to see the real spirit of what is being born. In fact, the nightly television news is more likely to document the dying of the old world than the birth of the new. A real listener – a real co-creator of the world Cayce predicted for the 21st century – senses the elements emerging for a new paradigm. He or she then acts in response to what has been noticed. That person is able to give expression and form to the new assumptions about life.

This sort of person (who is within us all as a potential) is also able to put aside fears. He or she is able courageously to accept that moment of void we encounter when we have let go of the old and yet the new isn't yet fully within our grasp. We might wonder what it is that most scares people about times of change and paradigm shifts. Do we fear that the future might be worse than the past has been? Or rather, are we more afraid of the void – of that moment of uncertainty and vulnerability – when the old assumptions have faded but we are not yet clear about the new? We need the confidence of a trapeze artist who has let go of one swing and momentarily hangs helplessly out in space before grabbing on to the next: he knows his own momentum will carry him forward to meet the swing he trusts will be there.

In many arenas of life, people confront the difficulties posed by that void – for example, in their vocations and in their choices about close personal relationships. Many individuals stick with an old job even though they cannot imagine having any other job that would be more distasteful to them. But they are afraid to quit – oftentimes not so much worried that they would remain unemployed as because they cannot stand the thought of being in that uncertain, vulnerable void for any amount of time. It takes courage to move on to a new vocation, a new set of friends, or a whole new set of assumptions for living. The capacity to overcome the fear is within each of us.

Another characteristic of the person who embraces the new paradigm is an alchemical type of skill. The alchemists of ancient times attempted to turn lead into gold. Or, more accurately, they tried to transform the base or earthly aspects of human consciousness into enlightenment. A version of this skill belongs to the pioneers of the millennium. Some things viewed as weaknesses by the old set of assumptions can be seen as strengths by the new paradigm.

Cayce was especially skillful at showing individuals how this transformative principle could work at a personal level. He often described how a fault could be lifted into a strength. For example, one man who came to Cayce on many occasions was known to be extremely talkative, often to the annoyance of those around him. However, Cayce pointed out how this fault could be alchemically transmuted into a great strength as he became an eloquent and eager spokesperson for spiritual truth.

Certainly not everything held in low esteem by the old paradigm will suddenly be much admired in the new one. It's the skill of the co-creators of a new world to recognize and work with those qualities that are good candidates for the alchemical change. Let us consider two examples.

One candidate is sensitivity. In the old world it's often considered a weakness to be sensitive. In the competitive worlds of our vocations, the sensitive person is likely to get ulcers. Sensitivity generally runs counter to the assumption that there are limited resources and one had better be tough to struggle hard for his own share. But in a new paradigm, sensitivity can be transformed from weakness to strength. For example, a requirement for leadership in the 21st century may be sensitivity to others.

Another candidate is interdependence. This is a good illustration of the process at work on a global scale. In the old paradigm, it's weakness for one nation to be dependent on another nation. For example, we say that the United States has a weakness in requiring the oil of the Persian Gulf countries. We say that Belgium is a weak nation because it's dependent upon France, Germany and the United States for military protection. And by old world assumptions these instances and many more are true. However, with a new paradigm the assumptions have changed. Now we can see that we are one people on planet Earth. What benefits the people of one nation can potentially benefit those throughout the world. Our interdependence becomes a strength, alchemically transformed into a stimulus for cooperation. A characteristic once held in low esteem can become something that is newly admired and appreciated. Cayce described this principle to one man, intent on being a leader in the creation of a new world: "... as has been given of old, 'That stone that was rejected of the builders has become the cornerstone ... '" (#900-318). Such is the work of the builders of a new world – to recognize and nurture the qualities of life that can go through such a dramatic switch.

Finally, the pioneers of 21st century culture that Cayce envisioned will treat with respect the elements of the old paradigm. They won't be angry or full of hatred, simply allowing the old worldview to run its course and die. Instead it's with love that they take the elements of the old ways and find new places for them. It's a crucial point to understand. Remember that when we moved to a new gestalt (for example, seeing the two faces instead of the goblet), the literal elements of the scene did not change. Instead it was our way of ordering them that was altered. We created new priorities, putting the background into the foreground. Or when we stretched a square into the higher dimensional life of being a cube, we did not destroy the square. We merely changed the relative importance and priority of its position.

The same must hold true if we are to move properly from a world run by the old paradigm to a world run by the new. Many of the elements of living will remain. The challenge is to arrange, order and relate them to each other based on a new set of rules. Cayce's prophecies about the 21st century and beyond make clear that we will still have families, businesses, governments, schools and agriculture. The shift in paradigms doesn't mean eliminating business just because it may have been poorly operated under the old set of assumptions. Nor does it mean throwing out the idea of governments just because wars and hatreds were created when governments operated under the old rules of the game.

Inner millennium shift is essentially a changing gestalt, a new way of arranging priorities and relationships. This is far more challenging than just watching the old world die. The current transformation isn't so much one in which the individual elements of the scene change; it's rather the emergence of a new gestalt that sees those elements in entirely new relationships. And with this new set of priorities, a different and more productive way of living can also be born. That's what the 21st century, as Cayce saw it – inner and outer – is really all about.

CHAPTER 7

CAYCE'S VISIONS FOR
FIVE ANCIENT RIDDLES

Twenty-first century consciousness is about practical spirituality, a term that neatly sums up Cayce's vision for how we will live in the new millennium. But practical spirituality isn't just a matter of remembering to think positively about real-life challenges we face in the modern world. It's also a willingness to deal creatively with some of the long-standing riddles and mysteries of what it means to be a human. In fact, Cayce's prophecies about 21st century consciousness suggest that we are ready for a quantum leap in terms of how humanity has dealt with ancient questions such as "What is time?" and "Can I get angry and still be on a spiritual path?"

In this chapter we will explore five of these profound, mysterious problems of the human condition. In each instance, we will find that Cayce had important insights that could potentially transform the ancient riddle.

The Riddle of Time

Hence the *necessity* of patience, of living in the soul, seeing all time as *one* time, that ye may know whereunto thou hast been called. (#696-3)

All force is one force, all time one time, all energy one energy, radiating in its different sphere, phases, or the modifications of the different conditions, see? (#900-362)

Time travel is one of the favorite plot devices of science fiction novelists and moviemakers. They know that we are drawn to the idea of getting beyond the limits of time. Commonsense logic tells us that the past is unchangeable and the future unknowable. But something else stirs in us to suggest otherwise. Maybe ... just maybe ... time isn't as linear and rigid as we normally think.

We get hints of the deeper mystery of time in subtle ways. A precognitive dream. A déjà vu experience. If we pay close attention to our inner and outer lives, there seem to be a clue hinting that time is more than we've thought.

I remember when I first encountered Edgar Cayce's perspective on the nature of time. I had trouble knowing what to do with repeated statements such as "All time is one time - see? That is as a fact..." (#294-45). I vigorously resisted the notion. It seemed to me that if we throw out the familiar concept of time, then a lot of other concepts have to be dismissed also – things like soul development and accountability. They appear to depend on a past that is over and done with, and a future that is yet to be created. My problem was further compounded when I heard Edgar Cayce's son Hugh Lynn say in lectures more than once: "In a sense, all of our 'past lives' are happening all at once."

Over the years I have slowly come around to accept the idea that a radically new idea of time is required if we hope to understand how the universe is structured and how we meet the practical challenges of spirituality. In spite of the way that it seems to fly in the face of commonsense, the evidence simply seems too strong to dispute. Time must be far more complex than the one-dimensional timeline on which the great and trivial events of history are irrevocably ordered.

But what are our chances of truly understanding how time works? Modern physics presents a dizzying analysis of time, one that leaves room for relativistic time frames that move at different paces and, more mystifying, the possibility that time can in essence move backward. Can we really figure all this out, or would it require us to have the mind of God? Perhaps it is ultimately beyond our reach. Huston Smith, author of *The Religions of Man*, offered an apt analogy at his lecture at the educational center of the Cayce work several years ago: The gap between human consciousness and divine consciousness is probably like the gap between the canine consciousness of our pet dog and the consciousness of a human. There are simply some human things that dogs are never going to be able to understand.

But I don't think we ought to be willing to give in quite so quickly on this question of understanding the higher dimensions of time. The very fact that the Cayce readings repeatedly offered this challenge to understand that "all time is one time" suggests that there is something practical that we can do with the idea, even if it explodes our normal worldview. The consciousness predicted for the 21st century and beyond is capable of working with a new understanding of time.

Consider what it means if time has a second dimension. By analogy, that means that time isn't just a *line*, it can be a *surface*. And with a surface to work with, time can turn back on itself and create a *circle*. Hence we have the possibility of cycles of time or recurrent patterns of time – something found in many indigenous cultures. To make it even more challenging, maybe time has a third dimension, as P.D. Ouspensky and others have suggested. Our analogy can become not just a circle with its repetition of opportunities but now a *spiral*, which combines cycles along with progression.

Consider some of the issues of practical spirituality into which all this enters. Perhaps it is possible to change the past. Maybe forgiveness isn't merely a change of attitude about something that happened long ago. Instead, there might be a profound kind of forgiveness in which *our consciousness actually experiences something different taking place in "the past."*

Or consider the human desire to experience "eternity." What does that really mean? Is it the desire to live for a long, long time … maybe forever? A different understanding of "eternity" emerges once we let go of our simplistic idea of time as only a line extending back into the distant past and forward into an endless future. *Eternity has more to do with the quality of how we experience the present moment.* It is the experience of the infinite that cuts perpendicularly through every possible moment on the timeline of history. Just imagine how our lives would change if we could redirect some of our worrying-about-the-future energy into trying to awaken to eternity right now.

These are riddles of time and the soul. And as modern science and spirituality come closer and closer in the 21st century, perhaps the merging of these two streams of understanding can help us gain new insight on this fundamental mystery of our lives.

The Riddle of Good and Evil

There is so much good in the worst of us, and so much bad in the best of us, it doesn't behoove any of us to speak evil of the rest of us. (#3063-1)

How do we understand and respond to evil? That's a question that has come to the forefront in the early years of the 21st century, especially when thoughtful people try to live in "the real world" and still maintain some kind of spiritual presence. The specter of the terrorism of September 11, 2001 brought us face to face again with the terrible riddle of good and evil.

Too easily our recognition of the reality of evil slips away, only to have us shocked back to an encounter with it in the form of some awful deed. Andrew Delbanco, in his book *The Death of Satan,* suggests that the very idea of evil seems incompatible with modern life, from which "transgression" and "personal accountability" are quickly receding. The tendency is perhaps even more pronounced in "new age" circles where evil is sometimes dismissed as an illusion of the unenlightened mind. *But an invisible evil is the most dangerous of all.* As Debanco points out, "If evil ... escapes the reaches of our imagination, it will have established dominion over us all."

Cayce treats evil as very real, and two points from his philosophy are worth considering. First, evil has many "faces," many ways that it presents itself to us in daily living. Unless we are prepared to deal with its multi-faceted ways of encountering us, we are sure to become overwhelmed and confused by what swirls around us, especially in the turbulent times in the early 21st century.

Second, we recognize and deal with evil in the *outer world* only to the extent that we undertake the distasteful and courageous work of meeting it *within ourselves.* Cayce borrowed a passage from Bartlett's *Familiar Quotations:* "There is so much good in the worst of us, and so much bad in the best of us, that it hardly behooves any of us to talk about the rest of us." And so, even though our self-justifying minds are quick to point out that we don't do the atrocious, abusive things that we see on the nightly news; nevertheless there *are* ways that each of us – perhaps in small scale ways – act out some of these same themes in our own lives.

To see our personal roles with evil, it's useful to return to the first point: there are many "faces" to evil, some of them no doubt more alive in us personally than are others. In Cayce's philosophy, there are at least five "angles" on how we can understand and relate to evil (or "bad" as he sometimes refers to it). The emerging human consciousness of the new millennium requires sensitivity to all five.

A lack of awareness. Sometimes evil can be understood as a deficit in consciousness, a state of being "asleep" spiritually. There is the constant tug from the influence of evil to become less and less conscious, more and more distracted. The temptations are all around us daily.

Extremism. If, as Cayce sometimes put it, the Christ Consciousness is the meeting point between extremes – that is, the middle path – then one "face" of evil is to go off to an extreme, even denying the validity of any counter-balancing point of view. And surely our world is full of extremists right now. What's a little harder to see is our own tendency to go extremes.

Aggression and Invasion. We think of these words in terms of their connotations to warfare but all human relations contain the potential for evil in this form. It is a matter of trying to subvert the free will of others by overpowering them with your own will. In his under-appreciated book about evil entitled *People of the Lie*, Scott Peck writes, "Evil has to do with killing, and I do not mean to restrict myself to corporeal murder. Evil is also that which kills the spirit." However, there is still a place for genuine self-assertiveness. One gift of authentic practical spirituality is the capacity to stand up for oneself (and one's ideals) with integrity, but without becoming aggressive and invasive in the process.

Just Under Good. Here is a particularly hopeful way of viewing evil or "bad." It is something that is just falling short, just missing the mark. "How far, then, is ungodliness from godliness? Just under, that's all!" (#254-68) That doesn't mean to ignore that bad or evil falls short, but it does give a powerful reason to stay engaged with elements of life that are "ungodly" and keep working with them.

Rebellion and Willfulness. This is Cayce's most fundamental idea about evil. Not only are we given the choice daily between good and evil influences in our own lives, but *the choice itself somehow makes conditions "good" or "bad."* We are co-creators of one or the other by our very decisions! "For there is daily set before thee good and evil, life and death, and with thy choice ye make it good or bad." (#3285-2) Perhaps what tips the scale toward evil is whenever the decision is based on a kind of "rebellious willfulness," as Gerald May refers to it in *Will and Spirit*: "Evil seeks to mislead or fool one into substituting willfulness for willingness, mastery for surrender."

And so, the choices are constantly ours – in the big and little decisions we make each day in response to the many "faces" of evil. As concerned as we need to be in the 21st century about evil on the scale of national and international affairs, practical spirituality demands we look at our own relationship to these very themes.

The Riddle of Healing and Spirituality

Sometimes medicine and spirituality seem worlds apart. It's not easy to find, even here in the 21st century, a physician with whom you can also speak about your spiritual values and interests. Not too many doctors see themselves as mystics. And yet that's exactly what Edgar Cayce was trying to pioneer for us, starting more than one hundred years ago. And in his visions for 21st century medicine it was the integration of these two streams that was seen as crucial. Spirituality and materiality can find a meeting ground in the human body. Mysticism and medicine can be two sides of the same coin.

In fact, the story of Edgar Cayce's life and work can largely be summarized by those two alliterative words. "Mysticism" speaks to the spiritual roots of Cayce's message; and "medicine" identifies the focus of his work – especially as we remember how he was just as concerned about soul health and mental health as he was physical health.

But Cayce was prone to pick up tag lines that reflected the sensationalistic side of his work rather than its real depth and meaning. And so we are more likely to hear about him in the mainstream media as "The Sleeping Prophet" or the "Miracle Man of Virginia Beach," whereas he was actually an intuitive healer and Christian mystic philosopher. And when we think of the Cayce prophecies for the 21st century, we are probably more likely to be curious about possible earth changes than we are about how healing will be done in the decades to come.

Mysticism is the direct experience of the oneness of all life. It's not intellectual speculation or abstract theorizing. When Cayce gave a reading, it wasn't a lecture or sermon. Instead, he put into words what he was *directly experiencing* from a higher level of consciousness.

To understand Cayce's mysticism and how it led to his medical clairvoyance, it's important to note two complementary aspects. First there is a *transcendent* element. Mysticism involves *disengagement* from our ordinary way of seeing things. Cayce's way of doing that was a prayer-induced, sleep-like state of consciousness which allowed him to leave the body – or, at least, to leave the familiar kind of consciousness that our bodies and our physical sensations create for us.

The other side of the coin is that Cayce's mysticism is *imminent* and *immediate*. It's here-and-now, and it's practical. He defines the purpose of life as the work "to make the infinite finite" – that is, to bring the transcendent *into* everyday life. Remember that two-thirds of his lifetime work as a clairvoyant focused on giving physical health readings. It's a powerful statement about how much he honored the importance of the physical world. And so, with the dual nature of Cayce's mysticism in mind, we can examine two principal themes that are at the heart of his "Mysticism and Medicine." There are two themes that he foresaw as essential to the times in which we are now living.

Love and intuition. Cayce's contribution to mystically inspired medicine is an outgrowth of love. A reading was essentially an act of love. He would virtually lay down his life for someone, and it was probably a lot more dangerous than we realize. But his love-inspired intuition was far more than the courage to go unconscious and trust that half an hour later he would be able to regain his normal mind. It was also a matter of how Cayce loved people. His ability to tune-in intuitively to their bodies, minds and souls was a by-product of his profound caring.

It may well be that all parapsychological phenomena will someday be appreciated for their dependence upon love. Psychic perceptions are expressions of oneness; and love is all about oneness, unity, and connectedness. The science of parapsychology rarely seems interested in such a notion, but it was significant that on one occasion the *Journal of the American Society for Psychical Research* published an article entitled "Parapsychology and Love" which attempted to make this very point. Surely Edgar Cayce's work is the very best example of this principle in action.

Images of the body. The mysticism and medicine of Cayce's work can also be captured by a series of symbolic images that can be used for the human body. First is an *automobile.* For example, when we dream of a car, it's often related to the condition of the physical body. But that's still a pretty mechanical image for the body. It's useful and may help us to interpret many a dream concerning practical health advice from the unconscious mind.

A deeper image is the body as a *temple.* In fact, Cayce was fond of using that biblical image, which connotes how the divine resides within the flesh. Just as God could be met face-to-face on special occasions by the High Priest within the Holy of Holies of the Jerusalem Temple, so can we find the presence of God residing inside our own bodies.

And yet as beautiful and useful as the temple symbol may be, it still has the flavor of an "imprisoned splendor," as the mystic scientist Raynor Johnson describes the divine element within us all. The "body as the temple" still doesn't quite capture the fullness of Cayce's "mysticism and medicine." An even more profound image – and true to the deepest teachings of Cayce about the human body – is a *bridge.* The body can serve as a connector between the material world and the spiritual world. It is *through the body* that we awaken to spirituality – not by discarding, ignoring, or escaping from the body, as some traditions would teach. It's that third symbol for the body that our 21st century consciousness needs to reach.

Keep in mind, then, how these two themes – mysticism and medicine – are relevant not only to Cayce's own pioneering work. They are just as important for *each one of us* trying to be mystics in ordinary life and finding ways to do our own life's work of practical spirituality.

The Riddle of Companionship on the Spiritual Path

"He that would approach the throne comes leaning on
the arm of a brother that has been aided." (#437-2)

For twenty years one of the focal points for my educational
work presenting the Cayce material has been "Discovering Your
Soul's Purpose." Books, television shows and conferences have put
me in touch with thousands of people who are trying to find a
spiritually motivated way to be in the world and be present to each
other. The heart of practical spirituality is this search to find one's
unique calling and way of service to other souls who are our
companions on the spiritual path. Surely the shaping of a new
planetary culture for the 21st century has something to do with finding
a spiritual approach for what it means to be companions along the way,
together.

A high percentage of the people who start on this self-
discovery process, "Discovering Your Soul's Purpose," hope to find a
new, spiritually-oriented career – *or*, if not a 9-to5 job then at least an
avocation that draws upon their soul talents in such a way to find
meaningful ways to be in relationship to others. And many of these
seekers do, in fact, gain a clear insight about a challenging, fulfilling
work that they can get started upon.

In particular, one pathway seems to come forth regularly
among the audiences with which I have worked. It takes on slightly
different descriptions from person to person; but fundamentally the
service that these people envision is *spiritual mentorship*. It is the
creative work of helping other people along the spiritual path.

Of course, the very notion of providing spiritual advice is
enough to give us pause. What a great mystery and riddle that has
been in human history. How can we support others without becoming
their bosses or taking on some kind of authority figure role. Surely the
21st century has more to do with finding ways to be *spiritual
companions along the way* than it does in finding new forms of priestly
duty over others.

For that matter, who among us is healthy enough – spiritually,
mentally and physically – to be telling others how to live? At first
glance the very idea of spiritual mentorship seems like it could be
presumptuous. But when we look closer, we see that befriending,

coaching, encouraging, and even advising fellow seekers may be the most natural outgrowth of our own spiritual striving.

Consider the most basic principle in Edgar Cayce's advice about how our own soul development is enhanced. "Aid others to know themselves better – for, as has been given, he that would approach the throne comes leaning on the arm of a brother that has been aided." (#437-2)   Of course, there are many ways to apply this call to service, but a very timely one for many of us now is the task of being a *spiritual guidance mentor*. In the confusing, complex world of the 21st century, there are millions and millions of very sincere people who are trying to take their next step toward becoming a whole person. Most of them could use the aid, encouragement and even wisdom of a fellow seeker.

Here is one very practical application of the Cayce legacy for the new millennium. We can train and support people who are ready to fulfill an aspect of their own soul-purpose by becoming spiritual guidance mentors. Those people would be prepared to help other seekers in ways such as:

- Meditation instruction
- Dream interpretation
- Coaching a person through the process of identifying a personal mission in life
- Consulting, interpreting *and* applying the spiritual guidance that can come from a wide variety of sources, including synchronicity, inspirational writing, and intuition.

Now we are looking at a profoundly promising new calling for people in the 21st century – whether it's seen as an occupation or merely an avocation. Spiritual guidance mentors are not intended to take the place of counselors and psychologists. However, they can provide a specialized kind of help and practical wisdom about soul growth that is often missing in today's world when people start looking around for help.

Think about this kind of situation. It is one that arises in various forms countless times daily. Someone is just getting started toward a more balanced, holistic life-style. Perhaps a book or magazine article has stimulated the first sense that there is a bigger story to how life works than she has ever before considered. Then she begins to have dreams that seem momentous, but they remain confusing and uninterpreted. She hears about meditation, and it sounds like just the sort of daily discipline that she'd like to try. However, she isn't sure how to begin, and merely following instructions out of a book doesn't feel like enough.

This hypothetical woman is just the sort of person who might benefit from the help of a mentor. The mentor could teach her the fundamentals of meditation and help her understand the experiences that arise. The mentor could also help her find ways to start interpreting her own dreams or the intuitive experiences she has started to have. And maybe even more important, when this woman feels that the time is right, the mentor can coach her through a process of evaluating her life and ideals, in order to see the spiritual mission for which she was born.

The very academic institution that Edgar Cayce co-founded – Atlantic University – has even developed a comprehensive training program to train people to serve in the capacity of companionship along the spiritual path. Of course it won't be the only way in which Cayce's vision for a new way of supporting each other will be manifest. But it's one key element in a fresh way of approaching this ancient riddle in human relations.

The Riddle of What to Do with Anger

One without a temper is not worth much, but one not able to control the temper is worth a great deal less. (#3507-1)

Affirming life is great, but sometimes we have to learn to say "no" before we can say "yes" to life. Hearing this, we may pause, fearing that we're about to enter down a pathway of negativity, and many have assumed that the "new age" is about positivity exclusively. They would ask, "Do we really want to honor negation in this way?" In fact, it may take a good measure of mental health to be able to set boundaries and define ourselves with a "no."

Consider one example of this principle, Cayce's bold advice to certain people: "So live each and every day that you may look any man in the face and tell him to go to hell! (#1739-6) People usually laugh nervously when they first hear this passage. Surely it's not Cayce, the life-affirming, positive-thinking spiritual counselor saying something like this! Perhaps it's just another example of his wry humor. Surely he didn't really mean for us to *live* that way. The world already has enough in-your-face, rude people. But Cayce was dead serious about the need for us to vigorously define and defend our boundaries, and sometimes that means telling someone to "Go to hell." But more often it probably suffices just to state a firm "no," letting it be known who you are and how you need to be treated.

It's a matter of affirming one's personhood. Beneath the negation there is actually a more significant *affirmation* of something. The point is this: *there is no love and no intimacy with others unless we can first define our own boundaries.* It's a matter of the most basic practical spirituality to say "no" when we need to. Then, from that position of relative strength, we can enter into relationship with another person. As strange as it may sound to our ears, loving someone may start by stepping back from them – saying "no" and defining oneself – and *then* finding the capacity to reach out and build an authentic bridge to that person.

This sounds a lot like "self-asssertion" as it has been taught in popular psychology, and Cayce himself sometimes advocated self-assertion. One good example was advice given to a 34-year-old machinist foreman who suffered from the social illness of letting other people take advantage of him. Cayce's blunt advice: "The entity because of his indecisions at times allows others to take advantage of him. The entity must learn to be self-assertive; not egotistical but self-assertive – from a knowledge of the relationship of self with the material world." (#3018-1)

Another example is Cayce's repeated description of just how important it is to be able to get angry. Anger is an emotion directly related to saying "no" to what's going on. Of course, Cayce didn't say we need to run around blowing our stacks daily, but he *did* emphasize the need for the personal power to get angry in the right way, when the occasion calls for it. "Be angry but sin not. For he that never is angry is worth little." (#1156-1) But then he adds the importance of having a *container* for that anger. "But he that is angry and controlleth it not is worthless." Note here that "control" does not mean "suppression" but instead "proper direction." It's a crucial distinction!

Maybe sometimes we're just trying too hard to be nice. In fact, "niceness" can be a mask for a lot of unresolved feelings, such as low self-esteem and fear. Admittedly niceness is sometimes an authentic expression of untainted love that arises out of inner strength. (And for a few very healthy people, "niceness" may be just that virtually all of the time.) But a majority of us suffer from some degree of compulsive niceness, and often it's the way we put off dealing with life head-on. We're nice because we don't want to hurt someone's feelings, when in fact they need something else far more than having feelings protected: they need genuine human encounter that is honest and purposeful. But that takes a lot of energy, and it's risky. It's usually the safer bet just to be nice – to avoid saying "no" and standing up for yourself – and let the situation pass.

So, if we follow a philosophy that isn't afraid to say "no," what kind of people would we become? What kind of world will we have in the 21st century if individuals are able *consciously* to get angry, to say "no," and to even occasionally to tell people to "Go to hell"? In many ways "conscious anger" would make for a healthy, saner world – perhaps even one with *less* antagonism and negativity, simply because we would have less bottled up and repressed energy leaking out in insidious ways. Of course, the key to this kind of practical spirituality is to stay in touch with something positive and life-affirming, even when circumstances challenge us to say "no." Negation outwardly can happen simultaneous to something very positive happening inwardly: the affirmation of our individuality, the connection with our own courage and strength, and the rededication to what we authentically hold as a personal ideal. When we understand that possibility, then we will have discovered the positive side of saying "no." What a transformation that can be for our society in the 21st century.

CHAPTER 8

A 21ST CENTURY APPROACH TO GUIDANCE AND DECISION-MAKING

It's all about decisions. That's the heart of Cayce prophecies for the 21st century. There may well be some strong patterns and likelihoods that allow a clairvoyantly sensitive person to see what may be coming. But choices and decisions are what ultimate selects from among the possibilities and creates a physical reality.

Not surprisingly, then, Cayce frequently emphasized the power that we have as individuals to shape 21st century culture. And that power is the result of lots of little decisions that we make in our lives.

When you face an important decision, how do you proceed? How do you go about making a choice when you realize that the decision can have an important impact on your own life and the lives of others? Perhaps you are the sort of person who likes to go with the first, intuitive impression. Or maybe you favor a deliberate, analytical technique that carefully considers every variable. These are but two of many examples of decision-making style; however, *every* style makes use of the human will in *some* fashion.

Cayce indicates that in the new millennium many people will incorporate some type of guidance procedure in the course of making an important decision. The guidance may come from inner, subjective sources (e.g., dream guidance, meditation guidance) or outer sources (e.g., counseling, psychic readings, etc.). To seek guidance is to recognize one's own limited perspective on the decision at hand. It requires a degree of humility on the part of the conscious ego-self as it sincerely receives help in making a choice.

Cayce also envisions a 21st century in which more and more people have found a healthy, balanced way to express their individuality. He even describes the goal of human experience to be coming "to know ourselves to be ourselves (i.e., enhanced self-awareness of one's individuality) *and* knowing ourselves to be one with the Whole." And surely the key to "knowing ourselves to be ourselves" is the discovery of right use of freedom and will.

To see the role that free will can play in guidance and decision-making, let's first consider the three broad strategies that can be used. Each of the three represents a different response to this question: "What are you looking for when you seek guidance?"

1. Looking for an answer. This is the most obvious and probably the most frequent response. But it isn't always the best approach. Using this strategy, you seek guidance which provides a specific solution to a specific question. For example, you might pose questions like these:

- Should I keep taking my medication despite its side effects?
- Should I finally tell my next-door neighbor what's been irritating me about his behavior for the past six months?
- What new type of vocation should I explore?

In each of these instances, the exact answer itself is sought.

What sources of guidance might you want to pursue in following this first approach? One effective method is to get advice from a professional – perhaps a physician or a counselor. Or, sometimes a trusted, knowledgeable friend provides just as much helpful guidance. But you might want to consider certain nontraditional methods as well – a psychic, an astrologer, a numerologist, etc. Obviously, your choice must be appropriate to your question. For example, an astrologer may be more likely to give helpful guidance on vocational choices than with medication side effects.

To what extent can these esoteric methods of guidance be relied upon? The philosophy in the Cayce readings provides two useful guidelines. First, remember that your life is not preordained. On a daily basis you are creating your future through the choices you make, and no esoteric art can define a predetermined future for you.

Second, esoteric arts are able to describe accurately about 20% of the significant influences. That 20% may make a significant impact on the problem at hand, but the remaining 80% of the influence rests with how you use your will. For example, astrology, numerology, and palmistry might be able to describe accurately 20% of the influences that should be taken into account when choosing a vocation. But it would hardly seem wise to base the decision entirely on this technique for receiving guidance. In fact, these approaches probably serve us better when they are part of the second strategy described below.

2. Looking for more information. This approach to guidance is to search for additional information so you can formulate your own answer at a later time. With this technique, you reserve the role of final decision-maker for your conscious will, but ask your unconscious self to give you more facts or additional perspectives which might lead to a better answer. Here are examples of questions which might lend themselves naturally to this approach:

- How should I respond to my boss? I don't know what he's feeling or why his actions are so confusing to me.
- What is best for my relationship with Richard? What kind of past-life experiences have we bad which make me so attracted to him?

In these two examples, the seeker is hoping to arrive eventually at a decision on how to act toward the boss or how deeply to get involved with Richard. Yet inner guidance is sought only to provide the *additional information* that might lead to a better conscious decision.

3. Looking for confirmation. This third approach seeks confirmation of a tentative conscious decision. In this instance the questioner looks for an inner sense of affirmation or warning concerning an intended course of action. For instance, one might pose these questions to the inner self:

- Will it be best for my daughter if I follow through on the decision to enroll her in a private school?
- Is the best financial result to be expected from following through on the planned sales of my automotive stock?

In these two examples, it's evident that the seeker has done some homework and has even arrived at a tentative conscious answer. Now the guidance is being asked to serve a role of supporting or warning against a specific course of action.

Cayce's psychology of decision-making is sophisticated, and it challenges us to recognize which approach fits best in a given situation. None of these three approaches is clearly superior to the other two for all situations, although some situations will be best suited to one of the three. In your own decision-making, focus as often as possible on the second and third approaches. In other words, you should be careful about turning the entire decision-making process over to the unconscious or to someone else.

Here's another way to say this: God wants you to learn how to make decisions. The plan for spiritual evolution for humanity involves more and more creative decision-making, and the 21st century is a significant moment in human history for a great stride forward on this front. Your personal will is to be awakened and used in a constructive manner. Yet, paradoxically, it is in your best interests spiritually to befriend and cooperate with your "soul," which is usually unconscious but always available to direct you wisely. The paradoxical nature of this principle can be frustrating. Nevertheless, you'll arrive at the best approach for attuned decision-making when you find a balance between two kinds of will: 1) your conscious personal capacity to choose and (2) the deeper understanding of a Higher Will within your unconscious.

The distinction between a conscious and an unconscious will has the potential to be the most significant breakthrough in psychology since a similar understanding emerged concerning the human mind. It can be one hallmark of the 21st century. Just think what an impact Freud and his contemporaries had on 20th century culture by convincingly demonstrating the reality of the *unconscious mind.* That hidden side of the mind may have been dimly felt and usually dismissed, but Freud and others showed its powerful influence in the early 20th century. The same qualities hold true of the *unconscious will.* We typically ignore its promptings and only dimly recognize its presence; and yet the unconscious will is potently active in our lives every day. *Learning how to recognize it and to follow its wise guidance is crucial for our planet in the 21st century.*

Comparing Cayce's Ideas to a Leading Psychiatrist

These concepts about an unconscious will are not mere speculation. Modern science in its own rigorous, experimental way has found evidence that much of what we call conscious decision-making is foreshadowed unconsciously in the brain just a moment before the decision reaches awareness. This may be suggestive of a broader and even more significant process in our unconscious life.

Dr. Leslie Farber, in his book *The Ways of Will*, proposes a theory which depicts the workings of two sides of the will – conscious and unconscious. Basing his ideas largely on observations from his psychiatric studies and practice, he calls the familiar, conscious will "Realm #2 will." It is characterized by the following qualities: It is immediately experienced, it is goal-oriented, and it employs conscious efforts. All of this sounds much like what Cayce would call "making use of what you have at hand," as well as "being persistent and consistent in our efforts." Clearly, this kind of free will – whether it's labeled "Realm #2 or something else – has an important role to play in daily life.

But then we need to consider the other side of will. In contrast to conscious will, Farber calls the unconscious aspect "Realm #1 will," which points to its more fundamental nature in the psyche. It is characterized by the following qualities: It is usually recognized only in retrospect (that is, only by looking back at life events and seeing how they unfolded), it focuses on a "process" or "way" instead of a specific goal, and it is generally effortless and linked to a "knowing" without necessarily having logical reasons.

Since Realm #2 will is already familiar to his readers, Farber devotes more attention to examples of Realm #1 will. He assumes that the workings of the unconscious will are a part of our experience, but we haven't known how to label these distinctive moments. He gives two especially clear examples which can be summarized in the following way.

1. When you examine your own biography, do you see situations in which you made a decision that, at the time, seemed rather trivial but in retrospect can be appreciated as momentous? With this retrospective view you may get the feeling that something unconscious within you knew the pathway down which that seemingly small decision would lead you. It may have been a decision to get in touch

with an old friend, which unexpectedly led to a new job opportunity and a move to a new city. Or it may have been a casual decision to pick an unusual book off the library shelf which later led to a new philosophy of life and a different circle of friends.

2. "Knowing" for no logical reason that you just have to do something, although you cannot give any good explanation why. Or conversely, it may be that you just "know" you cannot do something that your conscious mind and will are ready to do. It may be knowing that you cannot marry someone even though all factors look favorable. Or it may be knowing that you must get in touch with someone, even though there is no reason to expect a productive result.

These "knowings" sound like "intuition." In fact, Rudolf Steiner, a clairvoyant and spiritual philosopher living in Europe at about the same time as Cayce, described the way in which the three human faculties – thinking, feeling, and willing – can be transformed into higher modes of knowing as they are directed by Spirit. Transformed willing he called Intuition. (Transformed thinking he called Imagination; and transformed feeling, Inspiration.)

In addition to these two examples, it is helpful to note the high priority which Realm #2 will places on specific goals, accomplishments, and plans. In contrast, Realm #1 will tends to focus on a process or thematic way of approaching life. This is reminiscent of how many spiritual traditions teach that what's most important about life is the "way" in which we go about doing things. It's exactly like Cayce reminding us that ideals (which define a way in life) are ultimately more important than idea (or any sort of practical plans). Obviously, we need both; but prospects for a healthy society in the 21st century are enhanced as more and more people become sensitive to the importance of the *way* we go about doing things. This is especially where Realm #1 will can provide guidance.

All of this is also considerably like Cayce's emphasis on each person discovering and living their soul-purpose. Your soul-purpose in this incarnation is something to which Realm #1 will is especially sensitive, even though Realm #2 may not be. That soul-purpose is fundamentally a theme, a way of approaching life. (See Chapter 9 for lots more about this.) In other words, there is a kind of active willing within you which knows of the thematic way in which you can best contribute and grow for this lifetime. It operates rather unconsciously, but if its promptings are recognized, it still leaves much for the conscious Realm #2 will to do. Even if you begin to see the way or direction in which the deep unconscious will wants you to follow, many decisions still remain about how to accomplish it.

Practical Steps to Decision-Making

Building on these ideas about free will and decision-making, let's consider a multiple stage program for getting guidance and making decisions which respects both realms of the will. The following nine-step technique is one framework in which to experience such a creative balance. *This is exactly the way that Cayce indicated that spiritually-directed decision-making can be done in the 21st century*. Something like this needs to be found in the daily decisions we make in our personal lives; and just as surely an approach that incorporates these spiritual elements needs to be part of the decision-making process followed by our leaders.

Step 1. Set your spiritual ideal. This involves the conscious choice of an overall life direction. In a single word or a phrase, you describe the spirit you would like to have guiding and directing every aspect of your life. It is something to which you aspire in your spiritual growth, even if you rarely measure up to it now. Examples include "peaceful centeredness," "joyous service," and "oneness with the Christ spirit," just to name a few of almost countless possible wordings. What you choose must be highly meaningful to you personally.

Step 2. Feel the readiness of a question to be answered. The following seven steps can be successful only if the question you pose is one you are ready to have answered. In other words, there is a rightness of timing for virtually any life challenge. You, the seeker, must be sensitive to when a question is still in the process of emerging and when the timing is right for an answer. When you feel really ready to learn what is the best way to approach some problem, then the time is right to proceed to the third step.

Step 3. Carefully formulate a wording for the question. At Step 2, the challenge or difficulty may still be somewhat vague, but at this third step you must formulate a specific wording for the issue. On paper, write out what you seek to know. Clarify for yourself whether you're looking for a direct answer, more information, or confirmation (i.e., if you've got something you are already inclined to do).

Step 4. Consider all the factors bearing on this question. Look at all relevant facts of which you have some current knowledge. This step involves working with the conscious mind to list all information relevant to your question. Suppose your question was: "Should I move to Arizona?" In this fourth step, you would list all relevant information you already have, such as feelings of other family members about a move, job prospects in Arizona, considerations concerning the climate, local cost of living, etc.

Step 5. Arrive at a tentative conscious decision. Using rational common sense as well as your own feelings, weigh all the factors listed in Step 4 and formulate a preliminary answer to your question. Make sure that the tentative answer is in keeping with your spiritual ideal. Additional steps follow this one, but you need to feel good enough about your tentative answer to follow through on it without compromising your ideal.

Step 6. Obtain guidance from "outer sources" concerning your tentative decision. At this stage, you may want to turn to a trusted friend or professional counselor for advice. Or, you may want to use such esoteric resources as psychic readings, astrological readings, numerology, or the I Ching. Another form of outer guidance you may find helpful is the periodic occurrence of synchronistic signs and life events which can point toward guidance. Here is the first place where the unconscious will – Realm #1 – may start to come into play. By themselves, such meaningful coincidences may not be a reliable source upon which to base an important decision. Yet once you have arrived at a tentative conscious answer (i.e., Step 5) then synchronistic events may give you a feeling of confirmation or warning. As mentioned earlier, these coincidental signs may take the form of things you need to read, hear about or see, which, in an inexplicable way, seem to provide you with feedback on the issue which concerns you.

For this sixth step, work only with those forms of outer guidance with which you feel comfortable. Individuals may differ widely in their choice of outer resources.

Step 7. Look for guidance coming from "inner resources."
Many different avenues are available to each of us for tuning-in to a
higher wisdom and higher will. Some people receive these inner
promptings through imaginative reverie; others find that dreams
provide such guidance. But no matter what other avenues may be
pursued, be sure to include meditation guidance as a resource. Here is
a direct way to encounter Realm #1 will. In fact, meditation for
guidance should be one of the central aspects of living in the 21st
century.

Using meditation to receive guidance is quite simple.
However, you must not use your question as a kind of mantra or
affirmation, but rather you would complete a period of attunement
(including prayer for others) before turning to the question or problem
at hand. In other words, take several minutes at the end of your
meditation period to pose quietly in your conscious mind the question
you formulated (i.e., in Step 2 above). Hold the question in mind and
feel your sincere desire to resolve this issue. Experience your
openness to understand the question in a new light. Feel a readiness to
make whatever changes a deeper wisdom within you may require.

After silently posing and contemplating the question, begin to
listen. The listening must be broader than merely listening for a
voice, no matter how still or small. In fact, some people do receive
guidance through an inward kind of hearing (hence, clairaudience as
one form of psychic perception). However, most people receive their
guidance in some way other than by actually hearing words. The
listening process should encompass one's whole being. Listen with
your body. Listen with your imaginative forces. Listen with that part
of your mind which formulates new concepts and ideas.

What should you expect to receive? Although individuals
differ widely in how they experience guidance, people report the
following types of inner response:

- A feedback feeling or intuition of the rightness or wrongness of
  the tentative conscious answer (i.e., feedback on what was
  consciously decided at Step 5).
- A strong feeling, intuition, or image of what is likely to happen
  if the tentative decision is followed. In this case, the

unconscious will is not making any decision, but precognitively giving impressions of likely future events, leaving it to the conscious will to decide whether or not that is the desired result.

- A new, previously unconsidered solution. Although we may often hope for this result in seeking meditation guidance, it is not necessarily the most frequent result. A direct answer or solution is sometimes presented, but often it is merely a piece of the puzzle with the remaining parts left to be filled in by the conscious self. By way of analogy, imagine that you have asked a skilled mathematician to be your tutor in a difficult algebra course. Now you are stumped on one particular problem. The tutor doesn't provide you with the entire solution, but gives you a piece of the answer to get you started on finding the rest of the solution for yourself. Your unconscious will may work the same way.

- Impressions which provide a new perspective on the current question or problem. In other words, the insight received in meditation may not answer the problem but, instead, suddenly allow you to see the question from a new angle. Sometimes this new view can then quickly lead to understanding the appropriate way to respond.

- Recognition of another question to be dealt with before the original issue can be addressed. In other words, you may have posed a question you sincerely desire to have answered, and yet there are other issues to be resolved first. Suppose you've posed this question: "Should I go back to graduate school to obtain further job skills?" In meditation, you may receive impressions not directly concerned with an answer to this question. Instead it may awaken other questions that must be resolved first, such as "Are you making the best use of the skills you currently have?" or, "How have you contributed to the dissatisfaction you feel with your current job situation?"

It is highly recommended that before moving on to the next step, you seek meditation guidance more than once, particularly for an issue of great personal importance.

Step 8. Formulate a "guided" decision upon which you are

ready to act. Take into account the input provided from both outer sources of guidance as well as inner guidance such as meditation. Then reconsider the question and write down a revised version of your answer – one that you're ready to begin to apply. Make sure this decision is something you could conceivably follow through on and still be in keeping with your spiritual ideal.

Step 9. *Begin to apply the decision and yet respond constructively to obstacles which may arise.* Almost invariably, when you begin to put into motion a decision (no matter how meditatively you may have arrived at it), obstacles and resistances arise. Sometimes these obstacles can be traced directly to an origin within yourself, although most frequently you will experience them as coming from outside. Of course, the hope is that the guided decision will be easy to bring to fruition. Yet seldom is this the case.

When such obstacles arise, you are likely to respond in one of two nonproductive ways:

First, you may tend to try bullheadedly to force your way through the obstacles. Something within you says, "I've gotten my guidance and now I'm going to make it happen, no matter what anyone else says or does!" This kind of stubbornness very rarely leads to a happy ending. The mistaken use here is an over-activity of Realm #2 will.

The second frequent response is to give up. Something within you expects that, having tuned into a higher wisdom, everything should quickly fall into place. This lazy part of you doesn't want to have to make any persistent efforts.

A third and more productive alternative is better. It requires a willingness to persist with the conscious will in applying the guided decision. But it also requires a continued openness to the unconscious will, so that the obstacles or resistances can teach you and help you to refine the guidance. Think of it this way: Through guidance counseling, psychic readings, dreams, meditation or any other forms of guidance, you may have the basic theme of the best decision, yet not have a proper understanding of the right timing or way in which to proceed, or of the people who will be involved in bringing the decision to fruition.

The best approach carefully blends (a) consistent effort with (b) an open-mindedness that looks upon guidance as an *ongoing* process and not something that was resolved once and for all in Step 8. You must let life continue to instruct you. Continue to pay attention to your dreams and imaginative insights. Watch how your unconscious will may lead you into instructive situations. Continue to seek meditation guidance, even as you are already acting on your guided decision.

Conclusion

Cayce challenges us here in the 21st century to make this kind of decision-making process into a regular part of our lives. *How can we expect world leaders to do something like this with big decisions if we are not willing to do it with little ones?* Think of yourself as a spiritual researcher and try following these nine steps. Like any good research project, it may take some time. Don't expect this carefully constructed program to be a quick-fix shortcut. For some decisions, it may even take several weeks to complete all phases of the procedure. But you can be assured that you will have followed a program that leaves room for both sides of your will. By participating in this kind of personal research, you are helping to pioneer a crucial element of new age consciousness.

CHAPTER 9

SPIRITUAL "WORK" IN THE 21ST CENTURY

Cayce's prophetic sight envisioned a *positive* future for humanity in the 21st century. But it was never to be something that just "drops in our laps." It is going to take some intentional efforts – some "work," as it were.

The idea of work usually makes us a little bit uncomfortable. Maybe the discomfort stems from childhood memories of Saturday morning chores around the house, those jobs we had to do instead of being outside having a good time. Work also has the connation of having to making concerted effort. It usually means going against the flow of some resistive force, such as gravity. Remember, for example, the work involved in pushing a lawn mower uphill through thick grass. Not much fun.

Spiritual work, though, usually involves dealing with a resistance other than gravity. Instead, it's dealing with our habit patterns or our fears and doubts. And because spiritual work makes us more self-aware of who we really are, the resistance will always be some form of "unconsciousness" – that is, the resistance against which we have to work will make us tired, lazy, or dull.

What does Edgar Cayce mean when he says that we have work to do, as souls? What's behind this repeated principle: his teachings (and the application of them) are a kind of inner work? One part of the answer is that there is no real soul development unless we are willing to make an effort and deal with the patterns in the soul that keep us stuck. And as soon as we start dealing with those resistive patterns, it's going to hurt. As Carl Jung put it, "There is no growth in consciousness without pain," and surely the pain to which he refers is the byproduct of facing the resistive forces – forces in ourselves that prefer to keep things just the way they are.

Fulfillment of the hopeful side of the Cayce prophecies for the new millennium depends on a significant portion of humanity being willing to do a special kind of work to unleash creative potentials. It means having courage to actually *live* the ideals that we have set. One of the most insightful statements from Cayce asserts, "He without an ideal is sorry indeed; he with an ideal and lacking the courage to live it is sorrier still." (#1402-1) What a fabulous challenge is presented with those words – especially to our own times here in the early years of a new millennium. We have an ideal. We have been given an inspiring picture of what is possible for humanity. That vision has been presented by Cayce and many other prophets. *Now the question is simply whether or not we will have the courage to do the work to manifest that potential.*

This chapter explores some of the practical steps that are involved in personally taking on that sort of purposeful work. What has come earlier in this book has little real meaning unless we understand and act on what is found in this chapter and the one that follows (concerning a meditative life-style). These final two chapters address the most concrete steps that are needed if we are to be co-creators of the sort of world Cayce envisioned. That work is not going to be easy. There will be resistive forces, in ourselves and in the society around us. Inertia – in this case, the inertia to have things stay the way they are – is a potent influence. And not only will persistent, consistent effort be required for this sort of work; we will also need to adopt a long range timeframe because much of the transformation of our planetary society will take generations, not just years. Do we have the courage to work for purposes that extend beyond this lifetime?

Two aspects of the word "work" emerge in Cayce's readings as a whole. One is the grand quest that we are on collectively as souls: to become *whole*, to embrace all the parts of who we are and to fulfill our potential. Sometimes he spoke of this quest in terms of the way an organization – such as his Association for Research and Enlightenment – had tasks for becoming more whole and doing what it was capable of doing. And so, there are more than one hundred so-called "Work Readings," the psychic advice that Cayce gave to the organization itself.

The other aspect of the word "work" comes from the advice Cayce gave individuals about finding their own calling in life – the life work that would be fulfilling and also help the world in some specific way. In those nearly two thousand "life readings," Cayce coached individuals in a method for finding their own soul-purpose for this lifetime, of finding their own mission. Their "work" then became the journey to be more whole, to be healed, so that they could use their talents to contribute and make a difference in the world.

Finding the right sense of "work" is so important that when the stenographic records of Cayce's readings were transcribed, the word was usually capitalized, just to emphasize its importance. Let's first examine more closely the task that we all have to do – the big picture of "work" – and then the specific steps that we can follow in order to find our own sense of a soul-purpose here in the new millennium.

The Big Picture About Our Work

Making practical our spirituality was sometimes referred to as "the Work" by Cayce. But what, exactly, is this task all about? It's a journey, a quest, a striving; *and* it's effort – but paradoxically, a kind of effortless effort. Fundamentally our Work is really about development, and that means change. As individual souls, we are self-developing organisms who have to learn to adapt to change, even embrace it. We are on a cosmic journey, and there is no sitting down – at least not for long.

Sometimes Cayce described the Work in terms of awakening the universal Christ Consciousness. But we need to remember that attuning to the Christ Consciousness means engaging the *entirety* of what it means to be human. Evoking the universal Christ Consciousness within each one of us – and of equal importance, *identifying* ourselves with it – requires the ability to accept many competing or complementary sides of who we are.

For example, it's important to realize that the Christ Consciousness is not just a collection of static qualities of niceness – joy, peace, understanding. That is, certainly, a *part* of what's involved. But the Christ Consciousness which lives at the heart of our Work is just as surely exemplified by Jesus with the moneychangers and the Christ who comes with a sword. For us, that sometimes means facing our own shadow, the part of ourselves we are reluctant to look at. But that's what the Work requires – the courageous embrace of our dark side, as well as our light.

Many who are deeply engaged in the study of the Cayce material have had trouble with this point. There is a tendency to believe that we can more or less "meditate away" the wounded, untransformed sides of ourselves, the scary stuff that no one likes to face. One man claimed that all we have to do is "*starve* the shadow" – then it will disappear. Not so. The best observers of the depths of the soul have learned that such a notion is naïve. All of the stuff that lives within us is worth getting to know, understand, embrace, and ultimately transform.

Perhaps at its essence the Work is most clearly *a fierce devotion to the truth of who we are.* It's not so much a matter of fiercely defending the past or the status quo, but instead an uncompromising dedication to what is developing and emerging from within us *right now* in life. There is surely a universal impulse in our lives to grow and to transform, allowing an imprisoned splendor to emerge. Cayce and Jung and many other pioneers of soul psychology call it the Christ pattern. Other faith traditions have equally valid and meaningful names. Getting in sync with that impulse is the heart of the Work.

Let's consider just a little more deeply how the Work is fundamentally about soul development and the ongoing changes accompanying it. Many meditators often use a prayer of protection that is suggested in the Cayce readings – just the kind of affirmation that can be prayerfully said as we start the silence period of meditation. "As I open myself to the unseen forces that surround the throne of grace, beauty and might, I throw about myself the protection found in the thought of the Christ." It's easy to assume this means creating an image of a magical envelope of white light that encircles oneself as a guardian, ready to repel any *outside* nefarious force.

But maybe this prayer of protection can be seen in a very different light, particularly when we think in terms of the Christ Consciousness as the impulse to soul growth and change. Our own *internal* patterns can become the snag. One person reported a fascinating experience in this regard: "I had a hypnagogic experience as I awakened one morning in which I saw myself going down a chute that I knew symbolized the process of development and change. I was wearing a suit of clothing that had small, protruding hooks that were prone to snag on the passing walls of the chute. In fact, those walls had their own hooks which were always capable of catching hold of the hooks on my suit and thus halt my progress. I knew those hooks along the chute were things of my own making. Then I felt impelled to use the prayer of protection, and I experienced it creating a coating around me that kept the hooks from snagging as I sped down the chute."

That's the flavor of what we are looking for when we think about the Work. It's not about sitting still; it's about movement, development and change. But too easily we can become our own worst enemy, and our progress gets snagged on the hooks of our own self-doubts, fears, and wounds. More often than not that snag is a part of our own shadow-self, a piece of us that we haven't learned to see, understand and embrace. It's not easy stuff to go down that "chute." Maybe that's why Cayce called it "Work."

Living Your Soul-Purpose in the 21st Century

That "Work" has external forms of service also. We can identify a personal soul-purpose for this lifetime, a way to use talents to make a difference in the lives of others. As Cayce put it, "We all have a mission to perform," and there is no more important time in human history than right now for lots of us to see and apply those missions.

What specific part is yours to play in this emerging planetary culture that Cayce envisioned more than eighty years ago? Perhaps it seems presumptuous to assume that you and every other person have special roles – missions and purposes in living here in the early 21st century. But you don't really understand the Cayce prophecies unless you also grasp this fact about the purposefulness and potential of your *own* life in these special times.

Your soul growth, along the lines of your own destiny for this lifetime, begins with an ideal. In a deeply mysterious way, your encounter with a personal ideal is also a paradox. It is something you select, using your will's power to choose. However, a true, spiritual ideal is also something that chooses you – that reveals itself to you in surprising, wondrous ways. The following simple formula from the Cayce philosophy puts it most succinctly:

- Envision your ideal;
- Awaken and apply your will;
- And soul development is the result.

This brief affirmation summarizes a basic strategy for guiding spiritual development. Although it clearly shows that a proper and healthy use of your will is at the heart of soul growth, the entire approach depends upon a suitable starting point: your personal ideal.

Ideals can be subtle and ambiguous. Much of the confusion arises from the idiomatic meaning the word has assumed in our language. The word "ideal" has strong connotations of unreality and lack of pragmatism. There is a tendency to change the word to the form "idealistic" and to add a prefix, the word "just." To accuse someone of being "just idealistic" is a way of dismissing his or her ideas as (perhaps) admirable but obviously unworkable.

What is needed is a return to a deeper understanding of the original meaning of "ideal." In the Platonic sense, for example, the ideal (or ideal form) exists in a higher dimension and has a more essential and profound reality than what is perceived through the physical senses. In a similar way, it might be said that a significant aspect of your soul's ideal resides in the unconscious and is not immediately accessible to that part of you preoccupied with material life.

Several terms give an accurate feeling for the nature of an ideal. "Life direction" and "purpose" are two of them. Although some people are more immediately aware of this fact than others, we all live with some kind of motivation, and that creates a direction of personal development and a sense of purpose in living. For one person, it may be striving for fame; for a second, healing the suffering of humanity; and for yet a third, it might be creative expression. The array of possible motivations is virtually endless, but in each case it reveals the ideal of the individual.

Another word that may shed light on the meaning of ideals is "intentionality," a term sometimes used in theological writings, such as the work of Paul Tillich. In his classic book *Love and Will*, Rollo May builds on Tillich's notions of intentionality and relates it to the healthy functioning of free will.

Intentionality encompasses, but is not limited to, conscious intentions. Your conscious intention may be to make a new friend when you strike up a conversation with a stranger, but the broader intentionality includes your more fundamental orientation toward humanity in general. That intentionality includes deep currents of motivation and purpose which are largely unconscious to you at the moment you start the conversation. In this example, the intentionality (or ideal) may have the quality of oneness and interpersonal connectedness. However, other conscious intentions and intentionalities are equally possible. The immediate intention of starting the conversation could be to remove the boredom of the moment, with little real interest in the other person. In this instance, the intentionality bespeaks a view of other people as objects, to be used to satisfy personal needs.

The example of striking up a conversation with a stranger could include many other conceivable intentions and intentionalities. It is also rather simplistic; life never seems to confront us in quite so elementary a fashion. Nevertheless, the example points out the broader consideration that must be given to studying your own intentionality as opposed to merely your conscious intentions. Ideals (or intentionality) take hold of both conscious and unconscious life. The following three-part model shows levels of the ideal within us: Spiritual Ideal, Incarnation Ideal, and conscious ideal.

The Three Levels of Ideal

1. The Spiritual Ideal. Within the deepest recesses of your soul is a Spiritual Ideal. It is a given, an archetype of your spiritual makeup. In this sense the Spiritual Ideal is the same for all souls; rather than being something you have chosen or created, it has been placed within you by the forces of Creation.

The phrase used in the Cayce readings for this Spiritual Ideal is the universal Christ Consciousness; and in a sense, it is constantly active inside of us, even when we aren't paying much attention to it. Its impulse is felt most fully within your unconscious self, but it is a will toward your conscious enlightenment. This is exactly the discovery made by depth psychologists and psychiatrists like Jung, who have found that there is an impulse toward individuation which seems to have a life (and a will) of its own. The Spiritual Ideal is, therefore, a backdrop against which the next two levels of the ideal operate.

2. The Incarnation Ideal or Life's Mission. Nothing is more exciting and hopeful than the concept of a personal mission. The chance that your life could have a specialized purpose stands in stark contrast to the homogenized, depersonalized and desacralized ways that modern culture still often operates. Even so-called unique and unusual persons (i.e., the ones celebrated in certain magazines or television programs) in a more subtle way are really "norms" of the culture's value system.

Cayce spoke of the soul's mission and destiny for a lifetime. Your soul-purpose, chosen just before birth, exists as an Incarnation Ideal (or, for short, "Ideal," with the first letter capitalized) within your unconscious self.

In the "life readings" given by Cayce, there is presented to individual people not just a fascinating array of past-lifetime scenarios, but more importantly there is counsel regarding the specific purpose for the present lifetime. In the words of one such reading, each soul enters with a mission . . .we all have a mission to perform." (#3003-1) That purpose is something broader than merely working on one's own "bad karma." In other words, your mission has a quality of creativity that is life-enhancing and goes beyond just working on your faults.

To appreciate what Cayce's readings are saying about your soul-purpose, keep in mind the distinction he makes between two levels of your being. On the one hand, there is personality – a necessary component to function in the physical world, yet not the more essential you. That ingredient is provided by the individuality or real self. The personality is what you appear to be – your "persona" – or, more accurately, your array of personae, because the personality is made up of a collection of subpersonalities. It is the nature of your personality to operate by habit, in a rather automatic or reactive way. Sometimes that is helpful, but more often it stifles creativity and individuality.

The individuality is the spiritual "I" which has continuity from lifetime to lifetime. It is not yet perfected, but it is capable of growth and development. Whereas the personality functions by habit with little or no real conscious choice, the individuality operates through will. The individuality also has embedded within it the Incarnation Ideal which it selected before birth. That Ideal is to be lived with the personality as its vehicle of expression, but this requires that at least some aspects of the individuality first awaken to conscious life.

The recognition of your soul-purpose (or Ideal) is not an "all or nothing" thing. In other words, there are degrees of understanding and appreciation. The process unfolds through (1) systematic effort (i.e., use of your conscious will) in cooperation with (2) overtures from your deeper self (i.e., the initiatives of your unconscious will, or what was called in Chapter 8 "Realm #1 will). Gradually there is revealed to you the nature of your life's mission. A step-by-step program to make that discovery is described at the end of this chapter.

Your mission in life is something beyond just a professional label like bookkeeper, attorney, or social worker. The Ideal of your soul is to manifest a specific theme of being – a particular way of viewing life, responding to it and creating within it. Again, it should be stressed that your mission is not the repayment of negative karma. Certainly there is reality to limiting karma (i.e., soul memories of having misused physical life opportunities). In fact, the effects of karma must be dealt with and can even block the fulfillment of the real mission. However, your soul-purpose encompasses creative aspects far beyond compensation for past misdeeds.

If your life's purpose isn't exclusively a single occupation, then what is it? Here are examples of thematic statements of a life mission which were proposed to individuals in their own Cayce life readings:

- to be a spiritual leader through the arts
- to demonstrate the spiritual meaning of numbers and mathematics
- to be the transmitter and clarifier of ideas
- to be a spokesperson for the truth

In each of these instances there exists a number of different professional or a vocational possibilities (i.e., many souls fulfill a mission more through hobbies or free time interests, than through a career track). You should expect, as well, that at different points in your life span, there will be different ways to give expression to your soul-purpose. What is appropriate at age 35 to serve that Ideal may be quite different from what is best at ages 55 or 75 in serving that same sense of mission. Nevertheless, the Cayce readings present the concept of soul-purpose as something you can start doing at *any* point in a life span. Some people at or near retirement age were told in their life readings what their Incarnation Ideal was, and they were encouraged to work consciously with it, starting immediately.

In a way similar to Cayce's idea of a soul-purpose, G.I. Gurdjieff referred often to the individual's destiny. Gurdjieff is a fascinating character, born in the same decade as Cayce, yet living and working in Europe for virtually all of his life. Although he is not generally seen as someone who made prophecies, in many ways he was every bit as much a prophet as Cayce because he articulated a system of spiritual growth that is especially relevant for the 21st century. He, too, saw and referred to his teachings as "the Work," and he was uncompromising in his insistence that individuals seriously apply themselves to the tasks of soul development.

Gurdjieff used the term "personality" in an almost identical fashion to the way it is found in the Cayce readings, although he stressed one further feature of its origin. Gurdjieff pointed out that your personality is largely shaped by what you have taken on or learned through the imitation of other people. The imitation process began in earliest childhood until you now have an acquired side that is really "not you."

The other side of yourself is the key to understanding ideals and to recognizing your soul-purpose for this lifetime. As mentioned earlier, it's the individuality – the authentic soul-self. In Cayce's philosophy, this is the aspect of yourself that has continuity through reincarnation. This is the aspect of yourself that lives beyond physical life. Gurdjieff called it the "essence" of who we are, along with the "Real I" that lives through the essence. No matter what we call this more genuine part of ourselves, it's the place from which we can see and live the purpose for which we were born.

Complementing these ideas from Gurdjieff and Cayce about the Incarnation Ideal are statements made by Rudolf Steiner on the formulation of the soul's destiny for one lifetime. Steiner, born in the decade before Cayce and Gurdjieff, presented teachings that provide an elaborate theory of the soul's experience between death and birth, with a description of exact stages which are enacted as the soul draws closer and closer to physical reincarnation. He emphasizes the role played by more highly evolved beings of other realms in helping each soul digest the experience of the last lifetime and prepare for the next. These beings assist in the choice of a plan for the coming lifetime and they help each soul select an appropriate destiny. Then, this pattern is "knit" into the very structure of the higher bodies – the astral and etheric. According to Steiner, there is one last chance to preview the implications of the mission, which the soul has chosen. Stewart Easton, scholar of Steiner's work, summarizes Steiner's clairvoyant view of this process by writing:

> While still in the moon sphere and just as we are forming our etheric body, we have one last overwhelming experience that corresponds exactly to the tableau that passed before our vision after death while the etheric body was dissolving. This time, however, we have a prevision of the earthly life that faces us, not in all its details as in the vision after death, but in its general outline. This is the life we have planned for ourselves, including all the compensations for former wrongs that we now intend to right, and perhaps great but painful deeds that we intend to perform for the sake of humanity and future lives on earth. (*Man and World in the Light of Anthroposophy,* p.165*)*

But even with these purposeful patterns built into the bodies of the soul, the details of life experience are not predetermined. Destiny can work in wondrous ways to bring you into contact with promising opportunities, in the form of people or situations. But thereafter it is a matter of your choice and free will. Easton adds, "At the moment we meet someone with whom we are linked the element of destiny is at an end, and we are from that time onward on our own." (p.157)

3. The Conscious Ideal. The conscious spiritual ideal is the third level at which the concept of an ideal is useful. As the term implies, the conscious ideal is your best current understanding of who you are at your core, and that "best understanding" changes from month-to-month and year-to-year as you mature. Admittedly, a narrow, fear-based orientation to life may produce a conscious ideal, which is self-serving (e.g., fame or greed). However, anyone who has seriously considered that life has both physical and spiritual dimensions is likely to set a conscious ideal with spiritual overtones.

The consciously chosen spiritual ideal is a statement of personal aspiration. But it may also be a reminder of something you have already experienced, however briefly. It is an aspiration because the spiritual ideal calls you to be the self you rarely remember to be. But it also has the flavor of "remembering"; it's a recollection of personal experience because, without having had at least a fleeting taste of that different identity, the spiritual ideal remains a dry, theoretical concept in your life.

The notion of your spiritual ideal rooted in actual, personal experiences cannot be stressed too much. Certainly, it is fine to have hopes related also to things beyond the scope of personal experience. You may trust the words of others more advanced along the spiritual path than you are and have faith that some day you too will have similar experiences. No doubt, this kind of aspiration and hope is a powerful influence for spiritual growth. But the conscious spiritual ideal is best understood as something different from this kind of faith.

Something special takes place when you identify experiences from your past which have had a spiritually quickening effect upon you. When you choose a spiritual ideal which is related to a taste or glimpse that you have actually received of your individuality/essence/Real I, then there is no room for doubt about its reality. Admittedly, you may have questions about your capacity to sustain that sense of personal identity, but it is not a matter of doubting that that place in consciousness exists. Because you know so clearly and so personally that this spiritual ideal is authentic, you can at any moment use your will to call it back to mind, unfettered by doubt about its reality.

A spiritual ideal which is rooted in personal experience also allows you to avoid another pitfall in setting ideals. If you are like most others, there is a tendency to set your spiritual ideal in terms of the "shoulds" and "oughts" of key authority figures in your life, even spiritual authority figures. Something deeper within your soul, however, will not feel comfortable with this. It will rebel if your spiritual ideal is set in terms of what your parents or schoolteachers or church leaders have said your ideals ought to be. Actually it is a shortcut produced by your own personality to set a spiritual ideal in such a manner. Remember that your personality is largely the product of what you have taken on from other people. It tends to suggest a spiritual ideal made up of such "shoulds" and "oughts" which come from others. In fact, to allow your life to be guided by a spiritual ideal which has been determined in that way serves only to perpetuate the current form of your life.

Instead, your spiritual ideal is best chose personal identity that is uniquely you. Beyond habit a describes a place of clarity from which you are free to create your mission. It comes as a description of the quality of your o individuality self, at least as you best know it so far.

How to Discover Your Soul-Purpose

How can you find the exact nature of your soul-purpose? One approach is to ask a psychically sensitive person to attempt to "read" your unconscious life and identify the nature of your mission. The problems with this approach are (1) finding a reliable psychic and (2) evaluating what the psychic tells you. Another approach is to conduct a personal research project – an experiment with specific steps like those described in this chapter. But whatever approach you use, the mission statement you arrive at should be measured by these two questions:

- Does the stated purpose of my life ring true, does it strike a chord in my intuitive, feeling self?
- Does the stated purpose show fruits when I start trying to apply it?

Near the end of this chapter, we will explore the "fruits" of living your soul-purpose. But first let's examine a five-step program for self-exploration and the creation of a mission statement with application plan.

Step 1: Set Your Conscious Spiritual Ideal. Setting your conscious spiritual ideal allows you to take the first step toward identifying your mission for this lifetime. That spiritual ideal is your best, current understanding of the nature of your own individuality, the place from within yourself where the eventual soul-purpose is to be lived. In selecting a conscious spiritual ideal, let it be expressed as a symbol or a word (or perhaps a short phrase).

Step 2: Identify Your Soul's Assets. Having decided on a symbol, word or phrase for your conscious spiritual ideal, you are

ths, abilities, and aptitudes. The
this in astrological terms and past-
y serious and honest self-appraisal is
ilar kind of list. What works best is to
ten especially significant talents and
e within you. Some of them are ones you
(but perhaps not with as deep a sense of
is possible). Other talents you put on your list
ma, rarely, if ever, get a chance to use, yet you know
that abl. sible to you. Here is a list of sample talents and
abilities wh. er people have recognized in themselves. It may
help you get started on identifying your own.

friendly	sense of humor
innovative	articulate
sensitive	forgiving
creative	orderly
imaginative	kind
trouble-shooter	patient
good with animals	listening
good with plants	cooperative
good with children	playful nature
good with words	logical
energetic	motivator
psychic	financially adept
writing	loyal
decisive	artistic
empathetic	mechanically skilled
leadership	intuitive
practical	industrious
good cook	planning
wise	committed
teaching	musical

But before completing your list of talents, consider one
additional approach for finding soul strengths. Some of your most
significant abilities may lie hidden in your faults and weaknesses. You
can find a new orientation for some personal characteristics which you
have always labeled as faults. You may find a seed of great strength or

talent within a weakness.

For example, suppose that two of your personality faults are impatience and stubbornness. Buried within your tendency to be impatient might be a deep commitment to have things done right. This important strength of your soul may be twisted and misunderstood so that it comes out looking like impatience. Although the weakness still needs to be changed, this seed of something good should be recognized. In a similar fashion, the fault of stubbornness may contain at its heart the quality of persistence. However, when persistence is mixed with misunderstanding or fear, the result can be a fault like stubbornness. Nevertheless, the soul talent for persistence may have a key role to play in your life's mission.

This principle is a remarkable psychological insight offered by Cayce. In fact, the consciousness he prophesied for the new millennium is capable of seeing and magnifying such a strength-hidden-in-a-fault.

Try it for yourself. Make a list of three or four of your most noticeable personality faults. Now, one by one look at each weakness with new eyes. Can you find the seed of something good in that fault – perhaps a strength or talent which has become distorted? You may not immediately find something for every fault. But if you identify a hidden talent or strength in this way, add it to your list of soul strengths.

What you now have is a list of about eight to twelve talents and abilities you know are within you. Think of this as your list of candidates. All of them may have a role to play in living your soul-purpose, but a smaller number of them are crucial for identifying what that purpose is. From the total list of candidates, you will narrow the list down to about four or five which are most significant.

For example, suppose that your initial inventory yields a candidate list of a dozen talents and strengths. Eight of them are ones you at least occasionally use in daily life; two are talents you know you have within you, although they are rarely – if ever – used; and two are strengths which exist like seeds within your personality faults. For most people, the basic features of the soul-purpose are shaped by only four or five particularly important talents, and that's the average number Cayce identified for people in a life reading. All strengths and talents are probably used in some supportive role, but you can expect that about four or five abilities will be most significant in defining the mission.

The question remains, how do you narrow the longer candidate list down to this smaller number? In the example above, how would you pick the most important four or five from the original list of twelve? You can pose two questions to yourself that should help in this selection process:

- Which of these talents and strengths seem to be right at the core of your real self, your best self? That is to say, some of the talents and strengths on your candidate list will be recognizable as belonging to your essence. It would be hard for you to imagine being yourself without them. They are probably ones which began showing up in your childhood or adolescence. On the other hand, some of the talents and strengths on your candidate list may belong to your personality – to your "acquired, imitative self." Those talents and strengths have the "inner taste" or "inner feeling" of your having copied them from people you respect and admire. Even these acquired talents may have a helpful role to play in living your soul-purpose. But the first group – the talents and strengths of your essence – is most important in identifying the exact nature of that mission.

- Which talents give you the feeling that there are some additional ways that you can make use of them in order to be really fulfilled? In other words, which strengths on your inventory list seem to speak to you saying, "There is more that you are supposed to be doing with me," even if you have no idea as yet what that "something more" is.

You are ready to move on to Step 3 when you have made a tentative list of the four or five talents which you suspect are the key ones shaping your mission.

Step 3: Formulate a Mission Theme. The next step requires great intuition, imagination, and creative insight about your life. It also requires a willingness on your part to playfully adopt the role of a researcher. In this step you identify a tentative or hypothetical wording for your mission. It is only a likely possibility because confirmation awaits testing and application. Like any type of research there is an element of trial and error – an educated best guess which still needs to be tried out. Your "guess" of a thematic wording for your soul-purpose can be a highly insightful and even inspired one, but it still requires application and testing in daily life for validation.

It is possible, of course, to formulate an erroneous wording for your mission at this step. You may pick something that looks right, only to find in Steps 4 and 5 that things don't go right. Then, like any good researcher, you shall need to come back to Step 3 and try again. If you are fortunate, then your first, tentative wording for your mission may show good fruits when you put it into application. But if not, try to keep in mind how many of the great inventions of history (e.g., the electric light bulb) were developed by researchers who tested many mistaken hypotheses before hitting on the right one.

There are three exercises you are encouraged to complete in working on Step 3. Each one is designed to give you further clues, hints or pieces of the puzzle. One or two may be more helpful to you than another, and you can certainly complete them in whatever order you prefer. But each is designed to help you move from a point where you have a conscious spiritual ideal plus a short list of key talents to the point where you formulate a tentative thematic wording of your soul's mission.

Exercise #1 is a life review of special moments. Take ten or fifteen minutes of relaxed, quiet time to complete an unhurried review of your life. You may want to put on some soft meditation music to help you get into a reverie state. During your life review, look for times in your past when you did things which created strong feelings of "This is what I'm supposed to be doing in life – this is the real me coming through." Those moments may have happened years ago or very recently. They may have involved trying something out of the ordinary for you, or doing something familiar but in a new way or with a new attitude. During the reverie, as you recall one or more of these moments in your past, it is just as important to note *why* or *how* you were doing something, as it is what you were doing. Those specific memories may not tell you exactly what your life's mission is, but they may provide some helpful clues.

Exercise #2 is to re-examine your list of four or five talents. Take another look at your strengths and ask yourself these two questions: As a group, do they seem to point in any direction? Do they suggest a particular kind of service to the world or a creative way of living? Just by examining your list of most significant soul strengths you may get a clue as to the nature of your mission. Think of those talents as a team. What is that team especially well suited to do? You may be able to get some additional insight from this exercise by doing it with a friend who knows you well. With such a person, share your brief list of key strengths and ask that person what kind of life mission he or she sees as one which would draw upon those abilities.

Exercise #3 is to consider a list of example mission themes. The following list of sample statements of soul-purpose may prove to be helpful to you in creating a thematic wording for your own. Many of them are drawn from counsel given in Edgar Cayce's life readings. Others are taken from the self-exploration of individuals like you who were using these steps to find their own mission. Notice that the examples do not list professional labels like housekeeper, hair stylist, airline pilot, etc. Instead, each one gives a thematic description of a certain quality of consciousness or type of service to be done in the world. For each example, many possible occupations or hobbies might be considered as ways to put the mission into practical application.

Don't rush through this exercise. It is very important to invest some time in thinking about these sample mission themes. Take at least a minute to consider each one of these examples, and for each one ask yourself:

- Are there times in my life when I've lived with that sense of purpose, even for a brief period?
- If so, what were the inner and outer results of those efforts?
- Did I "resonate" to this theme? Does it feel right? Does it provide a good "fit" with the talents and strengths I have?
- Could I edit the wording of this example theme into something resembling it but more suited to me? Or, can I combine this example with another one?

Here are now some sample mission themes:

- To appreciate and reflect beauty
- To be an agent of inner and outer peace
- To be a healer of minds
- To be a unifier, one who synthesizes and blends the fragments of life

- To cooperate with Spirit in nature
- To be a catalyst for change and growth
- To be the innovator, the one who gets new things started
- To be a transmitter and clarifier of ideas
- To be a sensitive, receptive listener who hears the souls of others
- To be a motivator and helper of the undeveloped and immature to come to blossom
- To conserve and be a good steward of resources
- To be a spiritual inspirer through _____ [e.g., the arts, words, numbers/geometry]
- To be a finisher, one who brings things to a completion
- To make mechanical things work better to serve people
- To be the discerning, wise analyst of life
- To be a celebrator, a channel of joyous play
- To synthesize, blend, and unify the fragments of life
- To keep things pure
- To be a worker for justice in the world
- To be a balancer, one who keeps things harmonious
- To be a spokesperson for truth
- To manifest God's love through the family
- To show compassion for those less fortunate
- To be a healer of bodies
- To attract and channel material supply

After you have completed this third exercise and the previous two, it is time to decide upon a tentative theme for your life's purpose – a best, current guess with which you are willing to experiment further. But this is no wild guess or shot in the dark. Using both common sense and intuition, the tentative theme you select has a good chance of proving to be exactly what your soul intends for this lifetime.

Before arriving at your decision, you may want to include prayer, meditation, and dreams for guidance. Up until now in this discovery process, you have been making decisions with your conscious will. It may be time to listen for the promptings of a higher will. A strong feeling at the end of prayer and meditation may steer you in a certain direction as you decide upon tentative wording for your mission. Or, a dream may come in response to all your conscious efforts – a dream that reveals more of your soul's intentions, which have long been unconscious to you.

Step 4: List Applications of the Mission Theme. This step involves brainstorming for practical, new ways to express your mission statement. The focus is to make the best possible use of your key talents and strengths. One-by-one you can reconsider the four or five talents you chose for Step 2. What are the ways in which you could start using each talent in service to that mission?

For this step there are two categories of practical applications you should list. First, how can you use your talents and fulfill your mission by reaching out to other people? Second, how can you use those same strengths and live your soul-purpose by helping yourself? In other words, it's not selfish to invest time, energy, and talents in your own growth. In fact, it is one part of your soul's mission.

For Step 4 you can probably get the best results by writing down just two or three applications for one category (i.e., reaching out to others) and two or three for the second category (i.e., helping yourself). Sometimes a friend or family member can be of assistance at Step 4 – brainstorming with you the many possibilities. But then it's up to you to select just a few on which to work. Keep them practical and specific. The example below of Margaret illustrates a good approach.

Step 5: Test Out the Application in Actual Life. It may not be effective to try all your new applications at once. Pace yourself. Find a way to test the various new expressions as you reasonably have the time and opportunity. It involves an act of will, but a patient, persistent will.

What kind of "fruits" might you expect to see when you start applying your true mission in life? There are five signposts or indicators of things to watch for. They are reinforcements to show you that you are on track with your soul-purpose.

1. A deeper sense of wonder. Living your soul-purpose creates a feeling of life expanding and opening up before you, with surprise and awe. You feel the magical quality to life.

2. Others benefit as you creatively contribute to the world through some form of service. Sometimes the act of service and the benefit to others are quite direct (e.g., one of the so-called "helping professions," such as nursing, counseling, etc.). In other instances, the service may be just as real yet indirect (e.g., an artist whose creations later uplift and inspire others).

3. Feeling a greater closeness to God. Of course, how to recognize this is an ancient question. But, if God is understood as completeness and wholeness, then you can expect to experience the Presence as that which makes you more whole. So, begin by recognizing how you are not yet whole. What do you most deeply feel is missing in your life? For example, if you feel in darkness (i.e., confused) then greater closeness to God shall be experienced as light or profound understanding. If you feel trapped or limited, then God's Presence shall be felt as freedom. If you have been caught in a great loneliness, then God can especially be experienced as intimate companionship and support.

4. Seeing purposefulness in all of life. As you live your soul-purpose, it simultaneously awakens you to the recognition of purpose in the lives of others. You begin to be sensitive to the underlying reasons and opportunities inherent in life events all around you. Such a sensitivity may assist you in efforts to help other people consciously understand their missions in life.

5. A joyful attitude toward living. Perhaps the most evident characteristic of a person who is living his or her mission in life is joy. It may manifest as a bubbly, extroverted enthusiasm for life. Or, in other individuals, it may express in a quieter way. But, in whatever form it expresses through you, joy is the hallmark of a life which is fulfilling its mission.

Some of the signs may happen more dramatically for you than others. But if none of these signs occurs, go back to Step #3 and formulate a different mission theme.

An Example of Finding A Soul-Purpose Statement

The story of Margaret makes clearer the procedure involved in all these steps. She was a 41-year-old homemaker at the time she started working with this personal research project to find her soul-purpose. She had married at age 22 right after graduation from college with a degree in art. Soon after her marriage, she and her husband started their family, and Margaret hadn't worked outside the home since the birth of their children 16 and 14 years ago.

Feeling that her life was at a turning point, she started this discovery process by working on her ideals. After considerable self-study, she arrived at a wording for her conscious spiritual ideal: centered and hopeful compassion. Although this gave her a way of naming that place within herself called individuality, it did not yet tell her clearly what her mission in life was. Something more focused and applicable was necessary. How was she to go about living that ideal? What were her most important strengths? For what activities did these soul talents especially suit her?

Her next step was to create an inventory of her strengths, a list that turned out to have eleven entries. From that larger list she narrowed it down to four talents that had the feeling of greatest significance for her: artistic, optimistic, idealistic, sensitive to feelings. Interestingly, one of her key talents was a strength embedded in a personality fault. By her own admission Margaret was a dreamer, often coming up with schemes that had no hope of realization. Yet upon careful scrutiny, she saw that the essential seed within that weakness was a fierce idealism.

After completing the three exercises designed to help her arrive at a tentative wording for her mission, she selected this thematic phrase: to be the magnifier of aspirations and ideals. By those words she meant the work of recognizing and enhancing the highest calling in herself and others. She felt that it was her mission to assist people to believe in and trust those quiet, deep aspirations of the soul that so easily get ignored or explained away.

To test the validity of this hypothesis, she wrote down half a dozen practical applications she could start testing. Each practical application was a way she could imagine giving life to her mission.

Some of the applications to test involved direct service to others. For example, using her artistic strength, she resolved to (1) seek a part-time art therapy job and (2) start encouraging more family artistic activities. Her intuition was that art is one way in which people's aspirations and ideals can surface. To better use her talent for sensitivity to feelings, she resolved to test a way of planning her daily life so that it left more time just to be with people and listen to them, instead of always being in a rush. She was willing to test the possibility that if she made more room in her life for people, she would see opportunities to help them magnify their aspirations.

Some of her applications for testing, however, did not focus overtly on service to others. Some involved further development of a key talent. For example, she decided to sign up for a counseling course at the local college. She hoped that a structured attempt to improve her natural sensitivity to others would better equip her to serve.

Just as important, some of her planned experiments involved service to herself – the nurturance of her individuality. She knew it was important for anyone embarking on this discovery to keep that option in mind. If everything she wrote down as a practical expression of her soul-purpose was an act of self-sacrificing service, then it would be easy to end up with burnout. Surely some features of living her mission included using key talents to nurture her own best self.

With this principle in mind, Margaret resolved to keep a weekly time for her own creative art work, with special focus on letting her art give form to her ideals. This particular experimental application is an example of blending two talents into one commitment. In addition, she planned to use her soul strength of optimism to nurture her individuality identity. She planned to make it a discipline to believe in herself more deeply – regularly to affirm confidence in herself for meeting difficulties and challenges with creativity and love. She clearly saw that in the long run she would never be very effective as a magnifier of aspirations in others if she didn't use her strength of optimism in relation to herself.

The final step in the process for Margaret was to start testing these applications. Some could be put to use immediately. Others, like the search for a part-time art therapy job, took longer. As she applied and tested them, she looked for several things. As a researcher, she was seeking confirming, validating signs and remained alert to them.

One kind of evidence was a natural and unfolding flow to the efforts. Many verbal expressions capture this subtle feeling of life, and they all point to a certain intuitive rightness to what you are doing: "everything fell into place," or "being at the right place at the right time," or "finding that what's needed is provided." Of course, this doesn't mean that there are no problems or difficulties. Living your mission in life shall surely involve being stretched and challenged. But mingled in with the difficulties, you can expect to find reinforcing encouragement when you are on track with living your soul-purpose.

For example, at first Margaret couldn't find any part-time art therapy job. But rather than take this as an immediate sign that she was on the wrong track, she decided to take it just one more step before concluding that her hypothesis was in error. She volunteered to teach biweekly art classes at a nearby retirement community. Here "things fell into place" and began to unfold as if they had a life of their own. She experienced herself actually magnifying the best aspirations of people as she helped members of that community give their own (admittedly amateurish) expression to ideals through art. Eventually she created a paying part-time job for herself because her volunteer work was so well received.

Of course, not every application to be tested turned out with successful results. One experiment made use of her talent for optimism. She offered to teach the high schoolers' class in Sunday school at her church. She had always seen this group as full of cynicism and sarcasm, resulting from their self-doubts and low self-esteem. This application of her soul's purpose seemed like a natural. What a great chance to help others to magnify their ideals. She was given the job, but unfortunately she had a frustrating experience with it. She didn't give up easily, but was finally forced to conclude that for this time in her life, it was not a service situation that fit her soul's abilities and intentions. The discouraging results with this part of the experiment did not, however, invalidate the hypothesis that her soul's mission was "to be the magnifier of ideals and aspirations." Validating feedback came to her through the other applications she tested. But this "failure" did show her at least one parameter of her mission – it showed one point of limitation, at least for now.

Perhaps the most significant result of her testing period was the fact that certain qualities of life became more and more frequent experiences for her. In Margaret's case it was a greater sense of joy, a deeper feeling of the wonder of life, and a more frequent feeling of the presence of God. These features are among the five reinforcing signs previously described. More than anything else, the occurrence of these indicators convinced her that she had accurately chosen a thematic wording for her soul's mission.

But what if those reinforcing signs did *not* become a more frequent experience? What if the testing of her various applications had been accompanied by flatness, ordinariness or boredom? Or, what if virtually none of her applications created a natural flow to suggest the rightness of her efforts? Then, as a researcher, she would have been forced to conclude that her hypothesis was in error. She would have had to return to an earlier step and repeat it in a new way – probably to Step 3, selecting another wording for her soul-purpose.

With sincerity and persistence anyone can find his or her mission for this lifetime. If you are fortunate, you may have to go through the sequence of steps only once. But if you meet with initial failure or a mistaken notion, then a repetition of some previous steps is required. However, no investment of time, energy, and effort is more worthwhile than this discovery process. The sense of meaning in life and the possibility of fulfillment it offers are the greatest gifts you can present to yourself.

Conclusion

At first glance, perhaps this program for finding your soul-purpose statement seems far removed from learning about the Cayce prophecies for the 21st century. But it's really what Cayce said "the Work" is all about. Living in the material world here in the early 21st century, we have an extraordinary opportunity to help create the renewed planetary culture that Cayce said would be possible. But the success of that endeavor depends on people just like us doing what we were born to do.

CHAPTER 10

MEDITATION

The 21st Century Key To Powerful, Healthy Living

Twenty-first century life sometimes seems to overwhelm us. There is so much going on – so many forces feel like they push and pull us around – that we can fall into a sense of being powerless. What a miserable state in which to find ourselves. It easily leads to discouragement, self-pity, and even depression. So how do we get reconnected to power? And what *is* power, anyway?

The Qualities of Power

To answer the mysteries of power we need to begin with an assumption – one that is sometimes hard to swallow: Each of us is responsible for the conditions in our lives, and we have the capacity to change anything about those conditions, if we commit to it. It's a promise about power and a reminder that we are constantly co-creators of our life situation.

Often in the readings Cayce reminded people of the power they have access to, *if* they would simply understand what power is really all about. That's a big "if," as the saying goes. We fail to achieve self-empowerment largely because we don't grasp the deeper meaning of power. Our lives become enslaved to worries, limitations, and doubts, all in large measure because we've gotten tricked into buying into superficial explanations of power. Just think about this word and all the meanings it has in our modern world. No wonder we get confused about power and personal empowerment.

People crave power. The world respects it. Power is that elusive commodity that everyone promises, but no one seems quite to understand. Power is the capacity to get things done. It is energy – sometimes pure and raw, sometimes purposefully directed. Horsepower, atomic power, the power of love.

Power often connotes getting your way. Willpower, military power, people power. Other times, power is influence. It is a force that shapes, manipulates or controls – such as political power, the power of suggestion, and, yes, even a higher, spiritual power.

All these images of power suggest that it must surely be a paradox. It has two sides which may seem to contradict each other. For example, to have one kind of power, you must make an effort and work for it. But then, when you get it, you may find it turns on itself, and you may become corrupted by it – even becoming its slave. What a dilemma.

But consider another aspect of power, one that almost magically comes to you as you trust and surrender. A higher, spiritual power can move through your life only if you don't try to grasp it. Resurrection is possible only if there is first a release through crucifixion or surrender in some form. As Jesus taught, to save your life you must be willing to lose your life. The practice of meditation bring these principles directly into focus.

And so we have two ingredients, related and yet seemingly at odds with each other: personal power and a Higher Power. How can any sense be made of all these contradictions? Why does Edgar Cayce's approach to authentic empowerment have to be so complicated? Why couldn't he have simply given us a set of neat, efficient tricks-of-the-metaphysical-trade that are guaranteed to give us greater self-mastery, wealth, and enjoyment in life?

But these mysterious contradictions cannot be circumvented, not if we want to understand and live an authentic spiritual path. Paradox is the essence of spiritual teachings – be it teachings that come from Jesus, the Buddha, or any other genuine master. And so, the key to self-empowerment is simply this: always strive to do the best you can with what you have at hand, but also be willing "at-the-drop-of-a-hat" to surrender and give up all personal effort.

Consider this point from the perspective of Cayce's philosophy about the human soul. Each soul is made up of three attributes: spirit, mind and free will. The "center of gravity" for empowerment rests within the quality of will. Questions of power boil down to issues of how we are using the will. The key to understanding how power operates in human life is to trace how choice, decision, and freedom are being expressed. Will is the spark that gives power its dynamic, living quality. But just like power itself, the human will is a paradox:

1. A productive, meaningful life is impossible without the use of free will to affirm oneself, to show individuality, and to have strength.
2. A productive, meaningful life is equally impossible without a willingness to let something bigger than oneself work in and through the personality – to live with a measure of surrender to God's Will.

The key, then, is to learn how to integrate those two threads of life – truly an art form, especially in the chaotic, modern world.

One activity stands out above all the rest in helping us to weave together these two paradoxical qualities: Meditation, the theme for this chapter. In Cayce's philosophy, the only real empowerment comes from the regular practice of meditation, in some form (because surely there are many approaches and techniques). Meditation requires both aspects of the will – focused, individual effort, plus willing surrender to God. The result of a meditative life is exactly the kind of empowerment that allows us to be in the world, present to what is happening in the material conditions around us and simultaneously connected to the invisible world of spirit and its intentions for us.

Ancient Technique, Modern Application

Meditation is an ancient practice, so what makes it so central to living in the 21st century? Despite the fact that there's nothing new about meditation, nevertheless its practice here in our century has never been more vital. In times when stressful changes are going on all around us, we've got to meditate in order to maintain any connection to the invisible world of spirit.

Cayce's approach to meditation is ideals-centered. And, as noted earlier, he states clearly that knowing one's spiritual ideal is the most important thing we can do in life. Meditation is indispensable to the fulfillment of Cayce's prophecy that the Aquarian Age will be a time in which people have a direct connection to the spiritual world. For that reason alone, it warrants an entire chapter in this book. *Unless we learn to meditate and practice it regularly, there is really little point to studying the other prophecies that Cayce presented.* All prophecies point back to the transformation of the individual and the way that we live on this planet. All the prophecies come back to the interconnectedness of all life and the quantum jump that we are about to make in relationship to that principle. *Meditation, quite simply, is the way that each of us has a chance to participate in the consciousness that Cayce foresaw for humanity.*

And so, in considering the question "Why meditate?" we should realize that meditation moves us toward a new sense of what is truly valuable in life. Do you ever feel that life must be more than your body, your belongings, and your physical experiences? Are you looking beyond the standard symbols of success – money, possessions, fame, influence – for something that can reach deep within you and spark an inner light? If so, adding meditation to your life may be the most important step you ever take.

Meditation is a safe, direct technique for reconnecting to our spiritual selves. Furthermore, when this discipline is carried out on a regular basis, we can realize a host of physical and mental benefits. For example, here are some results reported in prestigious research publications:

- Meditation reduces stress and many forms of anxiety.
- Meditation can be an effective treatment for insomnia, hypertension, headaches, and chronic pain.
- Meditation promotes creativity, especially in the visual arts.
- Meditation just prior to studying or test taking may result in higher grades.
- Meditation may retard biological aging, especially in the areas of hearing, close vision, and blood pressure.
- Meditation practice correlates with positive marital adjustment.

Of course, the beginning meditator should not expect these kinds of results immediately, although effects such as feelings of relaxation and stress reduction may be felt early in the regular practice of meditation.

Meditation traditions typically take a long-term view of the benefits of the practice. For example, a study of Zen meditation published in the *Journal of Clinical Psychology* (Compton & Becker, 1983) reports that the desired effects of Zen meditation – most notably, an increase in individual self-actualization – result only after about a year of meditating regularly. This extensive learning period is consistent with Zen philosophy and practice.

Considering the enormous positive potential of meditation on all three levels of body, mind, and spirit – especially on a long-term basis – we should not be surprised to learn that millions of Americans and others in the Western world have begun the regular practice of meditation in recent years. It's a noteworthy confirmation of Cayce's visions about how people will live in the new millennium.

Both Eastern and Western sources stress the need for the meditator to consciously set a spiritual ideal for his or her life or, at least, to give considerable thought to the question, "Why am I going to practice meditation?" Lama Anagarika Govinda, in his book *Foundations of Tibetan Mysticism*, refers to this process of acting from the basis of a spiritual ideal as a re-orientation – the "turning about in the deepest seat of consciousness." This consists of letting one's life be directed by the inner, spiritual nature, instead of by the promptings of the outer, material world. While most seekers would agree that this inner-directed state would be desirable to attain, not all are willing to admit that one should consciously set an ideal for oneself as a step along the way towards this attainment. Some prefer to believe that, left to its own devices, the unconscious will eventually issue forth an integrated and enlightened personality – that the conscious mind has the responsibility only of getting out of the way and letting things flow. Govinda would disagree strongly with this attitude. As he puts it:

> Just as an artist will hold before himself the greatest
> masters as worthy examples, irrespective of whether

he will be able to reach their perfection or not, thus, whosoever wants to progress spiritually, must turn towards the highest ideal within the range of his understanding. This will urge him to ever higher achievements. For nobody can say from the beginning, where the limits of one's capacities are – in fact, it is more probable that it is the intensity of our striving that determines these limits. He who strives for the highest, will partake of the highest forces, and thereby he himself will move his limits into the infinite: he will realize the infinite in the finite, making the finite the vessel of infinity, the temporal the vehicle of the timeless.

The Need for a Purpose

What then is the purpose for meditation? Many of the sources warn against meditating to obtain something directly for ourselves (e.g., psychic ability or better health). Govinda even states that rebirth in the heavenly realms is not an aim worth striving for. Certainly these things may come as by-products of meditation and should be accepted and integrated into our lives. However, the real purpose for meditation should be to attune ourselves to the infinite nature of being – to allow the infinite to express in the finite. One who meditates simply to escape from this involvement with the material world and with other people fails to achieve the ultimate potential of the meditative process. In Govinda's own words: "For he who strives for his own salvation, or merely with a view of getting rid of suffering in the shortest possible way, without regard for his fellow-beings, has already deprived himself of the most essential means for the realization of his aim."

Most simply put, the language of meditation is the language of love. And love always speaks of giving and self-surrender, instead of getting and expectations. The best purpose for meditation – in fact, the best technique – is to enter with a sense of giving of oneself, rather than coming to get something. That doesn't come very naturally to us here in the 21st century, where we are bombarded daily with subtle and not-so-subtle messages that we need to always be on the lookout for what's best for oneself.

The language of love is a very subtle matter, because sometimes our wantings and expectations are for nice-sounding things. But the most profound experiences of meditation are probably reserved for those times when expectations are shed for personal reward or benefit. In its place is the feeling of having *given* of self.

When you want to evaluate the quality of your meditation, try the following method: Don't ask "What did I get?" That is not the language of love, even when you may have received remarkable things like greater energy, or a feeling of being out of your body, or a psychic intuition. Instead, do your evaluation by asking, "How deeply did I experience giving myself to something higher than myself?"

Describing "Spiritual Guidance in Contemporary Taoism," Erwin Rousselle points out that, from a psychological standpoint, meditation should have as its aim the creation of a new way of being. Writing this chapter on Taoism for *The Eranos Yearbooks, Volume 4*, Rousselle states that meditation changes the way we see ourselves and the way we see the world around us. However, it can do this only as we experience the union of the infinite (and, up to now, unconscious) forces expressing in the finite, and not just talk about it abstractly .

> To open the way for new and meaningful shifts in our psychological components is one of the essential aims in meditation. It is of fundamental importance that man should actually experience – and not merely note intellectually – the opposite pole in himself, his unconscious and his vital force.

In describing the psychological factors of meditation, Claudio Naranjo arrives at a similar conclusion in *The Psychology of Meditation*: that the purpose of meditation is to come to the awareness of a new way of being and then to give expression to it in the physical world. "Meditation is concerned with the development of a presence, a modality of being, which may be expressed or developed in whatever situation the individual may be involved."

Finally, those who have set a spiritual ideal and understand their purpose for meditating must have a sense of *devotion* if they are to succeed. Referring to the importance of such a frame of mind, Naranjo quotes the sutras of Patanjali which make the point quite simply: "[Samadhi] is closest to those who desire it intensely."

So, let's return to the question, "Why meditate?" We have identified some of the benefits of meditation for body, mind, and spirit. But ultimately you must answer the question yourself – by determining the spiritual ideal for your life and perhaps by answering another question, "What is my purpose in practicing meditation?" Answering that question is easier when you know more about meditation, what it is, and what conditions are necessary for its practice.

Conditions for the Practice of Meditation

Meditation is becoming more and more widely practiced in the Western world. An issue of *Time* magazine in 2003 even featured meditation as its cover story, largely praising its therapeutic value. Furthermore, some medical and psychological approaches for treating such ailments as stress, anxiety, hypertension, and headache include a form of body-mind relaxation, self-hypnosis, or "centering" – any of which may come to be identified as "meditation." Although often approached as a benefit for psychological or physical health, since ancient times meditation has been linked primarily to religious traditions. Cayce saw meditation as an activity which uniquely engages all three key aspects of who we are – body, mind and spirit.

Six conditions characterize the process of meditation. These six elements are drawn from both Eastern and Western sources, and all are necessary.

1. Meditation requires focusing one's attention. All forms of meditation have this trait in common. Sometimes referred to as "centering," it consists of two factors: concentrating one's energies, and finding the center – the point of integration – of one's being.

Meditation is not letting one's mind wander and not allowing one's attention to dwell upon fantasies or phenomena that may arise from the unconscious. As Cayce put it, "What *is* meditation? It is not musing, not daydreaming... (#281-41)

2. *Meditation requires letting go* – releasing thought patterns that have been controlling us and that have led us to a limited concept of our own being. This conditioning (i.e., the habit patterns of the mind) can even be seen as essentially one's karma; hence some ancient teachings of meditation suggest that it is the way that we break the cycle of continual reincarnations – an idea that harmonizes with Cayce's point of view. In meditation, we shift our attention and sense of identification to a more holistic and unlimited concept of ourselves and away from the limited and fragmenting nature of our habitual responses. Naranjo describes this as "a very precise unfolding of experience to which the individual opens himself as he lays aside his habitual patterns of thinking and feeling and his superficial identity."

3. *In the three-dimensional world, we experience ourselves as body, mind and spirit.* In meditation, the activities of body, mind, and spirit are brought into an attunement or state of unity. This concept is stated clearly in the Cayce readings: "As ye find your bodies made up of the physical, mental and spiritual, it is the attuning of the mental body and the physical body to its spiritual source. (#281-41)

4. *The real purpose for meditation should be to allow the infinite to express in the finite.* This experience must be part of the definition of meditation. In her book *Mysticism*, published in 1910 and still an important classic, Evelyn Underhill describes the purpose of introversion (i.e., meditation) with these words: "the breaking down of the barrier between the surface-self and those deeper levels of personality where God is met and known 'in our nothingness' and a mysterious fusion of divine and human life takes place."

5. *Meditation works toward making the enlightenment of consciousness a permanent state of being*, and it is not simply a transitory experience, as with mind-altering drugs. The ancient Taoist meditation text *The Secret of the Golden Flower* uses the phrase "making fast" to describe this meditative process: "Fixating

contemplation [i.e., meditation] is indispensable; it ensures the making fast of the enlightenment."

6. *Meditation is an habitual process,* not something done just once or occasionally. It becomes a positive habit. Govinda compares human consciousness to a musical instrument that frequently requires tuning anew. One of the most significant promises in *The Secret of the Golden Flower* refers to the *daily* practice of meditation, for even 15 minutes, which can permit an individual to move beyond karmic patterns that would result in coming back into the earth a thousand more times:

> Children, take heed: If for a day you do not practice meditation, this light streams out, who knows whither? If you only meditate for a quarter of an hour, by it you can do away with the ten thousand aeons and a thousand births. All methods end in quietness. This marvellous magic cannot be fathomed.

Thus, frequency and regularity of meditation appear to be a higher priority than length of meditation period.

And if we then take these six conditions – drawn from the many international traditions for the practice – it can lead us to this definition. "Meditation must be an habitual process in which the individual focuses attention and lets go of thought patterns, bringing body, mind, and spirit into attunement, thus allowing the infinite to express in the finite, all with the goal of the permanent enlightenment of consciousness."

The Practice of Meditation

Cayce asks us to imagine a world in which the regular practice of this important discipline is widespread among the human family. It's a wonderful prospect to contemplate for the 21st century. But how, exactly, do we go about the actual practice of meditation? What are the steps?

Whatever technique we use, it must help the individual focus attention and let go of thought patterns. On the issue of holding a focus, schools of meditation differ widely on the kind of mental activity to be made a part of the procedure. Some approaches emphasize mental images (e.g., mandalas, pictures of the Master), while others teach that all imagery should be ignored. But some form of mental activity is needed, at least in the initial stages of meditation. Images other than the chosen focal point are to be ignored or expelled.

Evelyn Underhill in *Mysticism*, for example, refers to the first stage of meditation as "recollection" and says it is the most difficult because it involves an act of will to go against the habits and impulses of the mind. An individual may spend years in this first stage:

> All the scattered interests of the self have here to be collected; there must be a deliberate and unnatural act of attention, a deliberate expelling of all discordant images from the consciousness – a hard and ungrateful task. Since the transcendental faculties are still young and weak, the senses not wholly mortified, it needs a stern determination, a "willful choice," if we are to succeed in concentrating our attention upon the whispered messages from within, undistracted by the loud voices which besiege us from without.

In *The Secret of the Golden Flower*, distracting images that may arise after reaching a state of stillness are referred to as the "fox-spirits." The text warns that to pay attention to these, no matter how beautiful they may be, is to settle for far less than the potential rewards of proper meditation. Instead, one must return to the chosen point of focus.

Naranjo identifies several characteristics of these points of focus which he found in his study of various approaches: First is centrality, such as in the cross and the lotus. These images evoke the notion of a center around which action flows, as well as a radiation or emanation. A second characteristic is an expression of giving or of self-emptying, as symbolized in the cross or as verbalized in portions of the Lord's Prayer. Finally, many of these focal points demonstrate lawfulness or order, as typified in the geometric order of a Tibetan mandala or in the symbology of the seed syllables of a mantra.

Cayce and Govinda provide very similar recommendations concerning the choice of a focal point for attention during meditation. Cayce refers to "affirmations" or verbal expressions of the spiritual ideal that has been chosen. His affirmations are usually from one to four sentences in length. Govinda's teaching is from the mantric tradition. However, the words of the affirmation or the Sanskrit syllables of the mantra do not work through any "magic power" within them. They come alive and aid in the transformative process only as the meditator dwells upon and experiences their *meaning*, as Govinda points out in *Foundations of Tibetan Mysticism*.

> Mantras are not "spells," as even prominent Western scholars repeat again and again, nor are those who have attained proficiency ... in them "sorcerers" ... Mantras do not act on account of their own "magic" nature, but only through the mind that experiences them. They do not possess any power of their own; they are only the means for concentrating already existing forces – just as a magnifying glass, though it does not contain any heat of its own, is able to concentrate the rays of the sun and to transform their mild warmth into incandescent heat.
>
> This may appear as sorcery to the bushman, because he sees only the effect, without knowing the causes and their inner connections. Therefore those who confuse mantric knowledge with sorcery are not very different in their point of view from the attitude of the bushman. And if there have been scholars who tried to discover the nature of mantras with the tools of philological knowledge, and came to the conclusion that they were "meaningless gibberish" because they had neither grammatical structure nor logical meaning, then we can only say that such a procedure was like pursuing butterflies with a sledge hammer.

Pronouncing the mantra correctly, as if the vibration of the sound had some special effect on the body, is not even important. Govinda points out that if the efficacy of Tibetan mantras depended upon the correct pronunciation, they would have all lost their usefulness "because they are not pronounced there according to the rules of Sanskrit but according to the phonetic laws of the Tibetan language."

Cayce states that Jesus gave the Lord's Prayer to His followers to be used as a focus for meditation. Its various parts are meant to affect particular spiritual centers within the body. Describing the way in which this prayer should be used in meditation, one Cayce reading says, "As in feeling, as it were, the flow of the meanings of each portion of same throughout the body-physical" (#281-29).

As the meditator says the words of the affirmation or the mantra, there is an inner response to its meaning. That awakening may be a feeling or a state of consciousness, but the meditator should focus attention upon that response. Most people find that in a very short time the mind will drift off and start thinking about something else. At this point, the affirmation or mantra should be repeated. On the other hand, one who *continually* repeats it is not taking time to be aware of what is being awakened from within during the meditation. Holding to the *form* of the words so tightly that one ignores the *spirit* behind them does not lead to deep meditation.

Most people find that various internal and external distractions are formidable problems in meditation. One becomes aware of the discomfort of the chair or of an itch. Outside sounds pull at one's attention. Perhaps the best technique to deal with these distractions is to *use* them as they come into awareness, rather than to fight them. In the words of *The Secret of the Golden Flower:* "To become conscious of the distraction is the mechanism by which to do away with the distraction."

The meditator may, for example, use the distraction as a reminder to return to the ideal or the spirit of the affirmation. To illustrate: An individual is focusing on the words from a Cayce prayer "Let me be a channel of blessings to others" and hears a plane overhead. The meditator can take a few seconds to pray for the people in that plane, letting the prayer bring the consciousness back to the spirit behind these words from which attention has been distracted. Such a technique takes practice and a degree of ingenuity to work with the mental associations that accompany various internal or external distractions. This is reminiscent of the Tantric tradition of turning a weakness into a strength. As one becomes aware of attention drifting off, the important response is not to fight the mind. This leads only to a cycle of frustration contrary to the consciousness we seek to awaken in meditation.

Breath Awareness

Along with focusing attention, *breathing* is an important issue to be considered in the practice of meditation. The relationship between consciousness and the breath has been noted by many sources. For example, our breathing patterns when we are startled or afraid are usually quite different from those in moments of tranquility. The meditator can use this principle to advantage in attempting to experience an expanded state of awareness.

Yoga exercises teach several breathing disciplines that many meditators have reported to be helpful when used in moderation. The Buddha's most fundamental method for meditation is simply resting one's attention on the flowing in and flowing out of the breath. From something even that simple, enlightened states of consciousness can emerge. As Govinda put it, "the process of breathing, if fully understood and experienced in its profound significance, could teach us more than all the philosophies of the world."

Cayce also was an advocate of using the breath to enhance meditation. As we will see shortly, he recommended a simple breathing exercise at the beginning of meditation. He also felt that in-depth work with breathing could be very beneficial, as long as the individual was clear about ideals and purposes and had done the necessary work to cleanse and prepare his or her body. A forty-four-year-old physics research director once asked Cayce for advice about advanced yoga breathing exercises. At the beginning of the reading, Cayce was encouraging, with comments such as, "These exercises are excellent... For breath is the *basis* of the living organisms activity."

But near the end of the reading, in response to a specific question, Cayce was somewhat more cautionary.

(Q) Considering the development of the entity, is further practice of the Yoga exercises of breathing and meditation recommended?
(A) By all means! if and when, and *only* when, preparation has been made; and when there is the knowledge, the understanding and the wisdom as to what to do *with* that gained! Without such, do not undertake same! (#2475-1)

Some of this emphasis on technique can begin to sound like too rigid a formula, even a technology of consciousness. And our 21st century is full of technology, not just mechanistic technology. More and more we see evidence of psychological technologies – and some would even claim spiritual technologies. But all this smacks of short-cuts, and Cayce felt strongly that there are no short cuts to soul growth.

Topics like how to hold focus, methods for overcoming distractions, and the secrets of breathing in meditation could be discouraging to a would-be meditator. He or she may wonder, "How can all of this ever be mastered? Surely there must be some easier way to achieve the benefits of meditation. But we must be careful not to get trapped in the Western attitude towards techniques that amounts to a desire for short-cuts to spiritual growth. Our culture has grown accustomed to quick changes, but the transformation of consciousness to a state of spiritual attunement is a slow process. We have discovered that we can manipulate nature with our machines, and we are tempted to try to manipulate the powerful forces that lie within the mind by techniques that promise quick results. Because of the Westerner's fundamental misunderstanding of the purpose of Eastern meditation practices, some teachers even believe that Oriental meditations are in large part unsuited to the European or North American. Perhaps that's too strong a statement; but Cayce would agree that we need to try to build upon the tradition in which we have been raised.

How to Meditate

Cayce offers an elegantly simple and highly practical technique for meditation. It is every bit as much relevant and practical here in the 21st century as it was in the 20th when he gave it. Of the dozens of meditation systems that exist, this eleven-step approach has a universal quality, drawing as it does upon recurrent themes and techniques found in Cayce's readings and other spiritual philosophies that share his perspective.

Step 1. Set a spiritual ideal for your life. Every meditation period should begin by taking time to remember a sense of purpose that leads you to the practice of meditation. If you have not recently taken time to formulate carefully the ideals that you want to have guiding and directing your life, now is a good time to do so.

What is meant by the word "ideal"? We have already explored this question earlier, especially in chapter 9, but it's worth re-examining in the context of setting the stage for meditation. As pointed out earlier, an ideal is not a "goal" (which refers instead to the product of our actions). An ideal connects us to the *purpose* for an action, or the *spirit* in which it is done.

Here is the question to ask yourself: "What spirit of living do I want directing every part of my life?" In other words, ask yourself what sense of meaning and purpose you want to strive for in the way you live your life? Admittedly, not every action, thought, or feeling will reflect that ideal, because in our humanness we often fall short. But each of us can aspire to a profound sense of meaning – a higher way of seeing life and others and self.

For one person, the spiritual ideal might be "loving freedom"; for another person, it might be "oneness with the Light"; and for still a third, simply "service." No matter what words you use, they should describe a place of consciousness within yourself that you have actually touched and tasted. A spiritual ideal must be something living for you – not merely a philosophical abstraction.

In setting a spiritual ideal this way, you may sense that even higher ideals are possible. In fact, one's spiritual ideal is, in effect, a statement which affirms, "This is the highest meaning and purpose of life that I know as reality, because I have personally been touched by it."

Once you have set a spiritual ideal for your life, begin each meditation period with a brief moment to remember that ideal and its connection to the meditation period. Meditation is a powerful technique for moving you more quickly in the direction of the ideal you hold.

Step 2. Set and maintain a consistent time of day for meditation, even if initially the length of each session is brief. It's the consistency that counts. That consistency should include the regularity of daily meditation, as well as the keeping of a particular time of day for the silence period.

Examine your life and the various kinds of demands you encounter in terms of time and energy. Taking these factors into account, at what time of day are you most likely to be able to still your mind and body, and keep your attention focused upon your spiritual ideal? That is the best time of day for you. For one person, it may be the first thing in the morning; for someone else, before lunch: for a third person, before bedtime; and for yet another person, it may best be done by awakening in the middle of the night.

By keeping the same time each day you can take advantage of a principle about the nature of the human mind: Your mind can be trained to make a change in consciousness at the same time each day. For example, you have probably already discovered that it's possible to train your mind to awaken at a particular time each morning to get ready for work. In this case, the training is to make the change in consciousness from the sleep state to the normal waking state. But the same principle can be used for moving from the normal waking state to the consciousness achieved in meditation. By keeping the same time each day for your meditation period, in effect you begin each meditation period "with a running start."

How long should your initial efforts at meditation last? A good length for beginners is just three or four minutes of silence. At first, even such a brief period will seem inordinately long. Yet with practice, you will get used to longer periods of keeping attention focused. Most meditators find that they want to build to at least 20-minute meditation periods. However, let such a length of meditation build up over the course of many weeks, increasing at a pace that best fits your temperament.

Step 3. Maintain long-term attunement practices as an ongoing preparation. Meditation is more than just 15 or 20 minutes each day. In a sense, you are always getting ready for your next meditation period by the way you treat your physical body and by what you feed your mind.

Each meditator needs to design a personalized kind of preparation program. Consider the way you treat your physical body as an essential ingredient to more effective meditation periods. For example, everyone has experienced the way changes in diet affect both mood and attention span. The simplest illustration of this can be observed after eating a large meal. A body preoccupied with digestion finds it difficult to stay consciously alert. However, the subtle effects of diet are probably even more important. Many meditators find that the elimination of certain foods is crucial to optimal meditation (e.g., eliminating or minimizing sugar, caffeine, alcohol, etc.). Each person must decide from careful experimentation what kind of diet preparation works best.

Most meditators also find that a regular physical exercise program becomes an ongoing kind of meditation preparation. Again it's important to determine what fits your life-style, but activities such as running, swimming, yoga, or walking are highly recommended for most people.

Each meditator should also identify ways of thinking that can be either an enhancement or an obstacle to meditation. For example, if you hold resentful feelings toward someone, until that pattern is changed, it constitutes a stumbling block toward more effective meditation periods. Of course, we should continue to meditate even though we have not cleansed ourselves totally of attitudinal and emotional stresses. However, the more we are able to monitor what we feed the soul through our daily attitudes and emotions, the better chance we have to obtain the deeper levels possible in meditation. As a first step in this kind of preparatory effort, identify just one or two attitudes or emotions that particularly need conscious work. Then do the necessary work!

Step 4. Just before each meditation session, use your own helpful aids for attunement. Here again, select those disciplines and activities that work best for you based on personal experimentation. Most meditators find that, when they first sit down to begin the meditation session, they still need some activities to help them enter the silence, even if they have been engaged in ongoing preparation (Step 3).

One kind of pre-meditation aid involves the physical body. For example, the Edgar Cayce readings recommend a simple head and neck exercise be done at the beginning of meditation. This exercise seems to alleviate much of the stress and tension we store in our necks and shoulders:

- Sit up straight and let your head drop forward slowly, and then bring it slowly back upright. Do this three times.
- Next, slowly move your head as far back as you can comfortably move it, and then slowly return your head to an upright position, a total of three times.
- Next, do three similar head movements to the right side.
- Then, do three to the left side.
- The exercise concludes with three circular movements of the head, first in a clockwise direction, and then in a counter-clockwise direction.

Another aid for attunement many meditators find helpful is to work with breathing. Although lengthy, somewhat forced deep breathing exercises are possible, it's also easy to use a more gentle approach to the breath. The simplest technique is to spend one or two minutes simply letting all of your attention dwell upon your breathing without trying to change the rate or depth of each breath. In other words, attention to the breath becomes a method for beginning to focus attention. Seemingly quite simple, this powerful technique is highly recommended.

Some meditators use a form of quieting or inspirational music at the beginning of meditation to evoke feelings of calm and uplifted spirits. Experiment with different kinds of music to find something that works for you. Some individuals also find that chanting is helpful at the start of a meditation session. Similarly, burning incense may create a physical stimulus that helps to both center the mind and evoke desired feelings.

Step 5. Begin with prayer. Remember that prayer and meditation are complementary. Beginning a meditation program for yourself does not reduce the importance and helpfulness of a prayer life. The two aid each other.

Spend several minutes in prayer before you begin to meditate. Remember that prayer is an *activity* of the conscious mind, whereas in meditation you will try to *still* the conscious mind. So during this prayer period let your conscious thought be active, but highly purposeful and directed. You may like to work with a prayer of thanksgiving, a prayer of petition, a prayer of praise, or a prayer of confession.

Many people working from a Christian orientation find this an especially appropriate place to work with the Lord's Prayer. The Edgar Cayce readings, for example, strongly encourage meditators to use the Lord's Prayer before beginning the silence period. The readings encourage us to say the prayer slowly, feel the meaning of each part of the prayer as it quickens and awakens a higher state of consciousness within the physical body.

Step 6. Repeat silently or aloud an affirmation corresponding to your spiritual ideal. Here "affirmation" is roughly equivalent to the Sanskrit "mantra." That is, the words chosen as a focus for attention need to have a powerfully evocative quality – able to awaken within us strong feelings of the ideal.

What words should you choose for your affirmation? You may take a favorite line from the Bible (e.g., "Be still and know that I am God") or from other sacred scripture. Or you may write your own short affirmation which encapsulates your spiritual ideal. Some meditators keep their affirmation quite brief and in fact use the short phrase they have selected to designate their spiritual ideal.

You may also find it helpful at the beginning of your meditation session to create in your mind some visual imagery that relates to your affirmation and helps you get in touch with it. For example, some meditators find it helpful to imagine themselves sitting in a special spiritual place. The image of that setting then allows them to identify more quickly with the life purpose which the affirmation represents.

Step 7. Focus your attention on the words of the affirmation and any images you're using, until you begin to experience the feeling and spirit behind the words. In this step, you are directing your conscious will to concentrate and keep your attention one-pointed. However, the effort you make to direct attention is not an intellectual effort to dissect the affirmation or analyze the images. Instead, let your attention rest upon the feeling and spirit the affirmation begins to call forth from your unconscious mind. This stage may require much practice because of the strong tendency for your attention to drift off to distracting thoughts and emotions.

Step 8. Release any images and the words of the affirmation and hold gently to their feeling or spirit. Once you have reached a point where you recognize that the affirmation has begun to do its work – that new feelings are being awakened – then drop the words and any images you have created. This is the silence of meditation. Here you rest in silent attention in the quiet spirit of the ideal your affirmation represents. At this point, words are unnecessary. They have done their job by getting you back in touch with another way of feeling and seeing yourself and life.

Step 9. When your attention drifts away, repeat Steps 7 and 8. In other words, you can expect that your capacity to stay in the silence will be limited. At first, you will probably find, after just 10 or 15 seconds of silently holding the feeling of your affirmation, that a distracting thought or emotion will grab your attention and pull you away. When you recognize you have been caught up in a distraction, go back to Step 7 and once again hold the words of the affirmation and/or image related to them in your attention until you re-experience their meaning and spirit. You may have to repeat this sequence many times in a single meditation session. Even experienced meditators have to go back frequently and reawaken to their sense of highest purpose by recalling the affirmation and then re-attaining the silence.

Step 10. Surrender all efforts to make something happen. Steps 6 through 9 include effort on your part to direct the meditation session. Even if you have no expectations or desires for some special experience in meditation, conscious effort and the exercise of will is necessary in Steps 6 through 9.

However, the last phase of your meditation should include a short period during which you fully surrender, discontinuing all conscious effort. When you have spent sufficient time holding in silent attention the feeling and meaning of your affirmation, and you feel permeated by its spirit, release even the affirmation.

A good way to experience the surrender called for in Step 10 is to refocus your attention on your breathing. In other words, once you have let the meaning of your affirmation permeate both your conscious and unconscious, then spend several minutes in attentive breathing. This breathing exercise at the close is not to alter your breathing or to attempt to force a change in consciousness by an extraordinary breathing technique. Instead, by letting your attention focus on something as simple as your breath, the power of what you have subconsciously achieved in the previous steps is able to touch you even more deeply.

The key to this tenth step is the word "surrender." There must be a sense of giving up (but not of "giving in") and letting go of all mental efforts to force something to happen.

Step 11. Conclude by praying for others. This will be the closing for most meditation sessions. After you experience the release and the silence of meditation and feel a rejuvenating, inner awakening, share what you have received through prayer. Since energy is directed by conscious intention and thought, through prayer for healing we can bless others for whom we have concern.

Unless a person has specifically asked you for prayer, merely surround with light the individual about whom you have concern. In so doing, you provide an energy and even a state of consciousness the person can draw upon when ready to make changes in his or her life. On the other hand, if someone has asked you specifically to pray for his or her own healing of a particular condition, then it's appropriate to pray for specific changes in the person's life. Always add to each of your prayers some form of "God's will be done." This distinction between prayers for individuals for whom we have concern and prayers for individuals who have asked for such help is meant to insure a respect for the free will of each individual soul.

Conclusion: Meditation for the 21st Century

Of course, the method Cayce outlined is just one of many ways to do this vital spiritual discipline. What's important is that we find *some* way of meditating that makes sense personally.

This point cannot be emphasized too much: *For the positive potentials of the Cayce prophecies to emerge, the world needs to have a meditative planetary culture.* Everyone does *not* need to have the same religion. In fact, the world might well be impoverished if we had only one, homogenized religion for the planet. But even with diversity of spiritual paths, we can have a common commitment to a meditative approach to life.

Without meditation, the habits and conditioning of our wounded personality selves take over – personally and collectively. Without meditation, the world of the 21st century can look forward only to deep expressions of discord and suffering. But with the widespread growth of meditation as a daily discipline, the opportunity for planetary cooperation and transformation becomes a very real possibility. That's what Cayce foresaw when he urgently encouraged those around him to have hope and to realize that someday the meditative, prayerful approach would reshape the way we do business with each other in the world. That's what he envisioned as the inspiring potentials for the new millennium. And to those who were pioneers of these efforts in the mid-20th century, he prophesied that someday their efforts would be appreciated. "For with the coming of the dawn, many will call thee blessed." (#254-43)

CHAPTER 11

WE CAN MAKE A DIFFERENCE

Cayce's most important prophecy unequivocally asserts that *we can make a difference* as humanity collectively creates its future. That's why this book has directed so much attention to the *inner millennium shift*. As we find creative ways to meet these personal changes, we help to build a more balanced, harmonious way for the outer shift to unfold. Cayce had a down-home way of making this point: "The little leaven can leaven the whole lump." It's a powerful principle: a few spiritually attuned souls can lift the consciousness of all humanity.

This philosophy has been called the principle of "critical mass." We're likely to have heard this term in a much more gruesome context: the explosion of an atomic bomb. To build a fission weapon, physicists know that it requires a threshold amount of certain radioactive substances, such as one form of uranium. If we have less than that threshold amount, no explosion can happen. But once we reach the threshold point – that is, the critical mass –something can suddenly start to happen.

The process is illustrated in the graph on the next page. The dotted line represents our common thinking, which states, "The effect I get out is in direct proportion to the amount I put in." In fact, many aspects of life follow this kind of relationship. However, in contrast, the solid line represents a process controlled by the principle of critical mass. If we look carefully, we'll see that other essential aspects of life follow this alternative rule.

Let's consider examples for each of the two. Some people find that the amount of food they eat has an effect on their weight, which roughly follows the broken line. Or, the number of dollars you pay per month in rent may be directly proportional to the quality of dwelling in which you live. Or, the amount of time you spend studying for a test will have a direct, proportional effect on your test score. (Of course, a more accurate depiction of many life experiences would be a curving line that would rise proportionately at first, but the concept of diminishing returns would set in and the line would begin to flatten out.)

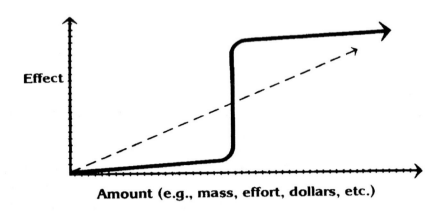

Amount (e.g., mass, effort, dollars, etc.)

But let's pause at the example of studying for a test. Suppose you are stuck in your learning by not understanding a particular key concept. If you study one or two hours, it may look pretty hopeless for the test tomorrow. Your score will be low, and furthermore, the difference will be very slight between having studied for one hour versus two hours. But imagine that it takes three hours to crack the difficult concept. Suddenly at the three-hour point that elusive concept becomes clear, and now you have the insight to be able to solve what had seemed to be impossible problems. Your score now is likely to be very high. Additional study beyond that may help a little bit more, but not very significantly. To put this into a chart we have:

Hours of study	Effect (i.e., test score)
1	45
2	47
3	85
4	87

This is a classic example of critical mass or the threshold effect. Here's another commonplace example: running water into a bathtub that has no overflow protection drain, and then measuring the amount of water that has spilled out onto the bathroom floor. For the first five minutes in which the faucet runs there is no spilling effect upon the floor. But suddenly the critical point is reached – in this case the seventy-five-gallon capacity of the bathtub.

The future of planetary consciousness will be shaped by a critical mass type of curve according to Cayce. And significantly, he never suggests that the future of the world will be shaped by a majority vote. It will not take 51 percent of humanity in order to create a dramatic change in planetary awareness. The critical mass effect can be initiated by a relatively small number of people. That "little leaven" which can lift consciousness in all humanity may be just a handful of people compared to the earth's population.

The teachings of the Bible, as well as the philosophy of the Cayce readings, indicate that this has happened before. Recall the story of Abraham at the time just before the destruction of Sodom and Gomorrah. God warns Abraham that this destruction will take place because of the selfishness of people in those cities. What is Abraham's response? He attempts to bargain with God. He wonders, "If fifty righteous people can be found, would the cities be saved?" God's response is yes, that for the sake of the fifty, the city will not be destroyed. And then Abraham proceeds to find out just how far God will go in His offer of mercy – forty-five, forty, thirty, twenty, ten? Yes, God says, even if only ten righteous people can be found, the principle of critical mass will produce a saving effect on the entire populace of the cities. Ten was the threshold amount. Unfortunately it appears from the story that even those few could not be located.

In another illustration, the Cayce readings speak of the ancient Jewish sect called the Essenes as having served as a critical mass. Historians tell us little about this group of people who lived before and during the time of Jesus. Much more is known about the larger sects of Jewish thought in those times: the Sadducees and the Pharisees. In fact, were it not for the discovery of the Dead Sea Scrolls near the ruins of an Essene community at Qumran, almost nothing would be known of them.

However, in Cayce's psychic vision of the past, the Essenes played a key role in the coming of the Christ. It was this group who prepared themselves as a channel for the Messiah's entrance. Over many decades of practicing physical, mental and spiritual purification, they became a leaven that acted upon the consciousness of the planet. According to the Cayce readings, it was largely through the work of this relatively small group – both Mary and Joseph among them – that the Christ incarnated as Jesus. Apparently there were problems later. Jesus was not exactly the sort of savior they had planned for, and there may have been a break between Jesus and this community as He reached adulthood. However, in Cayce's visionary view of history, the fact remains that a threshold number of people – far, far smaller than any numerical majority – had an impact that was profoundly far-reaching.

And what, we might ask, are the numbers we are working with as we consider the possibility of "critical mass changes" in our own times? Perhaps the quantity will be similar to those of the past. How many Essenes did it require to create a channel for divine incarnation? Perhaps there were only several hundred. We have seen that just ten righteous people were all that was required for a divine promise of mercy in biblical times.

Two passages from Cayce's prophecies – both given in June, 1940 – mentioned specific numbers as threshold amounts for a quickening effect on the mass consciousness. When Cayce addressed the issue of why there was so much turmoil in the 20th century world, he said that it was because people had forgotten God. It was not something that had to be, nor was it the karmic destiny of any nation or the planet as a whole. Then he went on to assert that the prayers of even a single individual can save a city.

In a second prophecy, given in that same reading (#3976-25), he promised a group of sixty-four people that they had the spiritual power to alter the course of America's destiny as World War II drew near for our nation: "For the prayer, and the living of same by those sixty and four who are here gathered, may even save America from being invaded – if that is what ye desire."

The first prophecy suggests that the threshold level for changing the future of a community or city is not even ten people, as the Old Testament story tells it. Instead, perhaps it is just one person who is attuned to God's will. The second passage is even more provocative. It was directed specifically to the sixty-four people gathered to hear a public reading by Cayce. This passage suggests a way of influencing the collective future of an entire nation. In this case, it was the threat that American territory would be invaded. We should note that World War II was already under way in Europe and the Far East, yet it was still a year and a half before the United States would be drawn in. Cayce's prophecy here in June of 1940 makes a bold assertion: if even sixty-four people pray and live in attunement with God's plan, then the likely future for the American people (an invasion) could be changed. Apparently the critical mass in consciousness was not achieved because the nation soon found its territory being invaded by aerial attack at Pearl Harbor less than two years later.

What's fascinating about this story is the report of one person who was present that day and recalls the discussion among the group members when the reading ended. Instead of questions like "what kind of prayer will be the right one?" or "At what time of day could we all be committed to praying?" the group members wondered aloud, "Where do you think the attack will come?" Fear had crept in and overshadowed the hopeful promise in Cayce's prophetic statement.

Looking back more than sixty years later, we may think of those people as having been foolish or fear ridden. We wonder how they could have missed the spirit of what was being promised, how they could have failed to see and grasp the spiritual opportunity being offered them. And yet don't we often do the same thing now? The principles and numbers are still the same. The situation may be a bit different. World War II has come and gone, but today there are equally threatening prospects for our world. But once again, sixty-four people might be enough to make the difference for a nation the size of America.

So what is our response? Do we wonder where the first earthquake will hit? Do we speculate on what kinds of riots will ensue if there is economic collapse? The opportunity is still there to be the little leaven that quickens the consciousness of the masses. This is a powerful concept, which says that a small group of dedicated people can have a tremendous effect on the course of the future. It is an idea that bestows on us a sense of promise and a challenge of responsibility. And we are more likely to feel some hope and accept that responsibility if we see clearly just how the magic of "critical mass" works in the realm of human awareness.

A Mechanism to Explain Critical Mass

How is it that ten righteous people or the prayers of just one individual could save a city? What forces and laws are at work to create such an extraordinary thing? Is it that God is placed in a dilemma? Perhaps in looking down on Sodom and seeing ten righteous people, God would feel "stuck." He could not afford to destroy His best followers, this line of reasoning would say, so He would be forced to let everyone else off the hook.

However attractive this kind of argument may be, it has little merit. It reduces God to a befuddled being who dishes out punishment and yet is easily manipulated and cornered. We can do far better than this lame and naive explanation of how the principle of critical mass works on human consciousness. We can identify the universal laws that are at work and that naturally govern this process.

Let's begin with the universal law of oneness, which Cayce proposed as the most fundamental principle in the universe. In fact, one Cayce reading says that the law of oneness is so fundamental to the way the cosmos runs that it should be the object of study for the first six months of spiritual inquiry. We might wonder how we could ever study that law for so long. It seems as if we could merely agree that all force or energy is essentially just an expression of the one life force. Then we could move on to more interesting topics. However, there is much more than this to the notion of oneness. There are many subtle ways in which it directs our experiences.

For example, the law of oneness provides us with a clue about how a threshold number of people can change the course of the future for all humanity. It's a key to understanding a mechanism that may allow the love of a few people to lift the awareness of humanity. The law of oneness begins by asserting that there are *not* two equal but opposing powers of good and evil that are battling for dominion of human minds. There is light and there is darkness, yes. Our experience tells us this, and no abstract law of oneness can deny this experience, which we all have. There are good works being done by some people, and there are evil-appearing, destructive works being done by others. The question, however, is this: what's the relationship between them, between light and darkness, or good and evil? Are they equal but opposing powers? If so, then we have majority rule when they clash, and nine units of good when confronted with ten units of evil will always result in a victory for evil.

But is that really what happens? When light confronts darkness, what is the result of their interaction? For example, if someone lights a candle in a darkened auditorium, doesn't the light permeate the entire room? Admittedly, that candle may illuminate the huge room with only a very dim light, but the fact remains that the darkness does not overpower the tiny candle flame. Light and darkness are not really equal but opposing forces. Darkness is better understood as an absence of light.

In other words, there is a fundamental oneness in the elements of this example. There is the one force, which in its full manifestation is pure light. It's possible to experience diminished or dimmed expressions of that one force – or even the absence of its expression. But the darkness is not a power that is independent of the light and could defeat it by superior numbers.

In the same fashion, the prayers of one person can work to save an entire community. The darkened consciousnesses of thousands of people do not constitute a power that can defeat a lighted prayer, despite numerical superiority. Of course, that one person who lives in a community of fear and selfishness may be psychologically affected by her surroundings. She may feel discouraged, drained and stuck in the thinking patterns of her neighbors. She may forget to pray or may doubt the value of prayer. In this sense the darkness can "win." However, the law of oneness holds that once that person remembers to pray and believes that healing work is being done. Then the darkened consciousness of the masses does not block the widespread impact.

In addition to the law of oneness, a second universal law helps us to understand the mechanism of critical mass. It's a principle from physics: the law of resonance. Perhaps you recall from high school physics the way in which tuning forks can demonstrate this law at a physical level. What happens if you strike a tuning fork and set it to vibrating and then move it near another fork of similar structure? It will set the second tuning fork to vibrating as well. Something similar happens at the level of human minds. It may well be that the vibration of consciousness can have a resonant effect upon other minds, recreating a sympathetic vibration or state of awareness.

Let's consider two ways in which the law of resonance may operate to explain the critical mass effect on human minds and behavior. First, consider an idea that Cayce and many others have suggested. Is it possible that there are many souls of advanced spiritual development who stand ready to help the earth in this time of transition? This aid may be through direct incarnation if appropriate parents can be found, or it may be through the infusion of ideas and knowledge, which could be telepathically transferred. Perhaps even without the receiver being quite sure where that inspirational insight came from! These ideas might be philosophical insights into the human condition, or they might be technological inventions, which could help humanity deal with threatened physical survival. The law of resonance would give us one way of understanding how this assistance would be received. If a certain number of people made themselves into receptive tuning forks of the proper structure, then they might be set to "vibrating" with a conscious awareness that is quite extraordinary.

What if instead of philosophical and technological ideas being transferred to receptive channels, it was certain vibratory frequencies of energy itself. The reception and expression of such energies might be used to heal physical bodies or perhaps even to heal and purify our polluted and sick physical earth. We can only guess at what kind of help might be available from conscious beings in other dimensions of God's creation. Of course, we cannot passively await their intervention and expect them to clear up the mess we have collectively created. However, there may be significant validity to the law of resonance. It probably applies to a lot more than just physical objects like tuning forks. As we work to shape our "personal structure" – by meditation, exercise, diet, etc. – we may some day find ourselves set to vibrating with energies or ideas that seem to come from beyond ourselves and which promise to help the world as a whole.

It could well be that within every person there are many "tuning forks." Each one of these tuning forks symbolizes a distinct outlook on life or a state of mind. (And anyone who seriously studies himself is quick to discover this inner diversity.) According to Cayce's philosophy, one such tuning fork within each and every one of us is special: the extraordinary state of mind he called the universal Christ Consciousness. Perhaps it has been buried away and forgotten in many people, but it's still there. However, it can be activated in one of two ways. The first is by conscious effort on the part of the individual – by seeking it out and making specific efforts to mobilize its vibration in physical life. It's probably safe to say that only a small percentage of the world's population is involved in diligently doing this now.

The second way is by the law of resonance. If someone nearby has set his or her own Christ Consciousness tuning fork to vibrating, it may create a sympathetic activity in similar structures in other people, just as surely as the experiment worked in high school physics class!

And how would people experience such a secondary awakening of Christ Consciousness vibrations? Since they are not voluntarily at work on the spiritual path, how would they receive the new vibrations mysteriously emerging from within themselves? These vibrations might appear as unfamiliar, new feelings about themselves and others. They might come as dreams or intuitions. They could manifest as a change in physical health – for some as a healing and for others as a temporary illness (as the old ways of treating their bodies can no longer be handled by a newly sensitized body and mind). Or they might appear as some sort of cosmic or supernatural physical phenomenon in response to these inner events in man's consciousness. Some people expect an outer, physical reappearance of the Christ – a Second Coming – as the manner in which this global awakening would express itself

Whatever the means or the appearance, we can expect that some people will be inspired by it. Because of what spontaneously happens to them, they proceed consciously to begin work on nurturing this newly realized spiritual dimension of themselves. However, others may be more frightened or stubborn about the process, and they would reject what they feel happening to themselves.

Here, then, is a scenario for how human consciousness will be transformed in the coming decades. It doesn't require the impact of outer earth changes – cataclysms such as earthquakes, wars or weather changes. This interpretation of Cayce's most essential prophecy is much less sensationalistic. It shows how relatively few people could work to bring on a new culture for our new millennium. The key ingredient will be a sufficient number of people dealing creatively with the stress of their own inner millennium shift.

The scenario supposes that even a small group – perhaps only several thousand people – will begin to handle the inner changes in a loving, creative, responsible fashion. These people will not be sucked into the darkened consciousness of the masses, which is cynical and fearful. Instead they will attune themselves; they will make themselves of such a "structure" that new energies and new ideas will set their minds and bodies to vibrating through the law of resonance. They will receive aid from the Christ Consciousness within themselves and perhaps also from spiritual beings in other dimensions. When the membership of this group reaches a certain number, then a critical mass point will have been reached – a threshold level will have been achieved and a tremendous new effect will come into play.

Now a second type of resonance will be set in motion throughout the planet. Perhaps within a matter of months – although it could be years – resonant vibrations will begin to stir to life the Christ Consciousness. It will happen in people of all faith traditions, and each person will find words out of their own cultural context to describe it. Even those who haven't been seeking inwardly or spiritually will begin spontaneously to have transformative experiences. This will be a remarkable event in human history. It will be a moment when humanity is on the verge of a quantum leap in awareness.

If that moment coincides with a period of catastrophic outer changes in the world, then the choices and responses will be even more crucial. But this scenario supposes that very large numbers of people will be inspired by the new ideas that they feel coming from within themselves. Remarkable dreams, intuitions and feelings will come to millions, even many of those who haven't been consciously seeking them. Certainly there will be holdouts, individuals who may fearfully hold on to the old ways. But we'll have turned the corner, and the momentum will have become unstoppable. Humanity will be at the dawn of what Cayce and so many others have predicted for the 21st century and beyond – a new paradigm for human living based on cooperation and peace.

The Politics of the Transition

It has been said that politicians are the last to respond to changes in mass consciousness. The spirit of the times is usually felt in art, science and religion before it finds expression in the power games of the governing process. How, then, we might wonder, will the transition to a new paradigm overcome the blocks created by world leaders who want to hang on to the old system? How can enlightened souls have an impact on the decisions being made, which affect all nations?

There is no point in claiming that by magic several thousand spiritually attuned people can cause world leaders to alter the quality and direction of their decisions. Instead of relying on magic for an explanation, let us consider by what mechanism spiritually attuned people can create what Cayce envisioned as an "invisible empire." Speaking in 1927 of those who might dedicate their lives to an expression of the universal Christ Spirit, Cayce called such individuals "those that would build an invisible empire within the hearts of men" (#3976-4).

The term "empire" is a blatantly political one. It refers to power and influence in human affairs that extend beyond the borders of any one nation. Historically, we might think of the Roman Empire or the Persian Empire, clear examples of political influences that spanned many regions and nationalities. When the Cayce readings refer to spiritually attuned people creating an invisible empire, they suggest that we can influence the decision-making process that governs the nations. And "invisible" suggests that the influence will come at the levels of mind and spirit.

But how can we really have an effect upon the decisions that shape the world – such as the choices of war and peace, or the decisions on how national resources will be spent? The answer lies in first considering who it is that is really in control of the world.

Before you respond that it's the presidents of the United States and Russia, or the chairmen of Exxon and Ford, think about this principle: *only those who can truly control themselves can claim to control things beyond themselves.* That means control over one's body, attitudes, emotions and actions. And the indisputable evidence is that most, if not all, of the so-called world leaders are actually controlled. This isn't a matter of some conspiracy in which multinational corporations secretly mold the decisions of governments. Instead it's a matter of world leaders not being enlightened, spiritually free beings. And so, they are controlled, but the influence comes from their own subconscious minds. Their desires, fears, insecurities, and habits shape the nature of their decisions, which in turn, affect millions of people. Often those controlling influences from within themselves are hidden or only dimly perceived.

Imagine, for example, how many important decisions are made by world leaders because of a feeling, mood or hunch. Suppose a national leader had to decide the next morning whether or not to invade a neighboring country. Consider but one factor: the quality and content of his or her dreams that night (remembered or unremembered) will likely leave that world leader with a particular mood or perspective in the morning, which could have a large effect upon the decision.

To the degree that world leaders are not yet enlightened beings that are free from the controlling influence of their own subconscious minds, we can exert a tremendous impact on their decisions. It is at the level of the subconscious mind that the apparent decision makers are directable. If Cayce is correct and all subconscious minds are in contact with one another, then we have identified a vehicle for creating an invisible empire. From a dimension beyond the three-dimensional, physical world, enlightened awareness has an influence. A world leader may never say, "I feel people praying for me and encouraging me to select the way of cooperation and peace." However, that may be exactly what is taking place.

In the past, patterns of fear or confusion may have existed within the subconscious mind of that leader which exerted a control and which led to choices of international tension and discord. But in the not-too-distant future, that same subconscious level may be the avenue by which the world leader is led to see matters a bit differently or to have new feelings and hunches about how to deal with old problems.

We can make a difference in the shaping of world events. We can make the difference. Just look at the arithmetic that can be extrapolated from some of the Cayce prophecies. Sixty-four people were once enough to change the destiny of the United States, a nation of 150 million people at the time. We could use the same ratios of influence applied to the modern world population of 6.5 billion. That would give us approximately 2800 as a target number for the critical mass to change the destiny of humanity. Perhaps as few as just 2800 people who truly live and pray in attunement with God's plan will be the threshold amount to trigger global changes for healing.

If we will just understand the power to which we have access, this can occur. If we will but look deeply and see what power is really all about, then we can judge in whose hands it actually lies. Yes, we can make the difference. By the way that a few of us prepare for and deal with the inner aspect of the millennium changes, we will largely determine what form the outer millennium changes will take. Just a handful of spiritually dedicated people can create a graceful, loving form of change in which all humanity will participate. And that, at its core, is the fundamental prophecy of Edgar Cayce. It should give us a great sense of promise about what is possible for the 21st century.

POSTSCRIPT

EDGAR CAYCE'S WORK
FOR THE 21ST CENTURY

Edgar Cayce's teachings and works are every bit as important to the 21st century as they were to the 20th. He was co-founder of three organizations, two of them still very much alive and active. Anyone interested in knowing more about the Cayce legacy can contact those two organizations.

In 1925 he first joined with supporters to create the Association of National Investigators. Its purpose was to provide a legal structure around Cayce's work and provide a framework for parapsychological investigation – especially in regard to medical clairvoyance. The A.N.I., as it was called, raised the money to build and run for two years (starting in 1928) the Cayce Hospital of Research and Enlightenment. But when the hospital failed for lack of financial support and discord among its leaders, the A.N.I. also collapsed.

Concurrent with the A.N.I., Cayce and several colleagues founded a small university in Virginia Beach. Atlantic University opened its doors to undergraduate students in the autumn of 1929. There were great plans for it to expand into a school of significant scope, influence and student enrollment. But after less than two years of operation, it too ran into severe financial difficulty and had to close its doors.

Whereas A.N.I. folded along with the hospital, however, Atlantic University was kept alive as a legal entity, chartered to offer advanced learning in the state of Virginia. It was some 40 years after Cayce's death before that dream began to be realized. In the mid-1980's it was re-activated as a small graduate school program and was given permission by the State Council of Higher Education of Virginia to offer a master's degree. The program – in Transpersonal Studies – is interdisciplinary and includes courses in psychology, philosophy, religious studies, health sciences, the arts, and parapsychology. Although it offers courses in residence at its Virginia Beach campus, the majority of its course enrollments are through computer and Internet-based distance learning, which makes its offerings available to students worldwide.

Atlantic University offers programs whereby students can study in-depth not just the Cayce materials but also a wide range of leading thinkers in a spirit-mind-body approach. The University maintains an extensive set of informational materials about its programs on the following web site: www.atlanticuniv.edu. It maintains accreditation through the Distance Education and Training Council, an organization authorized by the U.S. Department of Education to accredit schools that offer learning primarily via distance education.

The third organization co-founded by Cayce is also still active, and it is by far the largest of the three endeavors. Soon after the demise of the A.N.I., several of Cayce's most ardent supporters helped him start a new non-profit organization to continue his work, even though the treasured hospital project had been abandoned. The Association for Research and Enlightenment (A.R.E.) was created in 1931, and for more than 70 years it has served to make Edgar Cayce's work known to a wide array of audiences through membership, publishing, small group study, and educational conferences. In the early 21st century, more than 30,000 people worldwide are dues-paying members of the A.R.E., but literally hundreds of thousands of others are students of Cayce's work and make use of various resources of the A.R.E., especially its online materials at www.edgarcayce.org.

One prominent aspect of the A.R.E. is its publishing. Not only has A.R.E. Press issued a CD-ROM edition of all the Cayce readings and supportive documents, each year it also publishes several new books about how the principles in the readings can be applied in daily life.

Since 1931, the A.R.E. has also maintained a small group study program under the aegis of the "A Search for God" material – initially just one group that involved Cayce himself, and eventually growing to thousands of groups worldwide over recent decades. Cayce's teachings have found a welcome audience in dozens of foreign countries, many with their own organizations and book translations.

ABOUT THE AUTHOR

Mark Thurston, Ph.D. is an educator, psychologist, and author of eighteen books about practical spirituality. His previous publications include *The Essential Edgar Cayce, Discovering Your Soul's Purpose, Dreams: Tonight's Answers for Tomorrow's Questions*, and *Synchronicity As Spiritual Guidance*. He is also co-author of two highly practical guidebooks to the Cayce material: *The Edgar Cayce Handbook for Creating Your Future* (with Christopher Fazel) and *Twelve Positive Habits of Spiritually Centered People* (with his daughter, Sarah Thurston).

Dr. Thurston currently serves as a faculty member in transpersonal psychology and Director of Academic Affairs for Atlantic University in Virginia Beach, Virginia. His courses and classes include a training program designed to equip people to serve as spiritual mentors.

In 1998 he was executive producer and on-air host of *The New Millennium*, a series of twenty-six television programs produced at WHRO, the PBS affiliate for the Norfolk and Virginia Beach, Virginia area. Those shows, which were aired for two years on The Wisdom Channel, focused on the most important topics in the Cayce material.

Dr. Thurston is also the co-founder of the Personal Transformation and Courage Institute, a non-profit educational organization offering intensive courses in life purpose and transformational healing. He can be contacted at www.soul-purpose.com/courage

Other Books by Mark Thurston

The Essential Edgar Cayce

Twelve Positive Habits of Spiritually Centered People (co-author)

Edgar Cayce's Guide to Spirituality for Busy People

Synchronicity as Spiritual Guidance

Millennium Prophecies

The Edgar Cayce Handbook for Creating Your Future (co-author)

Soul-Purpose: Discovering and Fulfilling Your Destiny

Dreams: Tonight's Answers for Tomorrow's Questions

Paradox of Free Will

The Inner Power of Silence

Discovering Your Soul's Purpose

How to Interpret Your Dreams

Face to Face (co-author)

Understand and Develop Your ESP

Experiments in Practical Spirituality

Experiments in a Search for God

Meditation and the Mind of Mind (co-author)

The Artwork for the book cover was created by
"Daniel L. O'Byrne"

ABOUT DANIEL L. O'BYRNE

Photographing Nature and Wildlife

A self taught Artist and Photographer who has been an active member of the Renderosity community since 2002 posting in Photography and Mixed medium. He has undertaken various tasks writing articles on Photography for the Magazine as well as doing software reviews. He has been nominated as Artist of the month 3 times in Mixed Medium and in the Photographic Gallery. He has won awards for his artwork and photography, as well as producing images for book covers and album covers.

Daniel is a graduate of Portsmouth University, which he followed with Post Graduate studies at the University of Middlesex. He has a special interest in the field of Mental Health research. He worked in the Military for 23 years and was a Trauma Specialist there, both in the fields of general medicine and psychiatry and he has travelled widely.

Danny is working at present in Buckingham Mental Health Trust. He has been there for 10 plus years where he has spent time working with Rehabilitation and Community Care for people with enduring mental illnesses.

His hobbies include chess, golf, listening to music, and reading. An avid lover of nature and wildlife his interests in this has always been the inspiration for his art and photography. Daniel considers his use of lighting to be the very soul of his attempts to capture this within his work.

You can see some of Daniel's art and photography at:

http://www.renderosity.com/gallery.ez?ByArtist=Yes&Artist=danob

And:http://digitalartzone.co.uk/index2.htm